MARKETING MANAGEMENT

MARKETING MANAGEMENT

Amar Jyoti

genNEXT Publication

Marketing Management (PB)

Rs. 180

ISBN: 978-81-908675-9-7

Published in 2010 in India by
Gennext Publication
23 Main Ansari Road, Darya Ganj,
New Delhi-110002
E-Mail:GenNextpublication@hotmail.com
Phone: 23282060

Printed at: Young Art Press, Delhi

Contents

Preface

Marketing management is an important field for all companies. This is justified in a country like ours where huge number of consumers, big infrastructure, culture etc. makes the field of marketing very complex. This volume covers the field of marketing management in a very lucid manner and in Indian context. This book would fulfill the need for a text that covers the concepts of marketing management and their applications in day-to-day business.

Integration of marketing management functions is the underlying theme of the book. Building on an understanding of the consumer decision process, the book defines the roles of marketing strategies. This volume is a comprehensive textbook specially designed to meet the requirements of management students specializing in sales and distribution.

It highlights the major decision areas within sales and distribution and provides analytical models and approaches that will facilitate decision making. It gives an exposure to key concepts, theories and recent developments in sales and distribution and illustrates their applicability in tackling the challenges in business. Students shall find this book extremely useful for its treatment of the sales organization, sales management, territory management, designing a distribution system and distribution management. With its unique approach, generalized frameworks, elaborate research and extensive data analysis, this book will be of immense value to Marketing professionals of the Indian corporate sector and marketing departments of national and multinational companies in India.

The book gives real life examples in the areas of Marketing to provide experience of Marketing environment. It attempts to blend in theory with practice.

This volume is a comprehensive textbook specially designed to meet the requirements of management students specializing in Marketing. It highlights the major decision areas within Marketing and provides analytical models and approaches that will facilitate decision making. It gives an exposure to key concepts, theories and recent developments in Marketing and illustrates their applicability in tackling the challenges in business.

1

Introduction to Marketing

Production and marketing of goods and services are the essence of economic life in any society. All organizations perform these two basic functions to satisfy their commitments to their stakeholders - the owners, the customers and the society, at large. They create a benefit that economists call utility which is the want-satisfying power of a good or service.

There are four basic kinds of utility - form, time, place and ownership utility. Form utility is created when the firm converts raw materials and component inputs into finished goods and services. Although marketing provides important inputs that specify consumer preference, the organization's production function is responsible for the actual creation of form utility. Marketing function creates time, place and ownership utilities.

Time and place utility occur when consumers find goods and services available when and where they want to purchase them. Online retailers with 24×7 format emphasize time utility. Vending machines focus on providing place utility for people buying snacks and soft drinks. The transfer of title to goods or services at the time of purchase creates ownership utility.

To survive, all organizations must create utility. Designing and marketing wantsatisfying goods, services and ideas is the foundation for the creation of utility. Management guru, Peter F.Drucker emphasized the importance of marketing in his classic book, The Practice of Management as: 'If we want to know what a business is, we have start with its purpose. And its purpose must lie outside the business itself. In fact, it must lie in society since a business enterprise is an organ of society. There is one valid definition of business purpose: to create a customer'.

DEFINITION OF MARKETING

Continuous exposure to advertising and personal selling leads many people to link marketing and selling, or to think that marketing activities start once goods and services have been produced. While marketing certainly includes selling and advertising, it encompasses much more. Marketing also involves analyzing consumer needs, securing information needed to design and produce goods or services that match buyer expectations and creating and maintaining relationships with customers and suppliers. The following table summarizes the key differences between marketing and selling concepts.

Selling Vs. Marketing

Point of difference	Selling	Marketing
Starting point	Factory	Marketplace
Focus	Existing products	Customer needs
Means	Selling and promoting	Integrated marketing
End	Profits through volume	Profits through satisfaction

The difference between selling and marketing can be best illustrated by this popular customer quote: 'Don't tell me how good your product is, but tell me how good it will make me'. The American Marketing Association, the official organization for academic and professional marketers, defines marketing as: Marketing is the process of planning and executing the conception, pricing, promotion and distribution of ideas, goods and services to create exchanges that satisfy individual and organizational objectives.

Another definition goes as 'process by which individuals and groups obtain what they need and want through creating and exchanging products and value with others'. Simply put: Marketing is the delivery of customer satisfaction at a profit. The notion of exchange as central to marketing is reinforced by many contemporary definitions such as 'marketing is the process of creating and resolving exchange relationships' and 'marketing is the process in which exchanges occur among persons and social groups'. The essence of marketing is the exchange process, in which two or more parties give something of value to each other to satisfy felt needs. In many exchanges, people trade tangible goods for money. In others, they trade intangible services. Exchanges in marketing are consummated not just between any two parties, but almost always among two or more parties, of which one or more taken on the role of buyer and one or more, the role of seller. A common set of conditions are present in the marketplace, viz.,

1. Buyers outnumber sellers.
2. Any individual buyer is weaker than any individual seller economically, but
3. The total economic power of even a fraction of the buyers is enough to assure the existence of, or to put out of business, most sellers or groups of sellers, and
4. Consequently, the sellers compete to sway the largest number of buyers they can to their, rather than another seller's (competitor's) offerings. Finally and intriguingly,
5. The sellers in their attempt to meet competition and attract the largest number of buyers, are influenced as well, regularly modifying their behaviours so they will have more success, with more buyers, over time.

The expanded concept of marketing activities permeates all organizational functions. It assumes that the marketing effort will follow the overall corporate strategy and will proceed in accordance with ethical practices and that it will effectively serve the interests of both society and organization. The concept also identifies the marketing variables - product, price, promotion and distribution - that combine to provide customer satisfaction. In addition, it assumes that the organization begins by identifying and analyzing the consumer segments that it will later satisfy through its production and marketing activities. The concept's emphasis on creating and maintaining relationships is consistent with the focus in business on long-term, mutually satisfying sales, purchases and other interactions with customers and suppliers. Finally it recognizes that marketing concepts and techniques apply to non-profit organizations as well as to profit-oriented businesses, to product organization and to service organizations, to domestic and global organizations, as well as to organizations targeting consumers and other businesses.

EVOLUTION OF MARKETING

As noted earlier, exchange is the origin of marketing activity. When people need to exchange goods, they naturally begin a marketing effort. Wroe Alderson, a leading marketing theorist has pointed out, 'It seems altogether reasonable to describe the development of exchange as a great invention which helped to start primitive man on the road to civilization'. Production is not meaningful until a system of marketing has been established.

An adage goes as: Nothing happens until somebody sells something. Although marketing has always been a part of business, its importance has varied greatly over the years. The following table identifies five eras in the history of marketing: the production era, the product era, the sales era, the marketing era and the relationship marketing era.

Era Prevailing attitude and approach

Production:

- Consumers favor products that are available and highly affordable
- Improve production and distribution
- 'Availability and affordability is what the customer wants'

Product:

- Consumers favor products that offer the most quality, performance and innovative features
- 'A good product will sell itself'

Sales:

- Consumers will buy products only if the company promotes/ sells these products
- 'Creative advertising and selling will overcome consumers' resistance and convince them to buy'

Marketing:

- Focuses on needs/ wants of target markets and delivering satisfaction better than competitors
- 'The consumer is king! Find a need and fill it'

Relationship marketing:

- Focuses on needs/ wants of target markets and delivering superior value
- 'Long-term relationships with customers and other partners lead to success'

In the production era, the production orientation dominated business philosophy. Indeed business success was often defined solely in terms of production victories. The focus was on production and distribution efficiency. The drive to achieve economies of scale was dominant. The goal was to make the product affordable and available to the buyers.

In the product era, the goal was to build a better mouse trap and it was assumed that buyers will flock the seller who does it. However, a better mousetrap is no guarantee of success and marketing history is full of miserable failures despite better mousetrap designs. Inventing the greatest new product is not enough.

That product must also solve a perceived marketplace need. Otherwise, even the best-engineered. Highest quality product will fail. In the sales era, firms attempted to match their output to the potential number of customers who would want it. Firms assumed that customers will resist purchasing goods and services not deemed essential and that the task of selling and advertising is to convince them to buy. But selling is only one component of marketing.

Next came the marketing era during which the company focus shifted from products and sales to customers' needs. The marketing concept, a crucial change in management philosophy, can be explained best by the shift from a seller's market - one with a shortage of goods and services - to a buyer's market - one with an abundance of goods and services. The advent of a strong buyer's market created the need for a customer orientation. Companies had to market goods and services, not just produce them. This realization has been identified as the emergence of the marketing concept.

The keyword is customer orientation. All facets of the organization must contribute first to assessing and then to satisfying customer needs and wants. The relationship marketing era is a more recent one. Organization's carried the marketing era's customer orientation one step further by focusing on establishing and maintaining relationships with both customers and suppliers.

This effort represented a major shift from the traditional concept of marketing as a simple exchange between buyer and seller. Relationship marketing, by contrast, involves long-term, value-added relationships developed over time with customers and suppliers. The following table summarizes the differences between transaction marketing (i.e. exchanges characterized by limited communications and little or no on going relationship between the parties) and relationship marketing.

Comparing transaction-based marketing and relationship marketing

Characteristic	Transaction Based Marketing	Relationship Marketing
Time orientation	Short term	Long term
Organizational goal	Make the sale	Emphasis on customer retention
Customer service priority	Relatively low	Key component
Customer contact	Low to moderate	Frequent
Degree of customer commitment	Low	High
Basis for seller customer interactions	Conflict manipulation	Cooperation; trust
Source of quality	Primarily from production	Companywide Commitment

MARKETING FRAMEWORK

The basic elements of a marketing strategy consist of (1) the target market, and (2) the marketing mix variables of product, price, place and promotion that combine to satisfy the needs of the target market. Marketing activities focus on the consumer. Therefore, a market-driven organization begins its overall strategy with a detailed description of its target market: the group of people toward whom the firm decides to direct its marketing efforts. After marketers select a target market, they direct their activities towards profitably satisfying that target segment. Although they must manipulate many variables to reach this goal, marketing decision making can be divided into four areas: product, price, place (distribution) and promotion (marketing communication). These 4 Ps of marketing are referred to as the marketing mix. The 4 Ps blend to fit the needs and preferences of a specific target market. These are the four variables that a marketer can use and control in different combinations to create value for customers.

The product strategy involves deciding what goods and services the firm should offer to a group of consumers and also making decisions about customer service, brand name, packaging, labeling, product life cycles and new product development. The pricing strategy deals with the methods of setting profitable and justifiable prices. Marketers develop place (distribution) strategy to ensure that consumers find their products available in the proper quantities at the right times and places. Place-related decisions involve the distribution functions and marketing intermediaries (channel members). In the promotional strategy, marketers blend together the various elements of promotion to communicate most effectively with their target market. Many firms use an approach called Integrate Marketing Communications (IMC) to coordinate all promotional activities so that the consumer receives a unified, consistent and effective message. Marketers do not make decisions about target markets and marketing mix variables in a vacuum. They must take into account the dynamic nature of the five marketing environmental dimensions - competitive, political-legal, economic, technological and social-cultural dimensions. Marketers compete for the same consumers. So the developments in the competitive environment will have lot of repercussions. The political-legal environment includes the governing and regulatory bodies who impose guidelines to the marketers. Adherence to the law of the land is an imperative for a marketer to be a good and responsible corporate citizen. The economic environment dictates the mood in the target market who take decisions such as to buy or save, to buy now or later. The technological environment can spell life or death for a marketer with break-through technologies. Marketers often leap forward or get left behind owing to the changes in the technological environment. The social-cultural environment offers cues for the marketers to 'connect' well with the target market. Failure on part of the marketer to understand the social-cultural environment will have serious consequences. A marketers can not afford to rub a society/culture on the wrong side!

EXTENDING THE TRADITIONAL BOUNDARIES OF MARKETING

Until fairly recently, marketing focused primarily on exchanges of goods between individuals (business-to-consumer (B2C) marketing) and businesses (business-to-business (B2B) marketing). Industrial marketing deals with the organizational purchases of goods to support production of other goods or daily operations or for resale.

With the growth of the services sector, marketers realized that services cannot be marketed in the same way as the products. Certain characteristics of services posed serious problems for marketers who realized that services marketing must be done differently and not with the same marketing mix (4 Ps) variables. Service characteristics like intangibility (service firms don't sell a tangible thing, but a promise) inseparability (production and consumption of services take place at about the same time), heterogeneity (the problem due to the fact that no two service providers are like, nor are the service consumers) and perishability (service providers cannot maintain inventories of their products). To cope with these challenges, service marketers suggest additional 3 Ps - process, physical evidence and people.

The process is aimed at solving the heterogeneity or variability problem associated with the services by providing a service blueprint. The physical evidence solves some of the problems associated with the intangible nature of services. The physical evidence in terms of service environment, equipment, personnel and so on attempts to tangibilize the intangible. The final P - People - gives lot of attention to the service providers because they are, strictly speaking, part of the service provided. They can influence the perceived service quality in a big way.

With the world becoming a global village, marketers started targeting global audience for their products and services. International marketers implement the basic marketing framework discussed earlier. However transactions that cross national boundaries encounter an additional set of environmental factors. For example, differences in laws, economic conditions, cultural and business norms and consumer preferences other demand variations in marketing strategies.

The biggest challenge in international marketing is managing the international business environment. With many uncontrollable factors, sharing complex relationships among them, the international marketer faces the dilemma of whether to standardize or differentiate his marketing mix. Non-profit organizations encounter a special set of characteristics that influence their marketing activities.

Like for-profit firms, non-profit firms may market tangible goods and/or intangible services and operate in B2C and B2B markets. An important distinction is that profit-seeking businesses tend to focus their marketing on just one public - their customers. Non-profit businesses however must often market to multiple publics (say, their clients and sponsors), which complicates decision making regarding the markets to target.

Also a customer or service user may wield less control over the organization's destiny than would be true for customers of a profit-seeking firm. As a result, non-profit marketing must fine tune its marketing variables to adjust to these conditions.

FUNCTIONS OF MARKETING

Firms must spend money to create time, place and ownership utilities as discussed earlier. Several studies have been made to measure marketing costs in relation to overall product costs and service costs and most estimates have ranged between 40-60 percent. These costs are not associated with raw materials or any of the other production functions necessary for creating form utility. What then does the consumer receive in return for this proportion of marketing cost? This question is answered by understanding the functions performed by marketing.

In the following table, marketing is responsible for the performance of 8 universal functions: buying, selling, transporting, storing, standardizing and grading, financing, risk taking and securing marketing information. Some functions are performed by manufacturers, others by marketing intermediaries like wholesalers and retailers. Buying and selling, the first two functions represent exchange functions. Transporting and storing are physical distribution functions. The final four marketing functions - standardizing and grading, financing, risk taking and securing market information - are often called facilitating functions because they assist the marketer in performing the exchange and physical distribution functions.

While a product could represent many different things, a good, however, is a tangible object that can be seen and touched. A service, while a good and in sharp contrast to it, represents an intangible product that may involve human or mechanical effort in its delivery. Services are being consumed increasingly by personal and organizational consumers and constitute a very important part of the economics of developed and developing countries. More people are employed in service jobs than in those that produce goods.

CREATING A CUSTOMER

Essentially, 'creating' a customer means identifying needs in the marketplace, finding out which needs the organization can profitably serve and developing an offering to convert potential buyers into customers. Marketing managers are responsible for most of the activities necessary to create the customers the organization wants, These activities include:

- Identifying customer needs.
- Designing goods and services that meet those needs.
- Communication information about those goods and services to prospective buyers.

- Making the goods and services available at times and places that meet customers' needs.
- Pricing goods and services to reflect costs, competition and customers' ability to buy.
- Providing for the necessary service and follow-up to ensure customer satisfaction after the purchase.

THREE CONCEPTS

Since the later part of the 19th century, marketing has gradually evolved through various marketing orientations. These stages in marketing evolution present a generalised picture and a sufficiently significant number of companies have adopted the most modern marketing concept or philosophy.

THE PRODUCTION CONCEPT

This concept, viewed as one of the oldest of managerial orientations, typically aimed at achieving as high an output as possible. This philosophy assumed that customers would be more interested in acquiring conveniently available, reasonably priced, and well-made products. Keeping in view the market behaviour prevailing in times when customers did not have much choice, it was a sound approach. The focus of managers, generally having backgrounds in manufacturing and engineering, was to concentrate on achieving increasingly higher efficiency in production, lower production costs, and more intensive distribution. Even today, this approach seems to be quite sensible in relatively underdeveloped and developing economies because customers are more interested in owning a product and not overly concerned about finer features and aesthetic appeal. In general, one important condition seems to be favourable to adopt production orientation: when the masses look for a cheaper product and demand far exceeds production. In India, The National Textile Corporation (NTC) and all its subsidiaries are sticking to this philosophy while producing textiles for the huge, poverty-stricken population in this country.

Their philosophy and positioning is reflected in their ad, "Clothiers of the nation with affordable prices." In the global scenario, for nearly three decades Intel Corporation focused on achieving increasingly high production output of its successive generations of processors so as to bring down the prices of each improved version. The production concept is unlikely to get discarded for a very long time to come, because there would always be products and populations of such a nature that some companies would feel comfortable with this philosophy.

THE SELLING CONCEPT

Sales concept seems to be based on a lurking apprehension that customers will not buy the product in sufficient quantities unless aggressively pressurised. The selling concept was the major means of increasing sales and profits during 1920s to 1950s in the developed countries of that period. Companies believed that the most important marketing activities were personal selling, advertising, and distribution. Selling concept is geared towards converting existing product(s) into cash rather than first finding and then satisfying customer needs. Sales concept is often observed in practice when companies show heavy reliance on their promotional capabilities based on "hard sell" approach. It is obvious that if a company's products do not match the changing tastes and requirements of customers, with many alternative choices available, managers might be inclined to go for aggressive promotional efforts to sell enough quantities. In his book, The End of Marketing as We Know It, Sergio Zyman writes that the purpose of marketing is to sell more stuff to more people more often for more money in order to make more profit. Of late, this has been happening in case of some Credit Cards in our country. Generally, "hard sell" is often seen in case of products or services that people buy without giving much thought to the matter, such as non-essential goods, and tend to postpone such purchases. With ever intensifying competition, products becoming more standardised without any meaningful differentiation i.e., commoditization, heavy promotional efforts in all possible manners are bound to remain the practice, in order to grab more share of the customers' purse. The consequences of "hard sell" might harm the customer base to the extent that, in some cases, they might even bad-mouth the product if the product fails to match up to their expectations.

THE MARKETING CONCEPT

After World War II, the variety of products increased, people had more discretionary income, and could afford to be selective and buy only those products that more precisely met their changing needs and wants. However, these needs were not immediately obvious.

Sometime during the mid-1950s, there was growing recognition among American business people that merely efficient production and extensive promotion, including hard selling, did not guarantee that customers would buy products. With the passage of time, more knowledge, and experience, customers increasingly seemed unwilling to be persuaded. More and more companies found that determining what customers wanted was a must before making a product, rather than producing products first and then persuading them to buy. The key questions became:

1. What do customers really want?
2. Can we develop it while they still want?
3. How can we keep our customers satisfied?

Thus, the marketing concept era began. Marketing concept proposes that an organization should focus on customer needs and wants, coordinate its efforts, and endeavour to accomplish organizational goals. Geraldine E Williams reported that the CEO of Nike said, "For years we thought of ourselves as a production-oriented company, meaning we put all our emphasis on designing and manufacturing the product. But now we understand that the most important thing we do is market the product." The major focus of all sets of organizational activities should be satisfying customer needs. This requires carefully listening to customers as a student listens to a teacher. Stanley F Slater and John C Narver reported that there is positive relationship between market orientation and performance. Sometimes, philosophies that sound quite reasonable and appear attractive on paper, are difficult to put into practice.

To embrace the marketing concept as the guiding philosophy, the concerned firm must accept certain general conditions and manage some problems. Alan Grant and Leonard Schlesinger are of the view that market-orientation requires organization-wide generation of market intelligence across departments, and organization wide responsiveness to it. It means establishing a reliable information system to learn about real needs of customers and design the right need satisfying solutions. Setting up an information system can usually be an expensive proposition and requires committing money and time to its development and maintenance. Company-wide coordination may require restructuring the internal operations and overall objectives in case of one or more departments. Appreciating the critical role of marketing, the head of marketing has to be part of the top management team. Acceptance and implementation of marketing concept demands support of top management and other managers and staff. To inculcate a customer-orientation culture, it is necessary that employees at all levels in the organization should understand the value of the customer and the importance of the customer satisfaction.

Obviously, the internal customers (company employees at all levels) themselves should be satisfied and motivated to promote an organization-wide culture that puts high value on creating a satisfied customer. For this, the company has to ensure an appropriate work environment and take care of their legitimate needs. Benson P. Shapiro is of the opinion that a company is customer focused if the answers are "yes" to the four critical questions:

- Are we easy for customers to do business with?
- Do we keep our promises?
- Do we meet the standards we set?
- Are we responsive to customer needs?
- The marketing concept emphasises three main principles.

Customer-oriented planning and implementations

It should be the sole aim of all employees, irrespective of their department or functional area, to satisfy customers' needs. It would require carefully segmenting the market on the basis of the right criteria, targeting suitable segment(s), learning about customer needs and wants, analysing and spotting the right opportunities and matching them with the company's strengths.

Coordination of all organizational activities

Mainly product planning, pricing, distribution, and promotion should be combined in a sensible and consistent manner, and the head of marketing should be a part of top-level management.

Importance of Coordinated marketing in achieving organizational goals

The reward of doing the job well will bring in sales and profits because without profits, the firm cannot survive, neither would it be in a position to improve its offers. Marketing concept is significantly different from production concept and selling concept. Not long ago, Indian auto companies, Hindustan Motors, Premier Automobiles, and Bajaj Auto hardly showed any consideration for customers, producing obsolete models in large numbers (demand exceeded the supply). Though the prices kept on increasing, little was done to improve the models. Bajaj was the only manufacturer of scooters preferred by customers and to own one, customers had to deposit money in advance and wait for five to ten years before they could become proud owners. It is only after the entry of Maruti cars, with Japanese collaboration, that things started changing.

Premier Auto, and Hindustan Motors experienced major setbacks, sales declined and ultimately there were hardly any willing buyers. In the beginning, Maruti found it difficult to meet the demand and buyers willingly booked the car and waited for delivery. Bajaj Auto faced a similar situation as customers had many choices of two-wheelers. The position now appears as if almost every auto manufacturer is desperately trying to please customers. Customers have strong preferences for certain features and price ranges. Maruti has even started selling second-hand, reconditioned, and reliable cars from its outlets to customers looking for such deals, is order to expand its hold on the market.

In line with the marketing concept, it is imperative that the typical pyramid depicting an organization needs to be inverted to pursue marketing concept. In an inverted position, the customer will occupy the highest pedestal and top management will be at the bottom position. The communication flow will start from the customer, and the employees and executives will look up to learn what the customer wants and then respond to the inputs. This is the way to offer desired value, deliver more satisfaction, and help retain the customer.

Marketing concept is sometimes interpreted as a philosophy of attempting to satisfy all customers' needs with no concern for the cost. This would seem to be a sure way to financial disaster. The marketing concept is consistent with the idea of taking into consideration only those customer segments that the company can satisfy both effectively and profitably. The firm has to earn profits to survive, offer new and better products and services, and be a meaningful member of society. A company might therefore choose to offer less costly products and services to unprofitable customer segments, or even avoid them altogether. Being market-oriented pays dividends and has a significant effect on company performance.

RELATIONSHIP MARKETING

Companies in developed countries and many businesses in developing countries aim to satisfy customer needs and build lasting relationships. The issue focuses on reliability and trust between customer and organization. As a result of this customer focus, a whole new subject, customer relationship management is now studied in marketing courses.

According to Jagdish N. Sheth and Rajendra Sisodia, the term 'relationship marketing' refers to long-term and mutually beneficial arrangements wherein both buyer and seller focus on value enhancement through the creation of more satisfying exchanges. This approach attempts to transcend the simple purchase exchange process with customers to make more meaningful and richer contacts by providing a more holistic, personalised purchase, and use or consumption experience to create stronger ties. The new approaches to marketing such as experiential, permission, and one-to-one marketing can all be seen as means of creating stronger relationships with customers.

The emphasis is on developing long-term bonds with customers by making them feel good about how the firm interacts or does business with them by giving them some kind of personal connection to the company. Real relationship-marketing programme is much more than the use of database marketing to target customers more precisely. Its purpose is that each customer must feel she/he has received something in return for being a member of the partnership. Firms have found that Internet is an inexpensive, efficient and more productive means to extend a firm's customer services. Internet permits firms to ask consumers if they permit the company to send them targeted e-mail ads, promotions, or messages, before actually doing so. Some airlines, hotel chains, credit card businesses, and big retailers, etc., use relationship marketing techniques by awarding points to committed customers that can be used to obtain additional goods or services from the concerned company. To put it differently, relationship marketing is all about building trust between the company and its customers and keeping promises. These factors increasingly strengthen the customer dependence on the organization, as a result of which the customer's confidence grows, while the company better understands the customer and her/his needs and wants. Ultimately, this helps in cementing the relationship and encourages cooperative problem solving.

Relationship marketing is based on the principle that current customers are the key to long-term business success. According to Frederick F. Reichheld, the importance of customer retention can be judged by observing some of the following benefits it provides:

- Acquiring new customers can be five times more expensive than the costs involved in satisfying and retaining existing customers.
- The average company loses 10 per cent of its customers each year.
- A decrease of 5 per cent in the customer defection rate can increase profits by 25 per cent to 85 per cent, depending on the industry.

- The customer profit rate tends to increase over the life of retained customer.

Jagdish N. Sheth and Atul Parvatiyar are also of the opinion that it is to a company's advantage to develop long-term relationships with current customers because it is easier and costs less to make an additional sale to an existing customer than to make a new sale to a new customer. Neighbourhood grocery shop owners frequently reassure their frequent customers that if they are not satisfied with a consumable product, they can return it, even after some use and get the full replacement. They practice relationship marketing based on conventional marketing wisdom obtaining in India.

Acquiring New Customers vs. Retaining Old Customers

The telecom paradigm is perceptibly changing. As the focus shifts from increasing the customer base to growing the share of revenue, mobile phone service providers are focusing on a model where customer retention becomes the key focus area. In India, significant changes in the telecom scenario have influenced the strategy shift. To start with, we had two operators in every circle. Now six or even seven operators compete in the same service area. Then, telecom costs have been consistently sliding, leading to the cheapest telecom rates in the world. All this has led to an explosion in subscriber numbers. But they also increased customer churn.

Even acquisition costs per subscriber were going down (from between Rs. 5,000 and Rs 10,000 in the late 1990s, it is now about Rs 1,000 per customer). But break-even on new customers still takes 18 to 24 months. Given these dynamics, it is more profitable to retain an existing customer than fighting for a new customer. Today, non-portability of numbers in India acts as one of the biggest retention devices but this could be a temporary benefit. During the early stages of mobile telephony, customer retention typically meant providing basic customer services.

But when new entrants were actively wooing our customers, we recognised the need to focus on customer retention. We formed the Customer Asset Management (CAM) team, the business division parallel to our sales business unit. This team has a singleminded focus on retention activities with a direct say in all aspects of the business. We also started to focus on attracting the right quality of customers. Towards this, we fine-tuned our acquisition strategy. We are exploring alternative channels for selling. It is important for a service brand to create differentiation, which is an experiential sum of all its interactions with the customer. The total experience is our ability to deliver advanced products first in the market, providing an impeccable network quality and rounding off the product experience with a memorable service experience every time the customer interacts with us. According to Steve Schriver, research indicates that consumers are less loyal now than in the past due to the following reasons:

- The abundance of choice.
- Availability of information.
- Customers ask, "What have you done for me lately?"
- Most products/services appear to be similar - nothing stands out.
- Customers' financial problems reduce loyalty.
- Time scarcity (not enough time to be loyal).

These forces lead to consumer defections, complaints, cynicism, decreased affiliation, greater price sensitivity, and a tendency to carry on lawsuits.

The major differences between selling concept and marketing concept

1. The selling concept starts with the seller and its focus is on existing products, it being seller-oriented. The company believes in aggressive selling and other promotions. Customer value and satisfaction are no concern for the seller. The firm produces the products first and then figures out ways to sell and make profits. Different company departments operate without coordination.
2. Marketing orientation starts with the customer and the company strives to learn customer needs and wants, develops appropriate products or services to satisfy the customer. Business is viewed as a customer need satisfying activity. All departments coordinate their activities and the focus is on customer needs. Profits are an outcome of doing the job well by the company. It requires reliable companywide information system and maintains it. All departments are responsive to informational inputs. Everybody understands the critical role played by marketing, a fact visibly demonstrable when the head of marketing is part of top management.

THE SOCIETAL MARKETING CONCEPT

Marketing concept was accepted widely among companies in developed and some developing countries and continued to evolve and take on new meanings. Not long after this, criticism started about the nature of its social responsibility. The emphasis shifted to how marketing affected society as a whole in an age of depleting and increasingly scarce resources, environmental deterioration, etc. It was good enough to produce what customers needed or wanted, and for achieving organizational objectives, but in certain cases the concept could be in conflict with customers' and society's best long-run interests. Societal marketing concept is a management philosophy that takes into account the welfare of society, the organization, and its customers.

Adoption of this concept requires that marketing decisions be made in an ethical and socially responsible manner. Companies must pay attention not only to the short-term needs of customers but also to their long-term well being. This includes, for instance, excess fat content in ready-to-eat foods, toxic wastes, and environmental issues. The need is to strike a balance between the interest of customers, the company itself, and the society in which operations are conducted. Some responsible firms have started using recyclable packaging materials and products that do not harm the environment. Among the marketing tasks, demarketing is an approach that reflects the societal marketing philosophy.

Many companies encounter several hurdles in adopting the marketing concept. For some firms, it is simply too difficult to understand the underlying philosophy and they fail to implement it. Other companies face a conflict between short-term and long-term objectives and have no inclination to sacrifice short-term gains for the sake of customer satisfaction, simply because the customer is not the major priority of top management.

HOLISTIC MARKETING APPROACH

There have been major changes in almost every sphere of human activity over the last decade, like implication being that this requires fresh marketing thinking, a fresh approach to business, and this calls for a holistic marketing approach. This new thinking relies upon marketing research to define market segments, their size, and their needs. To more completely satisfy those needs, marketers need to have a more complete and cohesive approach to internal marketing, targeted marketing, relationship marketing, be visibly socially responsible, and make decisions about the controllable elements of the marketing mix.

MARKETING MIX

Marketing mix is a major concept in modern marketing and involves practically everything that a marketing company can use to influence consumer perceptions favourably towards its products or services so that consumer and organizational objectives are attained. Marketing mix is a model of crafting and implementing marketing strategy. Prof. Neil H. Borden first used the term "marketing mix" in 1949 to include in the marketing process factors such as distribution, advertising, personal selling, and pricing. Borden claims that the phrase came to him while reading James Culliton's description of the activities of a business executive:

(An executive) "a mixer of ingredients, who sometimes follows a recipe as he goes along, sometimes adapts a recipe to the ingredients immediately available, and sometimes experiments with or invents ingredients no one else has tried."

There are virtually dozens of marketing mix tools. However, Prof. E. Jerome McCarthy classified the "Marketing Mix Variables" in terms of 4 Ps: Product, Price, Place (distribution) and Promotion. These 4 Ps represent the tactical controllable factors and vary in case of different products and target markets. This classification is believed to be quite popular in marketing circles across the world.

Three other marketing mix classifications by: (1) Albert Frey, (2) William Lazer and Eugene J. Kelly, and (3) Mary Bitner and Bernard Booms are worth noting. Frey's two-factor classification includes:

1. The Offering: product, packaging, brand, price, and service.
2. Methods and Tools includes distribution channels, personal selling, advertising, sales promotion, and publicity.

The second classification proposed by Lazer and Kelly includes three factors:

1. Goods and Services Mix,
2. Distribution Mix, and
3. Communications Mix, and Bitner and Boom's includes 7 Ps.

However, the 4Ps remain the most popular classification in terms of marketing mix. A more recent marketing mix classification proposed by Robert Lauterborn focuses on customer's point of view and includes:

1. Customer Benefit,
2. Customer Cost,

3. Customer Convenience, and
4. Communication.

Lauterborn's view is that 4Ps correspond to customer's 4Cs.

McCarthy's Classification (4Ps) Lauterborn's Classification (4Cs)

1. Product. Customer Benefit.
2. Promotion. Communication.
3. Place (distribution). Customer Convenience.
4. Price. Customer Cost.

Marketing management strives to develop the most appropriate combination of marketing mix variables for each product to match the needs of the target market. Marketing mix elements are altered to accommodate the changing market conditions and changing marketing strategies adopted by competing companies.

Product (Customer Benefit)

In the marketing mix, the product or service is the most important element. There is an old saying in marketing: "Without a good product, you have nothing." Product is directly related to satisfying the customer needs and wants in the target market. Customers acquire products for the singular reason that they are perceived as the means to satisfying their needs and wants.

According to Philip Kotler, "A products anything that can be offered to a market for attention, acquisition, use, or consumption that might satisfy a need or want." In effect, according to this definition products include physical products, services, persons, places, organizations and ideas. Various product attributes such as quality, variety, design, brand, packaging, services, and warranties, etc., can be manipulated depending on what the target market wants. This may ultimately affect the product quality that can be kept high or low. Marketers also develop other product aspects such as service, packaging, labelling, instruction manual, warranties, and after sales service. Customers always look for new and improved things, which is why marketers should improve existing products, develop new ones, and discontinue old ones that are no longer needed or wanted by customers.

Promotion (Marketing Communications)

Promotion is a key element of marketing programme and is concerned with effectively and efficiently communicating the decisions of marketing strategy, to favourably influence target customers' perceptions to facilitate exchange between the marketer and the customer that may satisfy the objectives of both customers and the company. In reality, everything that a company does has the potential to communicate something to the target customers. For instance, the price of a product has the potential to communicate to target customers a certain image of the product. For example, a low-priced designer dress is unlikely to attract high-profit, well-heeled target customers, while less affluent buyers may find the designs too avant garde for comfort. The major elements of promotion mix include advertising, personal selling, sales promotion, direct marketing, and publicity. A company's promotion efforts are the only controllable means to create awareness among publics about itself, the products and services it offers, their features, and influence their attitudes favourably. It is critically important for marketing managers to create a strong marketing mix, because any weak element not complementing others can adversely affect the chances of a product's success in the market-place. All the marketing mix elements should complement others to communicate effectively with target market. The best products and high class promotional efforts would not sell it if they products are not available at distribution outlets.

Distribution (Customer Convenience)

Decisions with respect to distribution channel focus on making the product available in adequate quantities at places where customers are normally expected to shop for them to satisfy their needs. The aim of the management is also to keep the physical distribution costs (that would include inventory, transportation, and storage) as low as possible. Depending on the nature of the product, marketing management decides to put into place an exclusive, selective, or intensive network of distribution, while selecting the appropriate dealers or wholesalers. The right choice of these factors can give a company some competitive advantage. For example, a low-priced product consumed regularly on an ongoing basis should be available at as many outlets as possible (intensive distribution) otherwise consumers would buy any other substitutes that are more conveniently available.

On the other hand, for purchasing products such as CTV, washing machine, computer, or other similar durable items, consumers don't mind visiting some selected dealers (selective distribution), and for high-end, very expensive items such as Mercedes Benz cars, expensive and exclusive jewellery status watches and accessories, etc., customers are quite willing to visit exclusive dealerships, even if there are just one or two in the city (exclusive distribution).

Price (Customer Cost)

Pricing decisions are almost always made in consultation with marketing management. Price is the only marketing mix variable that can be altered quickly. Price variable such as dealer price, retail price, discounts, allowances, credit terms, etc., directly influence the development of marketing strategy, as price is a major factor that influences the assessment of value obtained by customers. Price can be kept as high or low, or at any level in between these two extremes. Too high would be the point at which any meaningful sales are not possible because the target customers won't accept the product, and too low would be the point at which company would incur losses instead of profits. Price is said to be an important competitive tool, and intense price competition between rival companies often culminates in a price war and the contestants generally end up gaining nothing. The customers, however, enjoy the benefit of low prices till such time that good sense prevails between contestants and prices are brought back to normal. In case of certain products, price becomes the indicator of product quality and helps impart an image to the product.

THE MARKETING MIX COHERENCY

Refers to how well the different elements of the mix blend together to accomplish the desired impact. For example, to sell an expensive luxury item in discount or bargain stores would show poor coherency between distribution and product offering.

THE MARKETING MIX DYNAMICS

Focuses on how the mix must be adapted to suit the changing business environment, changes in company resources, and the changes in product life cycle stages.

DEFINING AND DELIVERING CUSTOMER VALUE AND SATISFACTION

In developed and developing economies, consumers have several products or brands to choose from to satisfy a given need or a group of needs. Much depends on what consumers' perceptions are about the value that different products or services are expected to deliver. The sources that build customer expectations include experience with products, friends, family members, neighbours, associates, consumer reports, and marketing communications. Customer value is the ratio of perceived benefits and costs that the customer has to incur in acquiring that product or service. The emphasis here is on customers' perceptions and not the accurate, objective evaluation of value and costs, as customers often do not judge values and costs accurately.

Value indicates that a certain product or service is perceived as having the kinds and amounts of benefits (economic, functional, and emotional) that customers expect from that product or service at a certain cost (monetary costs, time costs, psychic, and energy costs). Thus, value is primarily determined by a combination of quality, service, and cost. The value to the customer can be made favourable either by increasing the total benefits at the same cost, maintaining the same benefit level and decreasing the cost, or increasing both the benefits and the costs, but the proportion of benefits is higher than the increase in costs.

Customers generally experience satisfaction when the performance level meets or exceeds the minimum performance expectation levels. Similarly, when the performance level far exceeds the desired performance level, the customer will not only be satisfied but will also most likely be delighted. Therefore, rewarding experience with a given product or service encourages customers to repeat the same behaviour in future (buying the same brand).

A delighted customer is likely to be committed and enthusiastic about a particular brand is usually unlikely to be influenced by a competitor's actions and is an asset to the marketer, being inclined to spread favourable word-of-mouth information or opinions. When a customer's perceived performance level is below expectations, it definitely causes dissatisfaction and the brand (product or service) will probably not be purchased on any future occasion. In extreme cases of dissatisfaction, the customer might even completely abandon the company and bad-mouth its products or services, a process over which a marketer has no control. In the true sense, marketing starts with the customer and ends with customer.

The key to inducing brand loyalty among customers can only be achieved by delivering higher value to delight customers than competitors. Satisfaction is basically a feeling of pleasure, and marketers should be aware of satisfaction delivered by competitors and try surpass that level in an attempt to delight customers. Delivering higher value can lead to delighting customers which, in turn, seems to be the key factor in developing loyalty, more so if the brand generates emotional bonding.

This emotional bonding is not just a preference based on rational content but is largely feeling-based.

VALUE CHAIN

The way to generate high customer loyalty is to deliver high customer value by designing a competitively superior value proposition aimed at a specific market segment backed by a superior value-delivery system. The value proposition consists of the whole cluster of benefits the company promises to deliver and is basically a statement about the resulting experience customers will gain from the company's market offering. The brand must present a promise which can only be kept depending on how the company can manage its value-delivery system. The value-delivery system includes all the experiences the customer will have on the way to obtaining and using the offering. In a hyper-competitive economy, a company's success depends on how it can create and deliver superior value. In order to do so, the company must develop the following five capabilities:

1. Understanding customer value
2. Creating customer value
3. Delivering customer value
4. Capturing customer value
5. Sustaining customer value

In order to succeed, therefore, the company needs to use the concept of value and a

value-delivery network. The value chain is a tool developed by Michael Porter for identifying ways to create more customer value. The value chain considers nine strategically important activities among the various activities of a firm; they create value and cost in a specific business. The primary value activities represent the sequence of bringing materials into the business, converting them into final products, shipping out the final products, marketing them and servicing them, apart from support activities such as procurement, technology development, human resource management and firm infrastructure, that are required for supporting the primary activities.

Primary value activities

- Inbound logistics: material handling and warehousing.
- Operations: transforming inputs into the final product.
- Outbound logistics: order processing and distribution.

- Marketing and sales: communication, pricing and channel management.
- Service: installation, repair and parts supply.

Support Activities

The support activities are handled in certain specialized departments.

- Procurement: procedures and information systems.
- Technology development: improving the product and process or system.
- Human resource management: hiring, training and compensation.
- Firm infrastructure: general management, finance, accounting, government relations and quality management.

BENCHMARKING

The firm examines its costs and performance in each value creating activity and finds out ways of improving it. The firm should estimate the leading competitor's cost and performances and install them as benchmarks against which to compare its own cost and performances. It should also study the 'best of class' practices of the world's best companies, in order to learn from them and improve their own performance. The firm's success depends not only on how well each department performs its work but how well it manages the core business processes. The core business processes include:

- The market sensing process: activities related to market intelligence.
- The new offering realisation process: activities related to developing and launching new high-quality offerings.
- Customer acquisition process: activities related to segmenting, targeting and prospecting of new customers.
- The customer relationship management process: activities related to building deeper understandings and close relationships with individual customers.
- The fulfillment management process: activities related to ordering, shipping and payment collection. To be successful, firms need to look beyond their own operations and create a superior value-delivery network (also called a supply chain) by partnering with specific suppliers and distributors.

DELIVERY NETWORK

The process consists of three parts. The first phase, choosing the value, represents the "homework" marketing must do before any product exists. The marketing staff must segment the market, select the appropriate market target, and develop the offering's value positioning. The formula "Segmentation, Targeting, Positioning (STP)" is the essence of strategic marketing. Once the business unit has chosen the value, the second phase is providing the value. Marketing must determine specific product features, prices, and distribution. The task in the third phase is communicating the value by utilizing the sales force, sales promotion, advertising, and other communication tools to announce and promote the product. Each of these value phases has cost implications.

CONCLUSION

Sales concept seems to be based on a lurking apprehension that customers will not buy the product in sufficient quantities unless aggressively pressurised. The selling concept was the major means of increasing sales and profits during 1920s to 1950s in the developed countries of that period. Companies believed that the most important marketing activities were personal selling, advertising, and distribution. Marketing concept proposes that an organization should focus on customer needs and wants, coordinate its efforts, and endeavour to accomplish organizational goals. The new approaches to marketing such as experiential, permission, and one-to-one marketing can all be seen as means of creating stronger relationships with customers.

Relationship marketing is based on the principle that current customers are the key to long-term business success. Marketing orientation starts with the customer and the company strives to learn customer needs and wants, develops appropriate products or services to satisfy the customer. Marketing mix is a major concept in modern marketing and involves practically everything that a marketing company can use to influence consumer perceptions favourably towards its products or services so that consumer and organizational objectives are attained. Promotion is a key element of marketing programme and is concerned with effectively and efficiently communicating the decisions of marketing strategy, to favourably influence target customers' perceptions to facilitate exchange between the marketer and the customer that may satisfy the objectives of both customers and the company. Pricing decisions are almost always made in consultation with marketing management. Price is the only marketing mix variable that can be altered quickly. Price variable such as dealer price, retail price, discounts, allowances, credit terms, etc., directly influence the development of marketing strategy, as price is a major factor that influences the assessment of value obtained by customers.

The value chain is a tool developed by Michael Porter for identifying ways to create more customer value. The formula "Segmentation, Targeting, Positioning (STP)" is the essence of strategic marketing. Once the business unit has chosen the value, the second phase is providing the value. Marketing must determine specific product features, prices, and distribution. The task in the third phase is communicating the value by utilizing the sales force, sales promotion, advertising, and other communication tools to announce and promote the product.

Note: APAC Customer Service provides customer care service and solutions to the clients in healthcare, business services, communications, publishing, travel and entertainment and financial services industries. The company primarily operates in the US. It is headquartered in Illinois, United States and employs 10,500 people. For detailed information related to this chapter reader can visit www.apaccustomerservices.com

2

Marketing Environment

INTRODUCTION

Marketing environment includes all the forces that directly or indirectly influence marketing operations by affecting an organization acquisition of inputs/creation of outputs such as human, financial and natural resources and raw material, information, goods, services or ideas. Sometimes a distinction is more between macro and micro factors of environment.

ENVIRONMENT ANALYSIS

Environment plays a critical role in business, especially in marketing. The marketing environment is constantly changing and thus presenting new opportunities and threats. A marketer's task is to correctly analyse the environment and design a marketing mix, which will fit the environment. The ultimate purpose of the environmental analysis is to facilitate the firm's strategic response to the environmental changes. The firm can attain its objective with strategic planning in order to encash on environmental opportunities.

THE STRUCTURE OF THE MARKETING ENVIRONMENT

The consumer occupies the core/central position of all business activities and hence occupies the centre of the marketing environment. The organization with its resources and having a policy and structure surrounds the consumer with its particular market offering as do its competitors, suppliers and other intermediaries. This microenvironment of marketing is again affected by the macro environment, which consists of the government, technical, political, social, economic factors.

THE MICRO AND MACRO ENVIRONMENT

There are two types of environmental forces, which influence an organization's marketing activities. Some of these forces are external to the firm and the organization has little control over them. The other type of forces comes from within the organization and can be controlled by it. Hence, the marketing environment can be divided into two major components:

- Macro Environment: consists of demographics and economic conditions, sociocultural factors, political and legal systems, technological developments, etc. These constitute the general environment, which affects the working of all the firms.
- Micro environment: consist of suppliers, consumers, marketing intermediaries, etc. These are specific to the said business or firm and affect its working on short term basis.

ENVIRONMENTAL SCANNING

Environmental scanning - also known as Environmental Monitoring - is the process of gathering information regarding a company's environment, analysing it and forecasting the impact of all predictable environmental changes. Successful marketing depends largely on how a company can synchronise its marketing programmes with its environmental changes.

The major components of environmental scanning are:

- External Environmental analysis
- Customer Analysis
- Competitor analysis
- Market analysis
- Company analysis

MACRO ENVIRONMENTAL ANALYSIS

DEMOGRAPHIC ENVIRONMENT

Factors relating to population, such as size, growth rate, age distribution, religious composition and literacy levels and aspects like composition of workforce, household patterns, regional characteristics, population shifts etc. need to be studied as they are all part of the demographic environment. The points to be considered here are:

- What demographic trends will affect the market size of the industry?
- What demographic trends represent opportunities or threats?

ECONOMIC ENVIRONMENT

Economic environment determines the strength and size of the market. The purchasing power in an economy depends on current income, prices, savings, circulation of money, debt and credit availability. Income distribution pattern determines the marketing possibilities. The important point to consider is to find out the effect of economic prospects and inflation on the operations of the firms.

GOVERNMENT ENVIRONMENT

Business is highly guided and controlled by government policies. Hence the type of government running a country is a powerful influence on business and marketing gets affected.

What changes and regulations are possible and what will be their impact?

- What are the political risks of operating in a governmental jurisdiction?
- What are the incentives the government may offer that might affect business?
- What are the taxes and duties that may be levied and might affect business?

LEGAL ENVIRONMENT

Firms prefer to operate in a country where there is a sound legal system such as in US.

Marketers must have a good working knowledge of the major laws protecting consumers, competitions and organizations. Laws like MRTP, Consumer Protection Act, Intellectual Property Right, FEMA, Labour Laws etc., can considerably affect business operations.

POLITICAL ENVIRONMENT

Political pressure groups influence and limit organizations e.g., the case of Enron in Maharastra and KFC in Karnataka. Special interest groups and political action committees put pressure on business organizations to pay more attention to consumer's rights, minority rights, and women's rights.

CULTURAL ENVIRONMENT

The beliefs, values and norms of a society determine how individuals and organizations relate to each other. The core beliefs of a particular society tend to be persistent, as the American value system of work, charity and honesty. It is difficult for marketers to change these core values, which have a major bearing on marketing operations in as much as they set the stage for marketing activity and consumer response.

TECHNOLOGICAL ENVIRONMENT

The most important factor, which is controlling and changing the human society and even impacting the future, is technology. Technology has literally transformed the way people think, work and relax. Man could realise his dream of putting an astronaut on the lunar surface, the moon, going to the other side of the globe within a few hours, and even exploring the mysteries of the solar system.

With the latest developments in genetic engineering, man is extending the human life span. Technology has changed the way people communicate with the advent of Internet and telecommunication system, and with the revolution in communications have come new ways of doing business. This is opening up new business opportunities while consumers reap the rewards of cutthroat competition among manufacturers. The following factors are to be considered for the technological environment:

- The pull of technological change
- Opportunities arising out of technological innovation
- Risk and uncertainty of technological development
- Role of R&D in a country and government's R&D budget

GLOBAL ENVIRONMENT

The global environment is also rapidly changing. The new concept of global village has changed how individuals and organizations relate to each other. The advent of worldwide terrorism has the power to turn a booming economy into a stagnant one within no time.

The new migratory habits of the workforce as well as increased offshore operation are changing the dynamics of business operation, while in the background, the WTO initiatives have changed the way nations do business with each other, opening up markets and heralding the coming of a new global economic order.

MICRO ENVIRONMENTAL ANALYSIS

This is also known as the task environment and affects business and marketing at the daily operating level. While the changes in the macro environment affect business in the long run, the effect of micro environmental changes are noticed almost immediately. Organizations have to closely analyse and monitor all the elements of microenvironment in order to adapt to rapid change and stay competitive.

CONSUMER

According to Peter Drucker, the aim of business is to create and retain the customer. Hence consumer occupies the central position in the marketing environment. The marketer has to closely monitor and analyse changes in consumer tastes and preferences and cater to (if not try and anticipate) their buying habits.

- What constitutes the consumer value system?
- What benefits is the consumer looking for?
- Who are the consumers?
- What are their buying patterns?

COMPETITORS

Competition shapes business. A study of the competitive scenario is essential for the marketer, particularly threats from competition.

- Who are the competitors?
- What are their present strategies and business objectives?
- Who are the most aggressive and powerful competitors?

COMPANY

Nothing can be as important as self-analysis by the organization itself.

"We have met the enemy, and he is us" - Pogo.

Understanding its own strengths and capabilities in a particular business, that is, understanding a business in depth should be the goal of a firm's internal analysis. The objectives, goals and resource availabilities of a firm occupy a critical position in the microenvironment of marketing. The company with its resources and capabilities surrounds the consumer in the microenvironment.

MARKET

The market is to be studied in terms of its actual and potential size, its growth prospect and also its attractiveness. The marketer should study the trends and development and the key success factors of the market he is operating. Important issues are:

- Cost structure of the market
- The price sensitivity of the market
- Technological structure of the market
- The existing distribution system of the market
- Is the market matured?

SUPPLIERS

Suppliers form an important component of the microenvironment. With their own bargaining power they affect the cost structure of the industry. They constitute a major force, which shapes competition in the industry. Also organizations have to take a major decision on "outsourcing" or "in-house" production depending on this supplier environment.

INTERMEDIARIES

Intermediaries exert a considerable influence in the marketing environment. They can also be considered as the major determining force in the business. In many cases the consumers are not aware of the manufacturer and buy the product from the renowned intermediaries as for example Wal-Mart in US, Pantaloons in India.

PUBLIC

Public constitute a major force in the micro environment and marketers have to very carefully study their opinion, values, beliefs and attitudes in order to design a proper marketing strategy for goods carefully tailored to meet the needs of the target consumer segment. In a sort of reverse engineering, marketers also use the media to shape consumer tastes and preferences.

CUSTOMER ANALYSIS

The important question for a firm is "Who are our customers?"

- Existing
- Potential

Hence, the first logical step in strategic market planning is to analyse the customer, i.e., to understand customer motivation, their unmet needs and how they can be segmented.

It's absolutely essential to the success of your business that you keep your existing customer base intact while you take time to find new customers.

If you appear to ignore your business's customers, they will be more likely to become influenced by the marketing efforts of would-be competitors and switch their loyalties to another business. And as you have experienced, this loss of customers tends to come without warning, and by the time you know they're gone, it's typically too late to do anything about their leaving.

A newsletter allows your business to communicate with customers directly and on a regular basis. As a marketing tool, a properly designed newsletter will contain information that is important to customers--things to which they wouldn't ordinarily become exposed that are nonetheless of more importance than just passing interest. When your customers hear from your business, they're less susceptible to your competitors' marketing efforts. By staying in communication with your customers, you are sending a message to them that they are indeed important to your business. This attention alone can make the difference between a loyal customer who stays with your business and one that feels neglected and ultimately decides to leave.

A newsletter should provide more than just news about your business. Although information such as changes in staff or product lines may be of interest to your customers, a newsletter allows your business to market in an entirely new fashion. Your business's newsletter can be an important marketing tool that not only encourages your existing customers to stay on as customers, but also motivates them to buy more of what they currently buy and/or to consider buying products that they haven't purchased to date. These additional sales (or "plus sales" as they're called) represent a real growth opportunity for your business.

There are many decisions that precede the actual publishing of a business newsletter, including: format of the layout, size and color, frequency of issue, the proper mix of information and sales promotional materials, who will actually receive the newsletter, and the distribution methods(s) to be used to get the newsletter into the hands of the right readers. In the past, newsletters have traditionally been sent via direct mail or as a handout at your place of business. But with the growth of the

Internet, both brick-and-mortar and e-businesses have been turning more frequently to e-mail as a cheaper and faster alternative.

Your goal should be to develop a strong following of customers who enjoy your business's newsletter on a regular basis and who, in return, remain loyal customers. By properly using a newsletter, your business can enjoy a greater degree of retention in its existing customer base, while at the same time encouraging them to buy more. This combination of retention and plus sales can make a significant positive contribution to your business's net growth. You'll lose fewer customers while selling more to those who stay!

Most companies constantly look for ways to expand their pool of profitable customers, with the ultimate goal of optimizing each customer's lifetime value. However, it can be difficult to match compelling offers with the right customers at the right time. Customers consume products and services via multiple channels, and they often have several products and accounts. Disparate customer databases also make it difficult to construct a consistent, consolidated view of each customer. Without a complete view of the customer and an understanding of which customers are profitable and why, it is impossible to determine which types of customers you should acquire and which ones you should seek to retain. The key to improved customer acquisition and retention is gathering and analyzing all your customer data in order to understand customer behavior and develop more effective marketing strategies.

Given the variable costs of service, it is important to concentrate on keeping and rewarding the most profitable and regular customers at the expense of everyone else. Some companies take this a stage further and get rid of their worst customers. This can influence the direction of marketing strategy. Instead of advertising to attract news customers with special offers, companies focus on loyalty programs to retain the small proportion of their customer base that provides the highest percentage of profits.

A customer loyalty program does not just help you hold onto customers, it can also shape the services you offer customers. Using data from loyalty programs, you can offer differentiated products and services based on customer preferences. A simple example would be customer mailings offering different discounts and offers based on individual spending levels.

The starting point for differentiated service is to profile your best customers. Your sales records can provide insight but, if you lack a comprehensive view of your customers, ask them directly for the information you need using surveys and feedback. This can help to make customers feel appreciated and increase their loyalty. Your top customers are likely to buy more frequently, spend more money, cost less per sale, and refer others. This can make an important contribution to profitability. Do not overspend to attract new business for the short term. Gain the attention and make a one-time sale to win new customers but, once they are sold, drive additional sales and build relationship by treating every customer as your best customer. That way you will not have to keep spending 5 to 10 times more to bring new customers in once. A fraction of that investment can keep customers coming back repeatedly.

CUSTOMER SEGMENTATION

- Who are the biggest customers?
- Who are the most profitable customers?
- Who are the potential customers?
- How could we segment the customers into unique strategic business groups?

CUSTOMER MOTIVATION

- What benefit offered by the product/service do customers value most?
- What are the customer's actual buying objectives, i.e., what needs do they want to satisfy?
- What are the customer's motivational priorities?
- What changes are taking place in the customer's taste and preferences?

Customer motivation analysis starts with the task of identifying motivations for a given segment and then to determine the relative importance of the motivations. Ultimately we have to identify the motivations that will play a role in defining the strategy of the business.

PRICE SENSITIVITY OF CUSTOMERS

There is a well-defined breakdown between those customers who are first concerned about price and others who are willing to pay extra for higher quality, better features and superior performance. Automobiles span the spectrum from Maruti to Mercedes. Airline service is partitioned into first class, business class and economy class. In each case, the segment dictates the strategy.

UNMET NEEDS

An unmet need is a customer need that is not being met by the existing product offering. Unmet needs are strategically important because they represent opportunities for firms to increase their market share, break into a market, or create new markets. Sometimes customers may not be aware of their unmet needs because they are so accustomed to the implicit limitation of the existing equipment. Unmet needs that are not obvious may be more difficult to identify, but they can also represent a greater opportunity for an aggressive business because there will be little pressure on the established firms to be responsive. The key is to stretch the technology or apply new technologies in order to expose unmet needs. For example Palm-top computers, blood-less operation, and commercial space travel are some of the examples of once unmet needs that have been met.

COMPETITOR ANALYSIS

"Nothing focuses the mind better than the constant sight of a competitor who wants to wipe you off that map" said Wayne Calloway, former CEO of Pepsi Co.

"Who really are our competitors?"

Is a tour operator is competing with a male outfit supplier? Is a business school competing with an insurance company? May be, the answer is yes, if we consider all of them to be fighting for a share of the consumer's purse.

So, the competitor analysis is the second phase of external analysis, in order to gain insights that will influence the product- market investment decision. The analysis is focused on identifying threats, opportunities or strategic uncertainties created by emerging or potential competitor moves. Competitor analysis starts with identifying current and potential competitors. After competitors are identified, the task is to understand them and their strategies, i.e., to analyse their strengths and weaknesses and strategic groups of competitors.

Who are the Competitors?

- Against whom do we usually compete?
- Who are our most intense competitors?
- Who are the makers of the substitute products?
- Who are the potential competitive entrants?
- What can be done to discourage them?

EVALUATING THE COMPETITORS

- What are their objectives and strategies?
- What are their entry and exit barriers?
- What is their cost structure?
- Do they have cost advantage or disadvantage?
- What are their strengths and weaknesses?
- What are their assets and competencies?

UNDERSTANDING THE COMPETITORS

To gain an understanding of the competitors, it is useful to analyse them on the basis of several dimensions, e.g., their size, growth and profitability, their image and positioning strategy, their level of commitment. It is useful to consider the characteristics of successful and unsuccessful businesses by studying data relating to key customer motivation, large cost components, mobility barriers, and value chain. Information on competitors can be obtained from market research and a variety of other sources such as trade magazines, trade sources, customers and suppliers.

MARKET ANALYSIS

"Imaging the future may be more important than analysing the past. I daresay companies today are not resource-bound, they are imagination-bound", says, C.K. Prahalad, University of Michigan.

Market analysis builds on customer and competitor analysis, its objective being to determine the market response to current and potential participants and also to understand the dynamics of the market.

Market Analysis is generally done on the following dimensions:

- Actual and potential market size: Important sub-markets, their size; the potential market includes the usage gap.
- Market growth rate: The driving forces behind sales, and forecasting of growth rate.
- Market profitability: The intensity of competition depends on five factors: existing competitors, supplier power, customer power, substitute products and potential entrants.
- Cost structure: To analyse the value added by the production stage and observe how it is changing and also the effect of learning curve.

- Distribution system
- Trends and developments
- Key success factors: What skills and competencies are needed to compete now and in the future
- The competitive nature of the market: The nature of competition among existing firms, if there is any potential threat from new entrants or the availability of substitute products, how powerful the customer and supplier groups are.

COMPANY ANALYSIS

The organization's performance in the marketplace is significantly influenced by the following three factors:

- The organization's current market position, how well it has positioned itself
- The nature of environmental opportunities and threats
- The organization's resource capability to capitalize on the opportunities and its ability to guard itself against threats.

Faced with a constantly changing environment, each business unit needs to develop a marketing information system to track trends and developments, which can be categorized as either opportunities or threats. The company has to review its strength and weakness against the backdrop of environmental opportunities and threats, i.e., to perform a SWOT analysis for the organization.

SWOT Analysis (Strengths, Weaknesses, Opportunities, Threats)- What to look for in sizing up a company's strengths, weaknesses, opportunities, and threats, is depicted in the following tables:

Potential Resource Strengths and Competitive Capabilities

A powerful strategy supported by competitively valuable skills and experience in key areas.

A strong financial condition; ample financial resources to grow the business.

Strong brand name, image/company reputation.

A widely recognised market leader and an attractive customer base.

Ability to take advantage of economies of scale and/or learning and experience curve effects.

Proprietary technology/ superior technological skills/ important patents.

Superior intellectual capital relative to key rivals.

Cost advantages

Strong advertising and promotion

Product innovation skills

Proven skills in improving product processes

Sophisticated use of e-commerce technologies and processes

Superior skills in supply chain management

A reputation for good customer service

Better product quality relative to rivals.

Wide geographic coverage and/or strong global distribution capability.

Alliances/joint ventures with other firms that provide access to valuable technology, competencies, and/or attractive geographic markets.

Potential Resource Weaknesses and Competitive Deficiencies

No clear strategic direction; poor quality of leadership

Obsolete facilities

A weak balance sheet, burdened with too much debt

Higher overall unit costs relative to key competitors

Lacking some key skills or competencies/lack of management depth/ a deficiency of intellectual capital relative to leading rivals

Subpar profitability; no cost control measures or cost accounting practices

Plagued with internal operating problems; no organizational studies done, poor structure

Falling behind rivals in putting e-commerce capabilities and strategies in place

Too narrow a product line relative to rivals; inadequate R&D.

Weak brand image or reputation; no efforts to improve quality of products/image

Weaker dealer network than key rivals and/or lack of adequate global distribution capability; weak logistics/communications.

Subpar e-commerce systems and capabilities relative to rivals.

Short on financial resources to fund promising strategic initiatives.

Lots of underutilised plant capacity.

Indifferent quality of supply chain, bought out components

Abnormally high staff turnover; inability to retain key personnel indicates weak HR policies, incentives and stability.

Behind on product quality and/or technological know-how.

Not attracting new customers as rapidly as rivals due to ho-hum product abilities.

Potential Company Opportunities

Serving additional customer groups or expanding into new geographic markets or product segments.

Expanding the company's product line to meet a broader range of customer needs.

Utilizing existing company skills or technological know-how to enter new product lines or new businesses

Using the internet and e-commerce technologies to dramatically cut costs and/or to pursue new sales growth opportunities.

Integrating forward or backward.

Falling trade barriers in attractive foreign markets.

Openings to take market share away from rivals.

Ability to grow rapidly because of sharply rising demand in one or more market segments.

Acquisition of rival firms or companies with attractive technological expertise.

Alliances or joint ventures that expand the firm's market coverage or boost its competitive capability.

Openings to exploit emerging new technologies.

Market openings to extend the company's brand name or reputation to new geographic areas.

Potential External Threats to Company's Well-Being

Likely entry of potent new competitors.

Loss of sales to substitute products.

Mounting competition from new Internet start-up companies pursuing e-commerce strategies.

Increasing intensity of competition among industry rivals . may cause squeeze on profit margins.

Technological changes or product innovations that undermine demand for the firm's product.

Slowdowns in market growth.

Adverse shifts in foreign exchange rates and trade policies of foreign governments.

Costly new regulatory requirements.

Growing bargaining power of customers or suppliers.

A shift in buyer needs and tastes away from the industry's product.

Adverse demographic changes that threaten to curtail demand for the firm's product.

Vulnerability to industry driving forces.

Dwindling sources of basic raw materials/suppliers

It has been criticized that after conducting the SWOT, analysis, managers frequently fail to come to terms with the strategic choices that the outcomes demand. In order to overcome this, Piercy argues for the TOWS Matrix, which, while using the same inputs (Threats, Opportunities, Weakness and Strengths) reorganizes them and integrates them more fully into the strategic planning process.

MODERN COMPLEX MARKETING SYSTEM

Before the industrial revolution, single individual produces - farmers, artisans, family based cottage or small enterprises - dominated the exchange process. They produced goods for nearby customers and secured orders for making ornaments, furniture etc. Further, producers and their customers were generally known to each other because they were all living in the same village or town. Therefore, selling was not a problem for producers.

The situation began to change fast as industrial revolution broke out in the last quarter of the eighteenth century. The invention of steam engine, electricity, telephone etc. propelled further development of human society. Newly built factories came up and they produced goods at cheaper costs in larger quantities. Factory production resulted in the emergence of towns and cities. People who lived in the villages hitherto migrated to towns and their way of living underwent dramatic transformation. They started buying factory made products. Companies and business enterprises came in all shapes and sizes in the last quarter of the nineteenth century. For instance, most of the multinational companies (MNCs) of today were born during the beginning of the 20th century. In India, many companies were founded during the second and third quarters of the twentieth century. For example, Birla group of companies came to exist during 1937-38 and they entered in many businesses after 1947-48. The TATA's ventured into three major Industries - Tata electric companies, Tata Steel companies and Indian Institute of Science - at the beginning of the last century.

Companies were organized as single proprietorships, partnerships, family owned companies and large corporations. They were either owned privately or publicly and were operated for making profits or providing service to the public. At the same time, companies also began to feel that the administration of all phases of a business operation was beyond the capabilities of a few individuals in the company. Therefore, authority was delegated to others and separate departments were created for different functions of a business operation.

The sales department, for example, looked after sales and market expansion. Companies also shifted a portion of their marketing functions to middlemen - retailers, wholesales, agents and brokers came to exist. The marketing activities conducted by the producers' sales department grew in importance as competition increased in the market and the task of sales department became increasingly complex. Marketing research, planning of advertising campaign, personnel selling, sales promotion etc. became inevitable functions of the sales and marketing division of a company. Companies also obtained specialised services from agencies for advertisement planning or marketing research. In this way, marketing research agencies, advertising agencies and media agencies came to exist.

Today, marketing is a complex activity. The single most reason that can be attributed for this complexity is rapid advancements in science and technology. The revolution in telecommunication and computer technology has changed the whole facet of the market exchange process. In order to generate and maintain demand, companies employ novel and sophisticated communication techniques to reach the target customers. In certain sectors, for example in the service sector, there is no face-to-face interaction between the service providers and the customers. The Internet medium has created digital relationships between customers and sellers. Online shopping is gaining momentum in recent times. Shopping complexes, supermarket chains, franchise retail chain outlets are emerging as important institutions in the marketing exchange process. The model of the modern complex marketing system outlines that many institutions participate and facilitate a firm's marketing function. For example, institutions such as advertising agencies, marketing research firms, retailing channels, banking and insurance companies, transport organizations and other innumerable service providers all play vital roles in the marketing efforts of a firm.

In fact, today's marketing manager has to coordinate several jobs before putting his company's products in the target market place. Let us consider a brief discussion on how the above said institutions make up the complex marketing system.

ADVERTISING AGENCIES

No product is sold without advertising backup. Advertising is a powerful tool in the hands of a marketer. In developing the marketing communication strategy of a marketing firm, an advertising agency plays a vital role. Marketing firms which are small and medium in size cannot afford to set up their own advertising departments or divisions. Moreover, advertising is increasingly becoming the job of specialists-copy writing, art-directing, cinematography, film shooting, editing, sound effect, animation, media planning, scheduling etc. Hence, marketing firms use the services of advertising agencies. Even large sized companies such as MNCs, nowadays, use the services of advertising agencies for the advertising campaigns. As a result, advertising has emerged as a major industry and at present, there are more than 430 agencies in India. As an industry, advertising has grown and developed phenomenally since independence. In the 1960's, the number of agencies had shot up to 280 with a total turnover of Rs 35 crores. The 1970's witnessed the birth of Vividh Bharati, a commercial programme on the All India Radio, and, at the turn of the same decade, Doordarshan came to exist. Television became a major medium for commercial advertisements. At the end of 1980, the press medium had a 80 per cent share and Radio and Television had a share of 15 per cent in advertising. The 1990's saw further growth in the advertising industry. Many periodicals and a lot of magazines made their appearance both in English and in many other regional languages. Technology in advertising has brought sophistication in the field of creativity. In order to retain clients, advertising agencies have dedicated service-cum-creative groups which are made available to a marketing firm (client) at call and they fully participate in all aspects of the firm's product- planning, product research, test marketing and advertising campaign planning.

MARKETING RESEARCH FIRMS

Modern business is very complex. Managers require data for decision making on marketing issues or to plan a marketing programme. Like the advertising agencies, marketing research agencies also provide specialised services to marketing firms. Medium and small sized firms utilise the services of marketing research agencies. Large sized firms, like Hindustan Lever, own their research divisions. There are many marketing research agencies in India. Some of the leading ones are given below:

- Operations Research Group (ORG). It was set up in 1960 at Baroda as an in-house research agency and it is the oldest market research agency in India. ORG's retail audit covers 75 consumer products. It has three major divisions- marketing research, public system and social research system - to deal with different research areas.
- Marketing and Research Group (MARG), Kolkata.
- Marketing Research Centre and Advisory Services (MRAS).
- Indian Market Research Bureau (IMRB), Mumbai.

In India, the marketing research industry has a short history and all research agencies have come to exist only in the last four decades. However, they have improved their client services keeping abreast with the changing environment and they serve up to the expectations of client companies. In a changed environment, marketing research has become a part of the marketing function of many companies and marketing research agencies play the role of consultant to many companies in India. The marketing manager of a firm has to decide his marketing programme according to the consultant's advice.

RETAILING

As a result of growing competition, every firm is trying for greater visibility for its products in the market place as well as premier shelf space at the showrooms or point-of-purchase (POP). So, retail management is also becoming a complex task to a marketing manager because retailers are all engaged in marketing their shelf-space. To avoid over dependence on retailers, some producers in the consumer goods market have set up their own retail outlets.

Another significant trend in recent years is that many marketing service agencies have Marketing Environment come up in the areas of financial services, marketing of consumer products etc. For example, Adishwar Marketing, a Bangalore based marketing agency, markets more than 100 consumer products under its own brand 'Worldstar'. The agency has entered into agreements with 45 industries to procure and market products in its own brand name. The agency is, at present, operating in the southern states - Andhra Pradesh, Karnataka, Kerala and Tamil Nadu.

FREIGHT TRANSPORTATION

Moving the products to the consumption point has made marketing a complex system. The marketing manger has to cope with several issues. Generally, freight transportation in India is dependent on roads and railways. In designing the distribution network of a firm, a marketing manager has to understand the commercial transport environment to minimise the cost of transporting the cargo.

DIRECT MARKETING

The development of direct marketing is another important feature of modern marketing. Many companies, particularly MNCs, use mail, telephone, fax, e-mail (Internet) to communicate with their target market directly. Tele shopping, on-line shopping and digital ATM services are all part of the direct marketing system. Marketers solicit a direct response from target customers through telephone or Internet (on-line shopping). Thus, telecommunication tools are used for direct marketing.

PUBLIC RELATIONS CONSULTANCY FIRMS

Independent public relations consultancy firms have come up in recent times. They offer packages for corporate communications. There is an 'International Public Relations Association' headquartered in London. In India, for example, Ritam Communication, (Kolkata), a private PR consulting agency, offers a total package of solutions for corporate communications. Ritam's clients are beverage giant Pepsi, Air India and many other consumer goods manufacturers.

EVENT MANAGEMENT FIRMS

Like any other organization, event management firms are coming up in India. They offer their clients services for organizing corporate events.

A marketing manager must be aware of event management as a tool of corporate publicity. Event management is not like advertising. Cathexis Pivotal, a Bhuvaneshwar based event management firm, differentiates between advertising and event management. In advertising, we do not know what the customers feel about the publicity package and the product at large. But, in event management there is a greater scope for immediate feedback. Generally, a marketing firm organizes corporate events to build up a corporate image and public goodwill. When a marketing manager does not have expertise in organizing a corporate event, he may appoint a free-lancer, temporarily, to organize corporate events. We now understand that marketing is essentially concerned with exchange and trade. Exchange has existed ever since mankind came into existence. The early process of exchange resulted in the setting up of village markets. Later, markets emerged in cities and towns to facilitate trading as a result of industrialisation. The advancement in science and technology, in later days, has manipulated the whole process of exchange and made it a complex system to manage.

CONCLUSION

The ultimate purpose of the environmental analysis is to facilitate the firm's strategic response to the environmental changes. The firm can attain its objective with strategic planning in order to encash on environmental opportunities. There are two types of environmental forces, which influence an organization's marketing activities. Some of these forces are external to the firm and the organization has little control over them. Economic environment determines the strength and size of the market. The purchasing power in an economy depends on current income, prices, savings, circulation of money, debt and credit availability. Income distribution pattern determines the marketing possibilities.

Technology has changed the way people communicate with the advent of Internet and telecommunication system, and with the revolution in communications have come new ways of doing business. Public constitute a major force in the micro environment and marketers have to very carefully study their opinion, values, beliefs and attitudes in order to design a proper marketing strategy for goods carefully tailored to meet the needs of the target consumer segment.

An unmet need is a customer need that is not being met by the existing product offering. Unmet needs are strategically important because they represent opportunities for firms to increase their market share, break into a market, or create new markets. Advertising is a powerful tool in the hands of a marketer. In developing the marketing communication strategy of a marketing firm, an advertising agency plays a vital role. Retail management is also becoming a complex task to a marketing manager because retailers are all engaged in marketing their shelf-space.

Note: EMC develops, delivers and supports a range of information infrastructure technologies and solutions. EMC is an information infrastructure company, providing hardware, software and services for managing and protecting data. The company primarily operates in the US. It is headquartered in Massachusetts, United States and employs 42,100 people. Reader can visit their site www.emc.com For a detailed study of connected to this chapter.

3

Changing Marketing Practices

INTRODUCTION

Marketing starts with customers and ends with customers. Creation of superior customer value and delivering high levels of customer's satisfaction are at the heart of present day marketing. It is a matter of common sense to appreciate the key marketing success factors. Marketing concept proposes that an organization should focus on customer needs and wants, coordinate its efforts, and endeavour to accomplish organizational goals.

CUSTOMER CONCEPT

Today many companies are moving beyond the marketing concept to the customer concept. In the marketing concept companies worked at the level of the customer segment, whereas in the customer concept the companies are shaping separate offers, services and messages specifically targeted at individual customers within the segment. It is this element of customization within the overall marketing strategy that has significantly impacted the way companies react to consumer needs and wants.

RELATIONSHIP MARKETING

Relationship marketing is based on building mutually satisfying long-term relations with profitable customers rather than opting for short-term, 'one-time profitable' transactions. In relationship marketing, the company creates a marketing network, which consists of the company, and it's supporting stakeholders, namely, customers, employees, suppliers, distributors, retailers, ad agencies and others with whom the company has built a mutually profitable business relationship.

CHANGINGBUSINESS ENVIRONMENT

We are operating in a most dynamic business environment today, one that is changing radically as a result of major radical societal forces, such as technological advances, globalization and deregulation, which have created new behaviours and challenges:

- Customers increasingly expect higher quality and service along with some customisation. They are also showing greater awareness and price-sensitivity in their search for value.
- Brand manufacturers are facing intense competition from domestic and foreign brands and rising promotion costs coupled with shrinking profit margins.
- Giant retailers are growing powerful and killing store-based retailers. They are marketing an 'experience' rather than a product assortment.

COMPANY RESPONSES AND ADJUSTMENT

Highly respected companies are adapting to the fresh challenges by:

- Reengineering the business process.
- Outsourcing from more competitive and cost effective sources.
- Attracting customers more effectively through e-commerce
- Benchmarking their activities, performances and cost structure.
- Building global network
- Becoming more market-driven

Marketers are also switching to new concepts such as:

- Customer relationship marketing
- Customer lifetime value
- Customer share
- Target marketing
- Integrated marketing communications

E-BUSINESS-SETTING UP WEBSITES

Websites have become much more creative than being simply online catalogues. Now they promote products and try to create brand images, use sales promotions, and even sell products and services.

The number of websites keeps on increasing everyday. What if a company creates a website that nobody visits. It is like opening a show room that no prospective customer comes to. Another situation can be, those who enter the showroom are not the target customers. They are not the ones who would buy the available merchandise. The number of websites is numerous and unless a company's website is visited by the right customers, it amounts to having wasted the money in creating the website. Search engines cannot keep track of all the available websites.

Visits to websites are deliberate and initiated by the visitors who can be customers, suppliers, or competitors, looking for particular products or information of their interest. In case of mass media marketing communications, such as advertisements, there is no passive exposure. What happens in case of traditional mass media marketing communications such as TV, or radio commercials, or outdoor media, people get exposed to them without really looking for such ads. In case of the Internet, the visitor initiative is very important. The Internet marketers have to make their websites attractive to the right target audience so that, they are motivated to visit their specific websites. Developing and maintaining a website requires considerable effort to attract visitors to the site and encourage them to return again and again requires creativity, effective marketing and regularly updating the site. Depending on the product category and the company's marketing objectives for the Internet, a website can be just a simple source of information about the company and its products or a powerful tool to build brand image, a means to offer samples, or generating sales leads.

In general, the communication objectives may relate to creating awareness, generating customer interest, provide information, help in building a strong brand, a powerful image or stimulate product trial by consumers. To accomplish their objectives, Internet marketers use many approaches, some of which include:

- Banners: A banner ad is a boxed-in promotional message that often appears at Changing Marketing Practices the top of the web page. If a visitor clicks on the banner ad, she/he is transported to the advertiser's home page. This is the most used form of Internet promotion. Banners can be used to create brand recall or recognition. Other names given to banners include side panels, skyscrapers, or verticals. Experienced web visitors ignore banners and many experts believe that their usefulness is very limited and their use seems to be declining.
- Sponsorships: This is another common advertising approach on websites. The advertiser is given a permanent place on

host's website and pays a sponsorship fee to the host. Some sites are targeted at specific segments, such as village is targeted at women. This site has many sponsors who offer special deals and offer advice to target visitors. The use of sponsorship sites is increasing and is more popular than banners.

- Pop-Up and Pop-Under: When a visitor accesses a web page, sometimes a window appears either in front or underneath the web page, the visitor is viewing. Pop-ups become visible as sooner the web site is accessed and pop-under becomes visible only when the visitor closes the browser. Pop-ups are usually larger than a banner but smaller than full screen. Website visitors often get irritated with popups and consider them as intrusion.
- Portal Use: Some portals give a prominent place to a company's offer for a fee. When a visitor follows directed search, the marketer's name appears prominently at or near the top of the list. For example, when anyone uses Yahoo's search engine to locate a toy marketer, the name of K-B Toys is displayed prominently.
- E-mail: Companies send e-mails to Internet users to visit the company web site. It can be effective only when the target customer is appropriate otherwise it becomes "junk mail."
- Interstitials: These ads appear on the computer screen while a visitor is waiting for a site's contents to download. The opinion about the effectiveness of interstitials is divided. Some believe they are irritating and a nuisance than a benefit, but some others believe that the recall rate of interstitials is better than pop-ups.
- Push Technologies: Some companies provide screen savers to its website visitors that allow the firms to directly "hook" the visitor to their websites. This is an approach to "push" a message to the consumers rather than wait for consumers to locate it. These new technologies are known as push technologies or web-casting technologies and open web pages or news updates and may also have video and audio content.
- Sales Promotions: Many companies effectively use sales promotions such as contests and sweepstakes to generate consumer interest.

Increasingly, more and more companies are using many of these promotional methods. However, attracting consumers is only one objective. Internet visitors are believed to be an impatient lot and holding them to the site is a challenge. Internet users in general, are comparatively more educated and from middle and upper income bracket and a larger percentage of young people using Internet live in urban areas. The use is gradually spreading to smaller towns and even some rural areas in India have been provided access. So far, the infrastructure facilities and costs of Internet are a major deterrent in its faster spread. Many companies are gradually spreading their network of broadband Internet services in different parts of our country and the future holds much promise. Use of the Internet to promote products is new and evolving. The businesses still have much to learn about how to attract visitors, keep them glued to the site for sufficient time, and sell to them. With more research input and experience, companies will develop more effective approaches about online marketing efforts.

Many companies initially thought, that web marketing could replace retail stores for customers or sales people in case of business-to-business selling. Over the years, experience has proved that it is very difficult to eliminate the services extended by middlemen. The major areas of concern for online marketers include tackling the problems associated with returned products, payment, and performance complaints. For example, eBay simply brings the buyers and sellers together to facilitate transactions and if a buyer was dissatisfied, the buyer has no place to go. These firms are making efforts to avoid or solve such sticky problems.

Service back up is also a major problem for companies aspiring to move into Internet marketing. Ann Grimes reports that quite a few successful Internet retailers combine online access with physical store and consider it the best formula. Security is also an issue. It seems that a very high percentage of people have never made an online purchase. Many experts believe that security and privacy are major issues and visitors fear that credit card numbers can be stolen because there have been many publicised instances. There also have been serious incidents when hackers have broken into marketers' databases to steal account numbers. The Internet is something impersonal unlike retail stores where consumers interact with store employees face-to-face.

This 'impersonal' characteristic makes consumers hesitant and less agreeable to share personal or credit card information. So far, ensuring complete security and secrecy on the Internet is very difficult for online marketers.

CONCLUSION

The societal marketing concept holds that organization's task is to determine the needs, wants and interests of target markets and to deliver the desired satisfaction more effectively and efficiently than competitors in a way that preserves or enhances the consumer's and society's well-being. Brand manufacturers are facing intense competition from domestic and foreign brands and rising promotion costs coupled with shrinking profit margins. A banner ad is a boxed-in promotional message that often appears at the top of the web page. If a visitor clicks on the banner ad, she/he is transported to the advertiser's home page. This is the most used form of Internet promotion. Companies send e-mails to Internet users to visit the company web site. It can be effective only when the target customer is appropriate otherwise it becomes "junk mail." Security is also an issue. It seems that a very high percentage of people have never made an online purchase. Many experts believe that security and privacy are major issues and visitors fear that credit card numbers can be stolen because there have been many publicised instances.

Note: CIBER is a provider of system integration and information technology (IT) consulting services to enterprise and government agencies. The company operates in around 18 countries including the US, Australia, New Zealand, India and Germany among others. It is headquartered in Colorado, United States and employs 8,300 people. For a very good study of "Changing Marketing Practices" see www.ciber.com

4

Marketing Information System

INTRODUCTION

Marketing Information System (MIS) assesses the information needs of different managers and develops the required information from supplied data in time regarding competition, prices, advertising, sales, distribution and market intelligence etc. Most of today's information systems are computer applications in a sophisticated data-driven age. These enable marketers to be more better informed about their customers, potential customers and competitors. New applications are being developed at a faster pace.

MIS

The term 'Marketing Information Systems' refers to a programme for managing and organizing information gathered by an organization from various internal and external sources. MIS assesses the information needs of different managers and develops the required information from supplied data in time regarding competition, prices, advertising expenditures, sales, distribution and market intelligence, etc. Information sources for MIS include a company's internal records regarding marketing performance in terms of sales, and effectiveness and efficiency of marketing actions, marketing databases, marketing intelligence systems, marketing research, and information supplied by independent information suppliers.

DATABASE

A database refers to the collection of comprehensive information about customers and prospects such as demographic and psychographic profiles, products and services they buy, and purchase volumes, etc., arranged in a manner that is available for easy access and retrieval. Databases allow marketers access to an abundance of information, - often through a computer system - such as sales reports, news articles, company news releases, and economic reports from government and private agencies, etc., that can be useful in making various marketing decisions.

INTERNAL RECORDS

Modern technology is making information required for marketing decisions ever more accessible. It is possible to track customer buying behaviour and better analyse and understand what customers want. The integration of various modern technologies is allowing companies to access valuable information. Ever increasing numbers of market researchers and managers are having access to e-mail, voice mail, teleconferencing, video conferences, and faxes.

Internal database is the most basic starting point in developing a strong MIS. Marketers, not just the growing numbers of large retailers in our country, need information about what is demanded more by customers and what is not. Internal record systems help in tracking what is selling, how fast, in which locations, to which customers, etc. Availability of all such information relies on reports available on orders received from sales people, resellers, and customers, copies of sales invoices, prices, costs, inventories, receivables, payables, etc. Getting inputs and designing systems to provide right data to the right people at the right time is critical for marketing decisions. Accumulated data about customers in various internal records is an important source to build database such as customer inquiries, existing customers and past purchasing histories of these customers. The key information in this regard consists of RFM (Recency, Frequency, and Money) variables. Recency refers to the time of purchase, frequency reflects the number of times the customer made a product purchase from the firm, and money denotes the quantity and monetary value of the purchase. RFM helps analyse and develop a customer index that reflects which customers are more profitable for the business. USP Age, in its September 2004 issue has reported that BPCL has been compiling its database for the past four years and has a formidable collection of more than 1.4 million customers. Shopper's Stop has been compiling data of its regular customers through its loyalty programme, First Citizen. Further, a company in India can obtain a database for as little as 50 paise to Rs. 5 per contact. Companies involved in Direct Marketing such as Catalogue Selling and Mail Order Marketing are heavy users of databases.

EXTERNAL SOURCES

Census Bureau is one key source of information regarding various demographic variables. Besides Census Bureau of India, other sources include Newspapers, Trade Publications, Technical Journals, Magazines, Directories, Balance Sheets of companies, Syndicated and published research reports. Various third party information suppliers offer a variety of information about customers as per marketer's requirements, for a price. For example, Reader's Digest markets a database covering 100 million households. It is one of the best databases to assess potential markets for consumer products. It lets Reader's Digest management know the likes and dislikes of many of its readers. Behaviour Scan is a single source information service that monitors consumer household televisions and records the programmes and commercials watched.

This source is an example that screens about 60,000 households in 26 US markets. Many companies develop their own databases. According to Laurence N. Goal, a single source providing information about household demographics, purchases, television viewer ship behaviour, and responses to promotions is called a single-source data. When consumers from these households go shopping in stores equipped with scanner-installed computers, they present their credit cards to billing clerks for payment. This permits each customer's identification to be electronically coded so that the marketer can track his or her purchases.

Some Important Data Sources

1. The Thomas Register: It is the world's most important industrial buying guide for industrial products. Thomas Register of Indian Manufacturers is available in print, CD, and through Internet. It has 120,000 listings of 40,000 industrial manufacturers and service providers covering 10,000 different product and service categories.
2. The Source Directory: Source Publishers, Mumbai publish this directory. Currently Mumbai and Delhi editions are available. It provides contact information on ad agencies and related services, marketing and sales promotion consultants, market research firms, music companies, telemarketing, and different media.
3. Yellow Pages: Tata Press and GETIT yellow pages are leaders. Currently, yellow pages publications are available for all cities and major towns of India. New Horizons is a joint venture

between Living Media and Singapore Telecom and have been publishing directories for specific businesses.

4. Internet: It is a source of extensive data on almost any subject. Different types of published data, research findings, statistics, and figures are available either free or on payment.

COMPUTER NETWORKS AND INTERNET

Present day computer networks enable marketers to access data sources and customers with immediate information about products and performance. Through such networks, marketers can exchange e-mails with employees, customers, and suppliers. Online information services such as Compu Serve and America Online typically offer their subscribers access to e-mail, discussion groups, files for downloading, chat rooms, and databases and other related research materials. Marketers can subscribe to "mailing lists" that periodically deliver electronic newsletters to their computer screens. This helps increased communication with a marketer's customers, suppliers, and employees and boosts the capabilities of a company's marketing information system. Online information services are available only to subscribers. However, the Internet allows global exchange of e-mails, discussion through newsgroups on almost any subject, downloading of files, chat rooms, etc. A well-maintained database enables a company to analyse customer needs, preferences, and behaviour. It also helps in identifying right target customers for its direct marketing efforts.

DATA MINING AND DATA WAREHOUSING

The term 'data mining' refers to automated data analysis of large amount of data stored in a data warehouse. This is similar to extracting valuable metals from mountains of mined ore. The purpose is to unearth - with the help of modern computing power - meaningful patterns of information that might be missed or remain undiscovered. Data mining creates customer database, which is extremely important for all narrowly defined target-marketing efforts. Data mining also leads to build database on resellers, distribution channels, media, etc. Data warehousing refers to storing subject-based, integrated, nonvolatile, time variant data in support of managerial decisions. It can be viewed as a central collection of clean, consistent, and summarised information gathered from several operational systems. With increasing computing capabilities, organizations are collecting large amounts of a variety of information or data possibly faster than they can use, and for this reason all the collected data or information needs to be sorted, classified and warehoused, so that it can be retrieved when needed in a meaningful manner.

MARKETING INTELLIGENCE SYSTEMS

In the current fast-paced business climate, keeping up with macro-environmental changes, and competition is becoming increasingly difficult. Marketing intelligence system refers to systematic and ethical approach, procedures, and sources that marketing managers use to gather and analyse everyday information about various developments with regard to competitors and other business trends in the marketing environment. This intelligence is collected from various sources such as newspapers, trade publications, business magazines, talking with suppliers, channel members, customers, other managers, and sales force people.

About competitive intelligence, the general idea is that more than 80 per cent information is public knowledge. The most important sources from which to obtain competitive intelligence include competitors' annual and financial reports, speeches by company executives, government documents, trade organizations, online databases, and other popular and business press. The company can take certain steps to obtain quality marketing intelligence. The company should take steps to train and motivate field sales personnel about the types of information to report regularly on any relevant developments in the marketplace. Besides sales force, the company can take steps to motivate channel members to pass along important intelligence. The company can also purchase competitors' products, and attend trade fairs. Some important questions that managers should ask about competitive intelligence are:

- How fast does the competitive climate in our industry change? How important is it to keep our knowledge about these changes current?
- What are the objectives of our company about competitive intelligence?
- Who are the important clients for competitive intelligence? To whom should the intelligence effort be reported?

With rapid developments in the area of software applications that run on PCs, it is becoming increasingly possible to keep track of client lists and the various kinds of contacts that are made with each client. Many such programmes keep track of clients' names, addresses, phone and fax numbers, e-mail addresses, personal details such as birthdays, likes and dislikes, product/brand usage, hobbies, club memberships, etc.

Most of today's information systems are computer applications in a sophisticated data driven age. These enable marketers to be better informed about their customers, potential customers, and competitors. This helps marketers to be more productive and establish and sustain competitive advantage. New applications are being developed at a faster pace. The ultimate focus of most such systems is to enable marketers to know enough about any given customer and the competitive context, to fine-tune their marketing efforts to better serve the target market so that customer's needs are met perfectly. This is the ultimate dream for every marketer.

MARKETING RESEARCH PROCESS

While the Marketing Information System has its focus on managing the flow of relevant information to decision-makers in the marketing department, marketing research is concerned with the function of generating information for marketing decision-makers. There are occasions when there are no easy answers for a variety of marketing situations that marketing managers face. Such situations may call for conducting formal marketing studies of specific problems and opportunities. Marketing research is intended to address carefully defined marketing problems or opportunities.

It helps in identifying consumer needs and market segments, furnishes information necessary for developing new products and formulating marketing strategies, enables managers to measure the effectiveness of marketing programmes and promotional activities, develops economic forecasting, helps in financial planning, and quality control. Research undertaken without precisely defining the problem and objectives usually results in wasting time and money.

For conducting marketing research, companies develop systematic procedures for collecting, recording, and analysing data from secondary and primary sources to help managers in making decisions. Marketing research is different from market research, which is information collected about a particular market or market segment. In the process of marketing research, companies collect a lot of different types of information. David G. Bakken is of the opinion that it is easy to think of all these in terms of three Rs of marketing:

- Recruiting New Customers.
- Retaining Current Customers.
- Regaining Lost Customers.

To recruit new customers, the researchers study different market segments to develop the right products and services consumers need and want. To retain customers, the marketer may conduct customer satisfaction studies. Marketers realise that good relationship with customers is important for long-term positive sales results. Regaining lost customers can be a formidable problem. It needs innovative marketing and outstanding communications. The information collected with respect to the first and the second Rs helps regaining the lost customers.

CONCLUSION

A database refers to the collection of comprehensive information about customers and prospects such as demographic and psychographic profiles, products and services they buy, and purchase volumes, etc., arranged in a manner that is available for easy access and retrieval. Internal database is the most basic starting point in developing a strong MIS. Census Bureau is one key source of information regarding various demographic variables. Internet is a source of extensive data on almost any subject. Different types of published data, research findings, statistics, and figures are available either free or on payment.

Note: The Procter & Gamble Company (P&G) is the world's largest consumer goods company that markets more than 300 brands in over 180 countries. The company is engaged in producing beauty, health, fabric, home, baby, family, and personal care products. The company operates in the Americas, Europe and Asia. It is headquartered in Cincinnati, Ohio, and employed about 138,000 people as of June 2008. For further knowledge regarding this chapter reader can visit www.pg.com

5

Marketing Process

INTRODUCTION

While there is lot of focus on the substance of marketing, particularly the marketing mix, an equally important aspect of marketing is the marketing process - how marketers do their job. The process is equal in importance to the substance because the process determines the nature and quality of the decisions made. A good process is likely to lead to a good decision. On the other hand, a faulty process will produce a good decision only on a random or accidental basis.

The marketing process can be divided in several different ways. One popular conceptualization of marketing tasks is:

1. Strategy formulation - the development of the broadest marketing/business strategies with the longest term impact.
2. Marketing planning - the development of longer-term plans which have generally stronger impact than the short-term programs.
3. Marketing programming, allocating and budgeting - the development of short-term programs which generally focus on integrated approaches for a given product and on the allocation of scarce resources such as sales effort or product development time across various products and functions.
4. Marketing implementation - the actual task of getting the marketing job done.
5. Monitoring and auditing - the review and analysis of programs, plans and strategies to assess their success and to determine what changes must be made.

6. Analysis and research - the deliberate and careful acquisition and examination of qualitative and quantitative data to improve decision making.

Though implied and considered as part of the overall corporate planning, the importance of situation analysis can never be undermined during marketing strategy formulation. Especially under product policies, but throughout the marketing mix elements, the company, customer and competitive scanning is so essential to marketing success. Situation analysis describes the process by which environmental assessment, marketing research and market size/growth estimates get done. It pays particular attention to environment scanning skills useful in forecasting and modelling consumer behaviour. It is important to note that each part of the process is intimately related to the other parts of the process.

FORMULATION OF MARKETING STRATEGY

Strategy formulation is the broadest, longest-term marketing activity. At this stage, complex and subtle integration with other corporate functions is required. All of the functional strategies must fit together into a business strategy. Because marketing deals with customers and the competitive environment, it is an early part of the total strategy formulation process. When done well, it is impossible to separate the marketing strategy from the corporate strategy.

The two meld into a unified whole. The strategic process is one of working with market dynamics (a particular segment or selection of the market) to achieve a solid positioning of the product/service offering that contains a clear 'benefit promise' to the consumer which is differentiable from the offers of the competition and which thus positions the firm well for potential competitive responses to its actions.

MARKETING PLANNING

Marketing planning involves objectives and plans with a 2-5 year time horizon and is thus further from day-to-day activity of implementation. Because of their broader nature and longer-term impact, plans are typically developed by a combination of higher-level line managers and staff specialists. If the specialists take over the process, it loses the commitment and expertise of the line managers who are responsible for carrying out the plan. The planning process is probably more important than the final planning document. The process ensures that a realistic, sensible, consistent document is produced and leads to important organizational learning and development in its own right.

MARKETING PROGRAMMING, ALLOCATING AND BUDGETING

This part of the marketing process involves a good deal of detail and focuses generally on the one-year time horizon. Programs can be related to either one element of the marketing mix such as distribution for one or more products or to all elements of the mix for a single product or market. To some extent, the choice will be determined by the nature of the company's organization. The more functional the organization (i.e. separation of marketing functions such as advertising, sales, etc.), the more likely it is that the programs will focus on one aspect of the mix across all products and markets. On the other hand, companies which organize around products or markets tend to also develop programs for each of them.

Allocating is a necessary function because there is never enough of any scarce resource such as advertising budget or distribution effort to meet the 'needs' of all products, markets and programs. In many ways, marketing is deciding what not to do: which prospects not to sell to, which products not to produce to, etc. Allocation is the formal process of choosing what to do and what not to do, as well as choosing how much to do. Because marketers tend to be optimists, they often underestimate the amount of effort which will be required to accomplish a goal. Allocation requires the stark realism to separate the clearly feasible from the hopeful. It forces the marketer to set explicit priorities and to make hard decisions.

Budgeting reflects the programs and allocations in a set of quantitative forecasts or estimates which are important within and beyond the marketing function. The budgets generally include financial proformas which are used by the control and finance functions to forecast cash flows and needs. They also generally include unit sales forecasts which are used by production scheduling personnel to 'load the factory' or service operation. If the forecasts are too low, customer needs are unmet and sales are lost. If the forecasts are too high, capacity sits idle and costs are much higher than they should have been.

MARKETING IMPLEMENTATION

Strategy formulation, marketing planning, and programming, allocating and budgeting all lead to marketing implementation. This is the execution phase which, in part produces the actual results. Poor implementation can ruin even the best strategies, plans and programs.

The total purpose of all that goes before implementation is to ensure excellent execution.

Implementation means different things to different people in the organization. To the salesperson, it means going through all of the steps of the selling process, while to the sales manager, it might mean reorganizing the whole sales force. Because of the relatively short time frame involved in most implementation activities, monitoring and auditing are generally easier than for the longer-term strategies and plans.

Implementation is very people-oriented. The results of implementation are manifested in people doing things - buying, selling, training, reorganizing, etc. Marketing implementation is unique compared to implementation in most other functional areas because the primary focus of marketing is outside the company. Thus marketing implementation focuses on prospects, customers, distributors, retailers, centres of influence (who are the influencers in a buying decision - they specify but do not purchase). But marketing implementation also includes dealing with other functional areas to gain support and to develop coordination. For example, product managers must implement their plans and programs through product development, production, service and logistics personnel in other functional areas.

Marketing implementation involves a very interesting tension between the structures the firm puts in place to guide marketing efforts and the skills of the managers doing the marketing job. In most firms, what happens is that over time the structures become rigid and dysfunctional to changing marketplace needs, which guides the firm to destinations it does not want to reach! It is only by the timely intervention of the marketers, using their personal skills to 'subvert the organization toward quality' that good marketing actions result.

MONITORING AND AUDITING

One reason to develop plans, programs and budgets is to have a set of goals or standards against which to measure performance. Marketing audits usually include two parts. The first is an assessment of performance against quantitative goals. The second part of a comprehensive audit reviews the processes and other non-quantifiable aspects of the marketing operation. Because marketing is a mixture of art and science, quantitative and qualitative, and because it involves so many interactive variables, it is hard to audit.

Standards are few and comparisons are difficult.

The audit raises a variety of important topics:

1. Who should perform the audit? Can the planners, programmers and executors audit their own performance without bias? If they cannot, who knows enough about the operation to perform the audit? Should outsiders such as consultants be involved and in what capacity?
2. How often should the audit be performed? Should it be on a regular basis or only at certain important points?
3. How comprehensive should the audit be? Should it involve all aspects of marketing or just some?

While auditing normally refers to an activity which is done only on certain occasions, monitoring generally refers to a more day-to-day review activity. It also often refers more to a review of external data than internal activities. It, too, is an important part of the total marketing process because it provides a frequent check of progress against plans and programs.

ANALYSIS AND RESEARCH

All marketing decisions should be based upon careful analysis and research. The analysis and research need not be quantitative, but it should be deliberate and should be matched to the magnitude of the decision being made. While formal analysis and research are important, nothing replaces common sense and good judgment. The marketer's kit has some very powerful analytical tools and the rapid development of decision support systems, mathematics including statistics, and other supporting disciplines such as psychology and sociology insure that the diversity and power of the tools will continue to increase. All of the tools must be applied carefully and intelligently to the decision at hand. It is a fine line, indeed between healthy scepticism and arrogant neglect of useful tools. The right analytical tool well applied can substantially improve marketing decision making.

Activities and Lateral connections have two dimensions, the first is temporal - it shows the natural development from strategy formulation through planning, programming, allocating and budgeting on to implementation. This process is not nearly as 'clean and separated' as the table implies. The activities are interrelated and contemporaneous. The second dimension is the lateral connection to other functional parts of the organization, such as production and operations, finance, control and human resources management. Each step has a company or business counterpart in the right-hand column. The marketing strategy thus becomes part of the total corporate strategy, which includes all functional areas. The marketing plan is often part of a broader corporate business plan. The marketing plan is usually the 'front end' of the corporate plan, because it spells out the operation, human and financial resources needed to support the organization's approach to its markets.

Marketing programs and budgets are usually part of the organization's fundamental operating documents. For example, the sales forecasts in the programs and budgets become the production schedule for the manufacturing function. Those, in turn, become the staffing programs for the human resource function and indicate the working capital needs to be supported by the financial function. If finance cannot support such a high level of inventory and accounts receivable, the sales forecast, production schedule and staffing program must be scaled down. In most organizations, great effort must be devoted to such lateral connections. The coordination needs are very high and the amount of conflict often great. Risk aversion and opportunity sensitivity differ among functions. Varying reward systems sometimes encourage different types of behaviour. The organization must develop formal and informal ways to foster good, open lateral connections.

SCHEMATIC OF MARKETING PROCESS

In general process of marketing strategy development there are five major areas of analysis (5 Cs) underlie marketing decision making - customers, company, competitors, collaborators and context. The questions to raise in each of these areas are:

- Customer needs - What needs do we seek to satisfy?
- Company skills - What special competencies do we possess to meet those needs?
- Competition - Who competes with us in meeting these needs?
- Collaborators - Who should we enlist to help us and how do we motivate them?
- Context - What environmental (say, cultural, technological or legal) factors limit what is possible?

This leads first to specification of a target market and desired positioning and then to the marketing mix (4 Ps). This results in customer acquisition and retention strategies driving the firm's profitability. In this schematic, value creation happens by identifying target segment, establishing a product/service positioning and developing the suitable product, place (distribution) and promotion for the chosen market segment. The pricing decision helps to capture value - for the company and for the customer. Value is sustained by acquiring and retaining the customers at a profit for the firm.

Note: The Black & Decker Corporation (Black & Decker) is a manufacturer and marketer of power tools and accessories, hardware and home improvement products, and technology-based fastening systems. The company primarily operates in the US and Europe. It is headquartered in Towson, Maryland and employs 22,100 people. For a very good case study regarding this topic, reader can visit company's website www.blackanddecker.com

6

Buyer Behaviour

INTRODUCTION

Why do people buy one product and not another? Answering this question is the basic task of every marketer. The answer directly affects every aspect of marketing strategy, from product development to pricing and promotion. Discovering that answer requires an understanding of buyer behaviour, the process by which consumers and business-to-business buyers make purchase decisions. Buyer behaviour is a broad term that covers both individual consumers who buy goods and services for their own use and organizational buyers who purchase business products. A variety of influences affect both individuals buying products for themselves and professional buyers purchasing products for their firms. This lesson focuses predominantly on individual consumer behaviour.

BUYER BEHAVIOUR

Consumer behaviour is the process through which the ultimate buyer makes purchase decisions. Here is a sample of popular definitions for consumer behaviour:

- The study of the buying units and the exchange processes involved in acquiring, consuming, and disposing of goods, services, experiences, and ideas' (Mowen)
- The decision process and physical activity individuals engage in when evaluating, acquiring, using or disposing of goods and services' (Loudon and Della Bitta)
- Reflects the totality of consumers' decisions with respect to the acquisition, usage and disposition of goods, services, time and ideas by (human) decision making units (over time)' (Jacob Jacoby)

The definition by Jacoby can be further illustrated. The totality of consumers' decisions include whether to buy or not, what to buy, why to buy, how to buy, when to buy, where to buy and also how much/ how often/ how long. The idea of consumption not only includes purchasing and using, but also disposing. The marketer's offering can mean many things - be it product, service, time, ideas, people and so on. The term decision making units obviously refers to people involved. In a typical purchase, many people may be involved and they play different roles such as information gatherer, influencer, decider, purchaser and user. In a consumer buying context, it may mean a family or group influence where as in the industrial buying context, it means a cross-functional team with each member of the team performing a particular role in the buying decision. The word 'time' could mean different units of time like hours, days, weeks, months and years.

MODELS OF CONSUMER/BUYER BEHAVIOUR

Consumer behaviour is a dynamic, multi-disciplinary process. The study of consumer behaviour builds upon an understanding of human behaviour in general. In an effort to understand why and how consumers make buying decisions, marketers borrow extensively from the sciences of psychology and sociology. The work of psychologist Kurt Lewin provides a useful classification scheme for influences on buying behaviour. Lewin's proposition is B = f(P,E) which means that behaviour (B) is a function (f) of the interactions of personal influences (P) and pressures exerted by outside environmental forces (E). This statement is rewritten to apply to consumer behaviour as B = f(I,P) (i.e.) consumer behaviour (B) is a function (f) of the interactions of interpersonal influences (I) such as culture, role models, friends and family - and personal factors (P) such as attitudes, learning and perception. Therefore inputs from others and an individual's psychological makeup both affect a consumer's purchasing behaviour. This model is further explained in the following sections of this lesson. There are many other models of consumer behaviour. The most generic model of consumer behaviour suggests a stimulus-response pattern of understanding the consumer's behaviour. The stimulus can be marketing stimuli (which can be manipulated by the marketer) and other external stimuli (like the economy, culture, technology and so on). The response includes the decision to buy, product choice, dealer choice and choices regarding time, quantity, etc. The consumer is at the centre of this model. The stimulus is applied to this consumer who in turn comes up with a response. The consumer has his/her own characteristics and a multi-staged decision-making process. There are also several influencing factors acting upon the consumer. The influencing factors may include personal and interpersonal influences.

DETERMINANTS OF CONSUMER BEHAVIOUR

Consumers don't make purchase decisions in a vacuum; rather, they respond to a number of external, interpersonal influences and internal, personal factors. Consumer often decide to buy goods and services based on what they believe others expect of them. They may want to project positive images to peers or satisfy the unspoken desires of family members. Marketers recognize three broad categories of interpersonal influences on consumer behaviour: cultural influences, group influences and family influences.

- Cultural influences: Culture can be defined as the values, beliefs, preferences and tastes handed down from one generation to the next. Culture is the broadest environmental determinant of consumer behaviour. Therefore, marketers need to understand its role in customer decision making. They must also monitor trends to spot changes in cultural values. Marketing strategies and business practices that work in one country may be offensive or ineffective elsewhere because of cultural variations. Hence cultural differences are particularly important and complex to understand for international marketers. Cultures are not homogeneous entities with universal values. Each culture includes numerous subcultures - groups with their own distinct modes of behaviour.
- Group (Social) influences: Every consumer belongs to a number of social groups. Group membership influences an individual's purchase decisions and behaviour in both overt and subtle ways. The influences may be informational and/or normative. Every group establishes certain norms of behaviour. Group members are expected to comply with these norms. Difference in group status and roles can also affect buying behaviour. The surprising impact of groups and group norms on individual behaviour has been called the Asch phenomenon because it was first documented by psychologist S.E.Asch. Discussions of the Asch phenomenon raises the subject of reference groups - groups whose value structures and standards influence a person's behaviour. Consumers usually try to coordinate their purchase behaviour with their perceptions of the values of their reference groups. Children are especially vulnerable to the

influence of reference groups. They often base their buying decisions on outside forces - what is popular with their friends, what is fashionable and trendy, what is popular, what are their heroes and role models (usually, celebrities) using. In nearly every reference group, a few members act as opinion leaders. They are the trendsetters who are likely to purchase new products before others in the group and they share their experiences and opinions via word of mouth. Other members' purchase decisions are affected by the reports of the opinion leaders. Closely related to reference groups is the concept of social class. A social class is an identifiable group of individuals who tend to share similar values and behaviour patterns different from those of other classes. These values and behaviour patterns affect the purchase decisions.

- Family influences: The family group is perhaps the most important determinant of consumer behaviour because of the close, continuing interactions among family members. Like other groups, each family typically has norms of expected behaviour and different roles and status relationships for its members. The traditional family structure consists of a husband and wife. Although these and other members can play a variety of roles in household decision making, marketers have created four categories to describe the role of each spouse: (1) Autonomic, in which the partners independently make equal numbers of decisions (e.g. personal-care items) (2) Husband-dominant, in which the husband makes most of the decisions (e.g. insurance) (3) Wife-dominant, in which the wife makes most of the decisions (e.g. children's clothing) and (4) Syncratic in which both partners jointly make most decisions (e.g. vacation).
- Consumer behaviour is affected by many internal, personal factors, as well as interpersonal ones. Each individual brings unique needs, motives, perceptions, attitudes, learning and self-concepts to buying decisions.
- Needs and motives: Individual purchase behaviour is driven by the motivation to fill a need. A need is an imbalance between the consumer's actual and desired states. Someone who recognizes or feels a significant or urgent need then seeks to correct the imbalance. Marketers attempt to arouse this sense of urgency by making a need 'felt' and then influence

consumers' motivation to satisfy their needs by purchasing specific products. Motives are inner states that direct a person toward the goal of satisfying a felt need. The individual takes action to reduce the state of tension and return to a condition of equilibrium.

- Perceptions: Perception is the meaning that a person attributes to incoming stimuli gathered through the five senses - sight, hearing, touch, taste and smell. Certainly a buyer's behaviour is influenced by his or her perceptions of a good or service.
- Attitudes: Perception of incoming stimuli is greatly affected by attitudes. In fact, the decision to purchase a product is strongly based on currently held attitudes about the product brand, store or salesperson. Attitudes are a person's enduring favourable or unfavourable evaluations, emotional feelings or action tendencies toward some object. Because favourable attitudes likely affect brand preferences, marketers are interested in determining consumer attitudes toward their products.
- Learning: In a marketing context, refers to immediate or expected changes in consumer behaviour as a result of experience (that of self or others'). Consumer learning is the process by which individuals acquire the purchase and consumption knowledge and experience that they apply to future related behaviour. Marketers are interested in understanding how consumers learn so that they can influence consumers' learning and subsequently, their buying behaviour.
- Self-concept: The consumer's self-concept - a person's multifaceted picture of himself or herself - plays an important role in consumer behaviour. The concept of self emerges from an interaction of many of the influences - both personal and interpersonal - that affect buying behaviour.

THE CONSUMER DECISION PROCESS

Consumers complete a step-by-step process to make purchasing decisions. The length of time and the amount of effort they devote to a particular purchasing decision depends on the importance of the desired good or service to the consumer. Purchases with high levels of potential social or economic consequences are said to be high-involvement purchase decisions. Routine purchases that pose little risk to the consumer are low-involvement decisions. Consumer generally invest more time and effort to purchase decisions for high-involvement products than to those for low-involvement products. For example, a car buyer will probably compare prices, spend time visiting dealer showrooms, read auto reviews and ask for advice from friends before making the final decision.

Few buyers invest that much effort in choosing between two brands of candies. They will still go through the steps of the consumer decision process but on a more compressed scale. Purchase decisions can be thought-based (cognitive) or feeling-based (emotive). While it is true that both cognition and emotion will be present in every purchase decision, either one of them will dominate the decision. As a result, we can construct a grid as follows to analyze different consumer purchase decisions.

Classification of Consumer Purchase Decisions

	Thought Based	**Feeling Based**
High Effort	Example: Investment Decisions	Example: Jewellery
Low Effort	Example: Home maintenance products	Example: Snacks

First, the consumer recognizes a problem or an unmet need. Then he/she searches for goods or services that will fill that need and evaluates the alternatives before making a purchase decision (and the actual purchase). After completing the purchase, the consumer evaluates whether he/she has made the right choice. Much of marketing involves steering the consumers through the decision process in the direction of a specific item. Consumers apply the decision process in solving problems and taking advantage of opportunities. Such decisions permit them to correct differences between their actual and desired states. Feedback from each decision serves as additional learning experience to help guide subsequent decisions.

During the first stage in the consumer decision making process, the consumer becomes aware of the discrepancy between the actual state ('where we are now' and the ideal state ('where we want to be'). Problem recognition motivates the individual to achieve the desired state of affairs. A marketer can stimulate problem recognition either by creating a new ideal state or by creating dissatisfaction with the actual state. In the second stage, the consumer gathers information related to his/her attainment of a desired state of affairs. This search identifies alternative means of problem solution. High-involvement purchases may elicit extensive information searches, while low-involvement purchases require little search activity. The search may cover internal or external sources.

MARKETING CHANNELS

One of the major purposes of marketing is to satisfy the human needs and wants by delivering products to buyers when and where they want them at a reasonable cost. One of the key aspects we find in this process is delivery. Over the past two decades, economic clout has shifted from the producers of goods to distributors of goods. The shift in economic power has been significant in the retail level of marketing channels, where mass merchandisers like Wal-Mart, Big Bazaar have become dominant players. As a strategic marketing tool, the distribution channels had for many years taken something of a backseat to the other three strategic areas of the marketing mix namely the product, price and promotion. Today there has been a shift in the emphasis and this has been credited to four developments, viz.

- Explosion of information technology and e-commerce.
- Greater difficulty of gaining a sustainable competitive advantage.
- Growing power of distributors especially retailers.
- The need to reduce distribution costs.

DEFINING DISTRIBUTION CHANNELS

Different people perceive marketing channels in different ways, some see it as a route

taken by a product as it moves from the producer to the consumer, and others describe it as a loose coalition of business firms that have come together for purpose of business. Customers may view marketing channels as simply 'a lot of middlemen' standing between the producer and the product. Given all these different perspectives it is not possible to have one single definition for marketing channels. Marketing channels can be defined as the external contractual organization that management operates to achieve its distribution objectives.

There are four terms in this definition that has to be given a special mention namely external, contractual organization, operates and distribution objectives. The term external means that the marketing channel exists outside the firm. Managing of the marketing channel therefore involves the use of interorganizational management (managing more than one firm) rather than intraorganizational management (managing one firm). The term contractual organization refers to those firms who are involved in the negotiatory function as the product moves from the producer to the end user. The function of these firms involves buying, selling and transferring of goods and services. Transportation companies, public warehouses, banks ad agencies do not come under these and are referred to as facilitating agencies. The third term operates suggests the involvement of management in the channels and this may range from the initial development of the channel structure to the day-to-day management. Finally the distribution objectives explain the distribution goals the organization has in mind. When the objectives change, variations can be seen in the external contactual organizations and the way in which the management operates. In simpler terms a channel then consists of producer, consumer and any intermediary.

Marketing channel strategy is one of the major strategic areas of marketing. In most cases eliminating middlemen will not reduce prices, because the amount that goes to the intermediaries compensates them for the performance of tasks that must be accomplished regardless of whether or not an intermediary is present. In simple terms, a company can eliminate intermediaries but cannot eliminate the functions they perform.

FLOWS IN MARKETING CHANNELS

As discussed a conventional channel of distribution consist of a manufacturer, a wholesaler. a retailer and the ultimate consumer. Not all the channels include all these marketing institutions. At times the product passes directly from the manufacturer to consumer. When a marketing channel has been developed a series of flows emerge. These flows provide the links that tie channel members and other agencies together in the distribution of goods and services. There are five most important flows namely

- Product flow
- Negotiation flow
- Ownership flow
- Information flow
- Promotion flow

FLOWS IN THE MARKETING CHANNEL

The Product flow refers to actual physical movement of the product from the manufacturers through all the parties who take physical possessions of the product from the point of production to the final consumer. In the negotiation flow, this represents the interplay of the buying and the selling functions associated with the transfer of title. If you note the diagram you find the transportation firm is not included in the flow because it does not participate in the negotiation function, also you can find the arrows flow in both the directions, indicating the negotiation is mutual at all levels of the channels. The ownership flow shows the movement of the title to the product as it is passed along from the manufacturer to the consumer, here as well we find the transportation function missing since the transportation firm does not take title or is actively involved in the facilitating function. It merely involves in transporting physical products.

In case of the Information flow, we can see that the transportation function has reappeared and all the arrows are two-directional. All the parties participate in the exchange of information. For example Coke may obtain information from the transportation company about its shipping schedules and the rates, while the transportation firm may seek information regarding when and in what quantities it plans to ship its products. Some times the information bypasses the transportation company directly to the wholesaler or the retailer when the information does not concern the transportation firm. If there is an offer, or a price reduction these information are not needed by the transportation firms.

Finally the Promotion flow refers to the persuasive communication in the form of advertising, personal selling, publicity. There is a new component that is added to the flow and that is the advertising agency and this actively provides and maintains the information flow. The organizations work closely with the promotional organizations so we find a two-directional arrow.

From the management view, the concept of channel flows provides a useful framework for understanding the scope and complexity of channel management. Changing scenario does make the role of the firms' complex, as a result of which innovative channel strategies and effective channel management are needed to make this happen.

FUNCTIONS OF DISTRIBUTION CHANNELS

Some of the major functions performed by the intermediaries are mainly physical

distribution, communication and facilitating functions. When we talk about physical functions, they include braking bulk, accumulating bulk, creating assortments, reducing transactions and transporting and storing.

Breaking bulk: One of the important role intermediaries perform is bulk-breaking function. Here these organizations buy in large quantities and break them into smaller quantities and pass them to the retailers, wholesalers or even to the customers. By doing so, the intermediaries reduce the cost of distribution for the manufacturers as well as the consumers. This particular function is also termed as 'resolution of economic discrepancies'.

Accumulating Bulk: At times the intermediaries also do the task of accumulating the bulk. The intermediaries may buy bulk from different small producers accumulate them and offer to those buyers who prefer large quantities. The intermediaries in accumulating the bulk are mostly found in the agricultural businesses, whereby the intermediary will procure vegetables from local farmers and assemble them and sell it to the wholesalers. Once the marketers accumulate bulk they start to sort the products identifying differences in the quality, grades and classify them into different categories.

Creating Assortments: The third important function of the intermediaries is creating assortment. When we take the case of magazines, on an average there are around thousands of magazines being published in a month and it is impossible for a particular newsstand to get it going, here big distributors and agents work in creating assortments and enable a speedy process. This needs a lot of teamwork and timing. Certain magazines become outdated within certain period of time.

Reducing Transactions: One of the biggest reasons that keep the economy moving and the customer smiling is the presence of intermediaries, they reduce the number of transactions necessary to accomplish the exchange of goods.

Transporting and Storing: Apart from breaking, accumulating, creating assortments and reducing transactions they also perform two key marketing functions namely transporting and storing. The final product has to be moved from the point of production to the point of consumption. This means it involves storing the product along the way till it is delivered. Most of the big retailers hold enough of the product in order to cater to the consumers

Credit Services: Apart from the function of physical distribution the intermediaries also help in offering credit services. Even though there are firms like Metro, which are predominantly cash and carry kind of intermediaries, most of the intermediaries provide credit facility or even paying in parts. Many intermediaries offer about 30 to 45 days to the retailers for paying back.

Risk Taking: one of the vital functions of the intermediaries is risk taking. Not every product finds favor in the eyes of the customer, much fallout within few months, as a result of which the intermediaries would be at risk. An uncontrollable factor like floods, earthquakes or even contamination or fire could pose a serious threat. The intermediaries have to bear these risks along with the market risks. These are some of the core functions intermediaries perform enabling goods and services to reach consumers at the right time.

CHANNEL STRUCTURE

Channel structure is distinguished on the basis of the number of intermediaries. There are different levels in a channel structure. The common levels are zero-level, one-level, two-level, three-level. Each level presents both opportunities and challenges for the marketer.

Zero-level structure is one of the simplest forms of the channel structure. Here organizations like Avon, Eureka Forbes use direct selling mode to take the products from their production houses to the consumers directly. A lot of money has to be spent in order to make this channel structure effective, as there is no third party to take your product to the consumer. Even a bakery can come as a firm, which bakes cakes and sells it directly to the consumers. Marketers who use the mailing services, toll-free numbers are also using this service.

One-level structure is one in which we have one intermediary acting as a link between the manufacturer and the consumer. Here the retailers procure goods directly from the manufacturer and supply it to the consumers. Retailers like Viveks, Wal-Mart deal directly with the manufacturer. In some cases in order to retain profitable and reputed retailers the manufacturers act as wholesalers. One of the advantages for the intermediaries is the customization and the discounts they receive.

Two-level channel has two people interceding before the product reaches the consumer. Here there would be a wholesaler and a retailer who takes the efforts for a speedy delivery and this is one of the most commonly used structures for consumer goods. In the case of Metro, most of the small retail and Kirana stores buy all the merchandise from Metro and in urn sell them to the consumer. One of the advantages of the four-level structure is the benefit of using the wholesaler in the distribution of services. Three-level channel happens predominantly when the firms plans to go global. When a manufacturer enters another country, it always holds good when he uses the help of agents to operate in that environment.

The agents are people who know the legal procedures and who can negotiate with the host country in case of a problem. Most of the airline firms that operate in different countries take the help of agents to penetrate the market.

When it comes for Business-to-Business operations, the channels differ from the consumer markets, in this structure, firms predominantly may use their existing sales force to sell the products to the customers, they may even use industrial distributors to take their products to the industrial customers.

Mark Andy is one of the big names in the printing machines industry. In India Mark Andy supplies its printing machines to the industrial customers through Heidelberg, an industrial distributor. It also has its own representatives who pitch in when the customer needs information. In case of Industrial Channel, the zero-level, one-level and two-level are the most commonly used method. When it comes for Business-to-Business channels agents become the integral point of the whole process, since the characteristic of the business-to-business market is oligopolistic and are huge buyers. In this digital economy, a shift has started in the channels on either side of the markets i.e. in both the consumer marketing channels and the business-to-business market channels. The web has created a platform whereby organizations can now directly communicate with the customers, as a result of which many of the channels are being disintermediated. This disintermediation does not necessarily mean that they completely eliminate the intermediaries, but rather when it comes to shipping the products it may outsource some of the distribution functions like the storage, transportation from third party firms.

DESIGNING DISTRIBUTION CHANNELS

Channel design refers to those decisions that involve in the development of new marketing channels or modifying the existent ones. The channel design decision can be broken down into six steps namely:

- Recognizing the need for channel design decision
- Setting and coordinating distribution objectives
- Specify the distribution tasks
- Develop alternative channel structures
- Evaluate relevant variables
- Choose the best channel structure

Recognizing the need for a channel design decision

First and foremost task for the organization is to recognize the need for a channel design.

An organization would go in for a new channel design for the following reasons namely

- When a new product or product line is developed, mainly when the existing channels are not suitable for the new line
- When the existing product is targeted to a different target market. This is common when an organization is used to catering the B2B, plans to enter the consumer market
- When there is a change in the marketing mix elements, when an organization reduces its prices on certain offering the channel worked out will be based on the price points, they may look in for discounters
- When facing major environmental changes namely in economic or technological or in legal spheres.
- Finally when the organization opens up new geographic marketing areas.

The list by no means is comprehensive, but gives a picture about some of the most common conditions when channel design decisions are worked out.

Setting and Coordinating Distribution Objectives

Once a need for a design is recognized the next task for the channel manager is to work out to develop the channel structure, either form the scratch or by modifying the existing one. It is necessary for the channel manager to carefully evaluate the firm's distribution objectives. In order for the distribution objectives to be effective and well coordinated the channel manager need to perform three tasks namely.

- Become familiar with the objectives and strategies in other marketing mix areas and other relevant objectives and strategies of the firm. In most cases the person or the group that sets the objectives of the other marketing mix elements will also set the objectives for distribution as well.
- Set the objectives and state them explicitly. A good objective is one, which is clear, and explicit, and has a greater role in achieving the firm's overall objectives. Some examples of a

good distribution objectives are as follows, at the start of the new millennium, Apple Computers set a distribution objective to reach more consumers with what it refers to as the 'Apple experience'. So, Apple reinvigorated and re-established relationships with large retail chains, which it had neglected in recent years. In the same way Coca-Cola seeks to broaden its penetration in schools and college markets, as a result of which it has entered into contact with many schools and colleges, whereby these institutions would sell only Coca-Cola products on their campuses.

- Check and see if the distribution objectives set are congruent with marketing and other general objectives and strategies of the firm. This involves verifying if the distribution objectives do not conflict with the objectives in the other areas of marketing mix or even to the overall objectives of the company. In order to cross check, it is essential to examine the interrelationships and hierarchy of the objectives of the firms.

Specifying the Distribution Tasks

Once the objectives are formulated, a number of functions need to be performed in order for the distribution objectives to be met. The manager therefore has to specify the nature of the tasks that needs to be carried out in order to meet the objectives. The tasks need to be precisely stated so that it meets the specified distribution objectives. For e.g. a manufacturer of a consumer product, say a high quality cricket bats aimed at serious amateur cricket players would need to specify distribution tasks such as gathering info on target markets shopping patterns, promote product availability to the target, maintain inventory, and timely availability, compile info about the product features, provide hands on experience using the product, process and fill customers orders, transport the product, arrange for credit provisions, provide warranty, provide repair and service, establish product return to make the offering readily available. Sometimes these functions may appear to be production oriented rather than distribution tasks, but when we talking about meeting customers, they are indeed distribution tasks.

Developing Possible Alternative Channel Structures

Once the tasks have been specified by the channel manager he should find out alternate ways of allocating these tasks. In most cases the channel manager chooses from more than one channel to reach the consumer effectively. Britannia would sell their biscuits thorough wholesale food distributor, departmental stores, convenience stores and even in pharmacies. Whatever may be the channel structure, the allocation alternatives should be in terms of (a) the number of levels in the channel (b) the intensity at various levels, and (c) the types of intermediaries.

The number of levels can be from two level upto five levels. The channel manager can think of going for a direct way of meeting the customers to using two intermediaries as an appropriate way. Intensity refers to the number of intermediaries at each level. Generally the intensities can be classified into three categories namely intensive, selective and exclusive. Intensive saturation means as many outlets as possible are used at each level of the channel. Selective means that not all possible intermediaries at a particular level are used. Exclusive refers to a very selective pattern of distribution. A firm like Parle may use intensive distribution channel structure, while Rolex may use high degree of selectivity. The types of intermediaries, third component has to be carefully dealt. The firms should not overlook new types of intermediaries that have emerged in recent years particularly the auction firms such as baazee, bid or buy as possible sales outlet for their products.

Evaluating the variables affecting Channel structure

Once the alternative structures have been outlined, each channel structure has to be evaluated on a number of variables. There are five basic categories namely, Market variables - marketing management is based on the philosophy of marketing concept, which stresses on the consumers needs and wants, the managers have to take the cues from the market. The subcategories that have a greater influence on the market structure are market geography, market size, market density and market behaviour

Product Variables - some of the most important product variables are bulk and weight, Perishability, unit value, degree of standardization, technical vs. non-technical and newness. Heavy and bulky products have a high handling and shipping costs relative to their value. The manufactures of such products have to keep in mind to ship in large lots to a fewer possible points. It would always be better if the channel structure remains short. Food products, flowers are considered to be highly perishable. When products are highly perishable, the channel structure should be designed to provide rapid delivery from producers to consumers. One important consideration is lower the unit value of a product, the longer the channels should be as low unit value leaves small margins for distribution costs. If the product flows directly from manufacturer or producer to the user the degree of customization is more, but as the product becomes more standardized it passes through many channels. Mostly the B2B machinery has a great degree of customization as it passes from the manufacturer to the industrial user, while many consumer market is predominantly a standardized one. When it comes for the technical component, the industrial products are mostly distributed through direct channels because of the technical expertise and service while many technical consumer products do use shorter channel structure. When the product is new and is in the introductory stage in order to capitalize on the aggressive promotion, a shorter channel is preferred to gain awareness.

Company Variables- the important variables that affect a good channel design are size, financial capacity, managerial expertise and objectives and strategies. Larger the firms in terms of size it enables them to exercise a substantial amount of power in the channel. The size does give flexibility for the firm in picking the channel structures. The same hold true when it comes for the financial capability. Greater capital available with a firm, less dependency is seen on the intermediaries. When a firm is into industrial marketing, it prefers to have its own sales force, warehousing, order processing capabilities and larger firms with good financial backing are better able to bear the high cost of these facilities. When a firm lacks quality managerial skills, a comprehensive channel structure ranging from wholesalers to brokers are needed to perform the distribution activity, once the firm gains experience it can change or reduce the number of intermediaries. The objectives and strategies a firm has may limit the use of intermediaries. These strategies may emphasis on aggressive promotion and may even alter the distribution tasks. Overall this is one of the prime variables used for evaluating.

,Intermediary Variables- the important intermediary variables are availability, costs and services offered. The availability is one of the key variables as this influences the channel structure. If we take the case of Dell Computers, due to lack of a proper channel structure he designed a direct mail order channel, which provided a strong technical backup as well. The cost is another variable a channel manager considers. If the cost of using a particular intermediary is too high compared the services it offers the manager may consider in minimizing the use of intermediaries. The services performed by the intermediaries is another integral component, a good intermediary is one, which offers efficient services at the lowest cost.

Environmental Variables- the uncontrollable or the macro environmental forces may affect the different aspects of channel development and management. Forces like the Sociocultural, economic, technological, legal forces have a significant impact on the channel structure. The other variables are those the organization can work upon or change to the situation but the environmental forces are those the organization has to cope up with.

Choosing the 'Best' Channel structure

In deciding the manager should choose an optimal channel structure that would offer desired level of effectiveness at the lowest possible cost. Even though there is not one set method to pick an optimal channel structure, it all depends on the orientation of the firm. If the goal of the firm were profit maximization, the channel structure would be in line with the goal. Most channel choices are still however made on the basis of managerial judgment and the data that is available.

MANAGING CHANNEL MEMBERS AND THEIR CONFLICTS

After a particular channel is selected, the marketer must manage or administer the channel members or intermediaries. Managing channel members include

- selecting intermediaries
- motivating channel members or middlemen
- controlling or managing channel conflicts, and
- evaluating performance of channel members

Selecting intermediaries: Selection of intermediaries or middlemen is a continuous process because some of them leave the channel or get terminated by the marketer. Hence it is not part of channel design. It is necessary for the marketer to determine criteria or factors for selection of intermediaries. These criteria differ depending on the type of middlemen and the firm's particular product/market conditions. Some of the common factors considered are financial standing, location, prior experience and type of customers served.

Motivating middlemen: The marketer must continuously motivate his intermediaries to achieve long-term success. Motivating the intermediaries to achieve top performance should start with understanding the middlemen's needs, perceptions and outlook. The quality of support from middlemen will depend on the motivational techniques used and incentives offered.

Controlling channel conflicts: Even though a manufacturer's channel design is well done, there will be some conflict because of the differences in the objectives and perceptions of the channel members. The conflicts or tensions between the channel members can damage channel performance. Marketers should periodically undertake surveys of intermediaries or conduct formal/informal discussions with them to assess the areas or sources of conflicts.

SOURCES OF CHANNEL CONFLICTS

The channel conflicts can be controlled or managed in several ways, including:

- Effective communication network
- Joint goal-setting
- Diplomacy
- Mediation
- Arbitration and
- Developing a vertical marketing system.

An effective communication network between the manufacturer and the intermediaries can be developed through periodic formal and informal meetings and cooptation of intermediaries in board of directors or advisory committees. In joint-goal setting, the channel members come to an agreement on the super-ordinate (or fundamental) goals they jointly seek. Such goals can be market share leadership, customer satisfaction or product/service quality in a highly competitive market where survival and success of channel members depend on their performance and cooperation. The channel members may resort to diplomacy, mediation or arbitration, when conflicts are sharp. Diplomacy is used when the conflict is resolved through discussions between the persons from both the parties. In mediation a neutral third party tries to conciliate the interests of the two parties. In arbitration, both the parties present their arguments to a third party (i.e. the arbitrator) and agree to accept the arbitration decision.

Evaluating channel members: It is a good policy for the marketer to evaluate the performance of each channel member periodically. An evaluation is useful to know which intermediaries are achieving favourable results and which are not. The intermediaries not performing well need to be counselled, re-trained, re-motivated or terminated. An evaluation data can also be used while deciding which type of middlemen to be used. The factors or criteria to be used for an evaluation of middlemen's performance can include sales achieved versus sales quota, average inventory levels, customer delivery performance, customer complaints, cooperation in market feedback, support for new products and new customers generated.

CHANNEL DYNAMICS

Like any other concept, channel systems do change according to the development and the need of the hour. With consumers becoming conscious of where they buy and how they want things to be delivered there has emerged different systems namely the vertical, horizontal and multichannel marketing systems. The conventional or the traditional marketing channel encompasses a producer, one or few wholesalers and one or few retailers. The objective of theses different players is to see that they make enough profits, they are highly independent and don't have control over other channel members. In contrast, the Vertical Marketing System (VMS) has the three members acting as one unified team, there is one channel member who owns the other members or allows franchising but ensures a greater role in the execution.

Many organizations have started to operate in this format as strong channel members try to dictate terms for the producer as well as when they found the objectives of different channel members differ from that of the producer. There are three variants of vertical marketing system namely corporate, administered and contractual vertical marketing system. In case of corporate the organization combines the production and the distribution under one roof. Organizations like Asian paints, Amul are not only involved in the production of the products but they also own a considerable no of outlets. An administered vertical marketing system coordinates the production and distribution efficiencies but use their size as a dominant influence. HLL commands a greater shelf space or Samsung gets better displays in retail outlets purely because of their size and the reputation they carry with them. The third variant namely contractual vertical marketing system coordinates the activities of individual firms at different levels integrating their programs at contractual levels. Firms like McDonalds, KFC use this type of vertical marketing systems for the integration of their businesses. The Horizontal marketing systems is one where two or more unrelated businesses come together pull in resources to exploit the emerging opportunities. Many private players especially banks have got into the act of tie-ups with retail stores or even with fuel outlets in order to gain greater market. ICICI bank has got tied with Big

Bazaar, and this has greatly enhanced the reputation of both these firms as well as increasing the customer base respectively.

The Multi-channel marketing systems as the term simplifies it is one in which a firm uses multiple channels to reach different customer segments. In the present scenario most organizations have started to use multiple channel method because it helps in the expansion of the market coverage, it costs little when the target segment is small instead of using a bigger channel and mainly helps in customizing the offering according the need of the segments. When distribution when goes overseas they are bound to face a lot of restraints and problems like the host country laws, the laws of the country to which the goods are shipped, the laws of the nations through which the goods pass must be abided by the company. Apart from this, other environmental factors do play an active role when considered from a macro-marketing perspective. In the next lesson, we deal with the role of retailers, wholesalers and logistics in this value chain and how do they facilitate the process of performing the channel function effectively.

Note: Dean Foods Company (Dean Foods) is a food and beverage company engaged in processing and distribution of milk and dairy products. The company's products are sold under well-known brands such as Land O' Lakes, Dairy Ease, Alta Dena, Barbe's, Barbers, Berkeley Farms, Campobueno, Celta, Country Charm, and Creamland. The company primarily operates in the US. It is headquartered in Dallas, Texas and employs 25,820 people. For detailed information & understanding more on "Buyer Behaviour" reader may visit this site www.deanfoods.com

7

Retailers and Wholesalers

INTRODUCTION

Retailing is one of the largest sectors in the global economy. It employees almost 23 million people in United States alone, generating about $3 trillion in sales annually. About 50 organizations in the Fortune 500 are from the retail sector. Retail is one among the fastest growing industry. Consider Wal-Mart, the biggest retailer in the world with approximately $250 billion in sales was started in the early sixties, while Fortune came with its annual ranking of top 500 organizations in 1952, a year when nobody would have dreamt about Wal-Mart. In the early nineties for the first time Wal-Mart became the top organization according to Fortune Magazine, which it still continues to hold. Retail is the buzzword today and this lesson explores the emerging retail scenario and the strategies available for different retail formats.

Wholesalers buy products from manufacturers and sell them to retailers while retailers take the product from wholesalers to the consumers. While the wholesalers try to satisfy the retailers, the retailers make all the effort in satisfying the needs of the consumers. Retailing has become an intrinsic part of our everyday lives that and this has been evident with the nations that have enjoyed the greatest economic and social progress have been those with a strong retail sector. Retailing encompasses selling through mail, the internet, door-to-door visits apart from brick and motor stores.

INDIAN SCENARIO

Retailing is the second largest industry in India next only to agriculture and contributes to about 11 percent of the GDP; it is likely that India will have about 220 shopping malls by 2006 up from 25 in 2003. The sector provides employment for 8% of the total workforce of the country. The sector is highly fragmented and is dominated by large traditional formats. Even though the total retail businesses are estimated at $180 billion only 2 percent comes from the organized sector. According to one of the sources, the size of the organized retail was estimated at about Rs 16,000 crores in 2002-03. India has the largest retail density in the world with 12 million retail outlets for a population of over 1000 million.

In the organized retail there are few big names like RPG's, Viveks, Rahejas etc who dominate the market to a greater extent. From what was once considered a conservative and a traditional society India has emerged as the hot pot for every organization that even firms like Reliance, Mahindra's are planning to foray into retail. According to the study conducted by the Euro-consumer study there has been an increase in the disposable income of the Indian middle class, apart from this the Indian middle and high income group is increasing by 10% annually over the last decade. Moreover the falling interest rates, easier consumer credits, varieties and different price points have all been credited to the booming retail market. The Urban customers have started to experience the western lifestyle, and they have become more demanding than ever before. Scenario has changed from what once was a forced way of buying has not led to the age where shopping is considered as an experience. The consumers are becoming highly knowledgeable and this in turn has had a positive effect on the consumers.

DRIVERS OF CHANGE

- Changing Demographics- One of the biggest reasons for the growth of retail in India is the changing demographics. The number of middle-income class and the people in the age group 18-35 has been ever increasing and this has changed the consumer's preference. According to a world study India is considered as one of the youngest economies and this is helping in the growth of the sector.
- Emphasis on Convenience - With the ever-expanding cities and upcoming towns, people are becoming choosier with the things they buy and the places they shop. This has resulted in the emergence of new retail ventures trying to be niche in some area.
- Explosion of Knowledge and Technology- With the emergence of internet, people have become aware of what's happening in the other part of the world and this has led him in comparing the prices, assortment, ambience etc. To cope up with this

knowledge explosion different retail formats have emerged and this has made shopping more of fun and a experiences.

- Added Experimentation- Back in the 1980s, people were highly loyal to the brands they bought and the outlets they shopped, but the present generation of consumers like to experiment. Long back people never felt shopping for vegetables and groceries at retail outlets were a good idea, but things have changed and vegetable retailing has grown by 35 percent

FUNCTIONS OF RETAILING

Retailers perform four major activities in the value chain. They are:

- Arranging assortment
- Breaking bulk
- Holding stock and,
- Providing service

Each of these activities holds significance when the product gets transferred from the manufacturer or the wholesaler to the retailer. We will discuss about each of the activities in detail and their contribution in the value addition to the offering.

- Arranging Assortment- an assortment is a retailer's selection of merchandise and this includes the length and breadth of the products. The assortment may include substitutable items of the same brands with different price points. Making decisions on the assortments is one of the crucial elements for a retailer; a small retailer makes decisions based on the perceptions he holds for a particular product and by past experiences. Those in the organized sector rely on future projections, past sales record and on detailed study on various factors that may affect the sales.

  Retailers need to consider other factors such as the store layout, the ambience, and merchandise mix to create an urge. Subhiksha one of the leading grocery and pharmaceutical chain in Tamil Nadu has an impressive assortment of only the fast moving brands and stock keeping units (SKU's) rather than all that is available, while Food World positions itself as a one stop shop as a result of which it holds multiple brands. Subhiksha works on its layout, price (value for money) as it's tool in reaching the consumer groups.

- Breaking Bulk- another activity that retailers perform is breaking bulk. Breaking bulk means physical repacking of the products by the retailers in small unit sizes according to the customer's requirement and convenience. The retailers procure goods from the wholesalers in large quantities in order to reduce transportation costs and time. They further break the products or arrange them into convenient units. The entire operation not only adds value to the end user but also send a positive word of mouth about the manufacturer or the supplier. This particular function is losing its prominence due to the advent of the different categories like the ready to wear segment.
- Holding Stock- the third activity retailers perform is holding stock. Retailers maintain appropriate levels of inventory. In the current scenario holding stock has got its own positives and negatives. Retailers have to face a negative consequence for holding unwanted stocks while at the same time keeping low stocks may affect the business. Based on the size of the retailer inventory decisions are worked. A large retailer uses specialized software's for maintaining inventory levels while small retailers use day to day transactions as a yardstick in maintaining the inventory
- Extending Service- the service the retailer's offer is more than just the core product. It may be an add-on to the core product itself. The add-ons may be the credit facility they may provide, after sales service or even providing information about the latest products to the customers. For the suppliers the retailers may provide with information pertaining to the trends in the market, information about a particular target group and even provide storing facility. Time zone, a part of the Titan group were the one of the pioneers in organized sector to some up with specialized people who were trained in handling any complexities in the instrument.

THEORIES IN RETAIL

Like every other industry new retail firms have brought innovative approaches in retailing. Retail development can be looked at from different theoretical perspective, as no one theory is universally acceptable. The reason for this unacceptability is mainly because of different market conditions, different socio-economic conditions in the market. This session deals with the following theories namely

- Wheel of Retailing
- Retail Accordian Theory
- Theory of Natural Selection
- Retail life cycle

Wheel of retailing

This theory talks about the structural changes in retailing. The theory was proposed by Malcomb McNair and according to this theory it describes how retail institutions change during their life cycle. In the first stage when new retail institutions start business they enter as low status, low price and low margin operations. As the retail firms achieve success they look in for increasing their customer base. They begin to upgrade their stores, add merchandise and new services are introduced. Prices are increased and margins are raised to support the higher costs. New retailers enter the market place to fill the vacuum, while this continues to move ahead as a result of the success. A new format emerges when the store reaches the final stage of the life cycle.

When the retail store started it started low but when markets grew their margins and price changed. The theory has been criticized because they do not advocate all the changes that happen in the retail sector and in the present scenario not all firms start low to enter the market.

Retail Accordian Theory

This theory describes how general stores move to specialized stores and then again become more of a general store. Hollander borrowed the analogy 'accordian' from the orchestra. He suggested that players either have open accordion representing the general stores or closed accordions representing narrow range of products focusing on specialized products. This theory was also known as the general-specific-general theory. The wheel of retailing and the accordion theory are known as the cyclical theories of retail revolution.

Theory of Natural selection

According to this theory retail stores evolve to meet change in the microenvironment. The retailers that successfully adapt to the technological, economic, demographic and political and legal changes are the ones who are more likely to grow and prosper. This theory is considered as a better one to wheel of retailing because it talks about the macro environmental variables as well, but the drawback of this theory is that if fails to address the issues of customer taste, expectations and desires.

RETAIL LIFE CYCLE

Like products, brands retail organizations pass through identifiable stages of innovation, accelerated development, maturity and decline. This is commonly known as the retail life cycle. Any organization when in the innovation stage is nascent and has few competitors. They try to create a distinctive advantage to the final customers. Since the concepts are new at this stage organizations try to grow rapidly and the management tries to experiment. Profits will be moderate and the stage may last for a couple of years. When we talk about our country e-buying or online shopping is in the innovation stage.

In the accelerated growth phase the organizations face rapid increase in sales, competitors begin to emerge and the organizations begin to use leadership and their presence as a tool in stabilizing their position. The investment level will be high as there are others who will be creating a lot of competition. This level may go up to eight years. Hypermarkets, Dollar stores are in this stage. In the maturity stage as competition intensifies newer forms of retailing begin to emerge, the growth rate starts to decline. At this stage firms should start work on strategies and reposition techniques to be in the market place. Supermarkets, cooperative stores are in this stage. In the final stage of the retail life cycle is the declining phase where firms begin to loose their competitive advantage. Profitability starts to decline further and the overheads starts to rise. Thus we see that organizations needs to adopt different strategies at each level in order to sustain in the marketplace.

CLASSIFICATION OF RETAIL FORMATS

Retailers have changed dramatically according to the changing trends and the evolving needs of the consumers. Different retail format have emerged over the years and each have been an improvisation over the earlier formats. Retail stores can be classified broadly based on store based and non-store based, the store based is otherwise the brick and the motor stores while the non-store based are those, which do not use the traditional format. Ownership in store based is further divided based on ownership and merchandise.

This section discusses some of the prominent formats under each classification:

Retail formats are broadly classified into store based and non-store based retail formats. The store based formats are the traditional models where you have brick and motor stores while a direct relationship with the customer is the trust area of the non-store based. The store based is further divided based on the ownership and the merchandise held by the stores.

CLASSIFICATION BASED ON OWNERSHIP

- An independent Retailer- these are retail stores which owns only one retail outlet. Usually the format is passed from generation to generation and this is has a proprietor who owns the store. 80 percent of the retail stores fall under this class in our country. From the paan shops to the kirana stores we find this type of stores in our country. Saravana stores is a good example.
- A Chain Retailer- they are otherwise known as the corporate chain where we find two or more outlets under a common ownership. These stores have commonality in merchandise, store layout, ambience etc. The advantage of this particular type of format is the economies of scale they enjoy. Here since they are scattered all over consumer preference may not be given greater importance. Some of the chain retailers are Mega mart and Nilgris.
- Franchising- this is a contractual agreement between two parties where the franchiser allows the franchisee to conduct the business under an established name in return for a fee. Some of the well-known franchisers are Mc Donald's, Archie's stores, Pizza Hut etc.
- Leased Departments- These is otherwise known as shops in shops. In this particular type a portion of a store is rented or leased to a third party. We see Coffee Day having outlets in Crossword bookstores or Pizza Corners in multiplexes.
- Consumer Cooperatives- these are retail institutions owned by consumers and this is mainly because of dissatisfied customers whose needs were never fulfilled by the existing retailers. Some of these are either owned by the government or backed by government. This helps in price negotiations and is one of the prime players when price quality is considered as an important parameter.

CLASSIFICATION BASED ON MERCHANDISE

- Convenience Stores- these are relatively small stores near residential area and are open for long hours. They carry limited line of high turnover products and have self-service formats. This format is emerging in India and they work seven days a week. BP's In & Out, HP Speed mart fall under this category.

- Supermarkets- These stores are relatively large and operate on low costs, low margins, high volume and offering a self-service format. The store houses food, laundry, and household maintenance products. Some examples for this format are Nilgiris and Food World.
- Hypermarkets- has it's origins in the US, these are stores that have a space of about 80,000 to 2,20,000 sq ft. the combine supermarket, discount stores and the warehouse principles in setting up them. They are usually situated on the outskirts of big cities and towns. In India the size is proportional and is not too big. Big bazaar is considered as a hypermarket.
- Specialty Stores- they are characterized by narrow line, with deep assortments in that particular product line. For the speciality stores a well-defined target market is essential. Personal attention, store ambience, customer service are important to the retailers. Music World, Gautier Furniture's are examples of this type of retailers. A new form of speciality stores have emerged and are called the category killers, who offer products from a single product line at economical prices. This particular concept has found tremendous appeal with the Indian market. Toys kemp in Bangalore is a classic example of this type of stores.
- Departmental Stores-This format originated in the mid-nineteenth century and is popular in many parts. They are large scaled retail outlets whose merchandise offer runs across different product lines. Apparel and home furnishing are the most common categories found in the departmental stores. The size of an average Indian departmental store varies between 20,000-40,000 sq ft, while that of the western stores are around 75,000 + sq ft. Some of the big players in this format are Life style, Globus, Ebony and so on.
- Off-price Retailers- In this format, the merchandise is sold less than the MRP. The retailers buy manufacturer's seconds or overruns as a result of which the merchandise may be in odd sizes or may be minor defects. Some off-price retail stores are manufacturer run and are called the factory outlets and

sell the manufacturer's products at lesser prices compared to other retailers. Mega Mart, Levi's factory outlets are some of the examples of this format.

- Catalogue showrooms- they are retailers who specialize in goods like jewellery, electronics. Customers have to check through a catalogue and then order the product they need. This concept s still in the nascent stage in the Indian market.

NON-STORE RETAILING

A form that is gaining ground in the non-store retailing, in this type of retailing the customers have a direct relationship with the retailers. The non-store retailing is broadly classified into direct selling and direct response marketing, which incorporates mail orders, television shopping and electronic shopping.

- Direct selling- this form of retailing is common for products like cosmetics, food products, educational materials and basic home appliances where the consumer will be in his place while the marketer brings the products to his doorsteps. Over the last decade the concept has grown leaps and bounds and according to the direct selling industry in India, there has been a 60-65 percent growth in sales turnover from this industry alone every year.
- Telemarketing- Using the telephone to sell directly to consumers has become the major direct marketing tool. Marketers use outbound telephone charges to help sell their products and services. Some telemarketing systems are fully automated. Marketers also use inbound toll-free numbers to receive orders arising from interactive marketing done through television and radio ads, direct mail or catalogs. Telemarketing is used in industrial as well as consumer marketing. The recent explosion in unsolicited telephone marketing has annoyed many consumers who object to the almost daily junk phone calls that pull them away from their normal routines.
- Mail order Retailing- this form eliminates personal selling and the physical store operations. This format is appropriate to speciality products or narrow product lines and where the target market is well defined. The main advantage of this type of retailing is the convenience they offer to the customers.
- Television Shopping- the television based retailing has received fair amount of success in India. With players like Asian Sky

shop, TSN products are advertised on televisions with features, warranties and prices discounts. Phone numbers are given for different cities where the customers has to give a call to the nearest place and order the products. The products are then home delivered.

- Electronic Shopping- the fastest growing medium to do retailing is electronic medium. Every brick and motor retailers are looking for click only models whereby customers can order products at the click of a button. This format virtually eliminates the physical infrastructure needed and can help in reducing the cost of operations. An effective supply chain is what these players need. It has been estimated that the Indian online shopping market is worth Rs.150 crores with 25% growth in 2005-06. The industry is expected to grow in the next 3-5 years. E-bay, rediff.com are some of the online shopping portals in the country.

ELEMENTS OF RETAIL STRATEGY

The retail strategy is an overall plan and guidelines that guides a retailer. A retail strategy is a clear and well-defined plan that the retail organizations outline to tap the market and create a long-term relationship with the customers. The steps that are involved in strategy formulation are the same in every industry.

- Situation Analysis- The first stage in retail strategy is establish the organizational mission. A mission statement acts as a motivator for the organization. The mission statement is one, which inspires the employees in the organization to stay focus on the goals of the organization. Evaluating ownership and management options like whether to go it alone or have a partnership or to buy an already existing organization has to be clearly outlined. Apart from this the merchandise that would be sold should also be evaluated.
- Objectives- these are the long, short and the mid term goals the retailer hopes to attain. The goals may be based on profits that may include ROI, sales which include market share, and the customer and the stakeholders' satisfaction. Te objectives need to be well defined keeping in mind the mission of the organization and should see that the strategies get translated into results.

- Identification of customers- Even though the strategy of a particular retailer may be executable and the mission of the organization looks inspiring, but if a wrong target market is chosen, it may prove a failure. It is essential for the retailer to understand the needs of the customer. A retailer has three options which he may choose according to his objective, he can try selling different product categories to a broad spectrum of customers which is known as mass marketing or work on one particular segment which is market segment or have two or more segments which is commonly called as selective segments.
- Overall Strategy- The overall strategy is broadly classified into controllable and uncontrollable factors. The location of the store, merchandise decision, communication, objectives come under controllable factor since the firms has a element of autonomy in deciding about them. In case of uncontrollable factors, the factors that a retailer must try and adapt like the technological changes, legal imperatives, cultural factors, economic situation get categorized. This step is one of the most essential steps in retail strategy because this stage demonstrates the firm's ability to adapt to different changing conditions.
- Specific Activities- this deals with the tactical decisions and the day-to-day operations of the firm. The firm's responsiveness to the environmental factors with the help of the marketing mix elements is the actual functioning of the firm's activities.
- Control- in the final phase of strategy formulation is the review of the firm's performance of a period of time. The firm's strategies and the tactics have to be evaluated to find the effectiveness and if it fall in place wit the organizational objectives and the with the firm's mission. In case if the firm finds that some of the tactics are time consuming and not much of benefit could be figured out the organization should ensure that such tactics have to be modified or be dropped from the firm's future course of action.

WHOLESALING

This includes all the activities involved in selling goods and services to those who buy for resale purpose. In the case of wholesaling this excludes manufacturers or producers who are involved directly in the production of the goods. They are the marketing intermediaries that buy from one source and sell it to another.

The main function of a wholesaler is facilitating the transportation of the product and at times in the transfer of the titles. The intermediaries' performing the wholesaling function is predominantly divided into two types namely merchants and agents. The difference between the two forms lies in if they take title to the goods they sell.

The classification is based on whether the intermediaries take title to the goods they sell. Taking title to the goods means the intermediaries own that merchandise and must be prepared to handle the risk associated with the ownership, including getting stuck with merchandise even if it turns out to be un-sellable.

CLASSIFICATION OF MERCHANT WHOLESALERS

The merchant wholesalers are independently owned concerns that take title to the goods they distribute. Some of the merchant wholesalers operate at the national level while some of them are more into regional levels. The merchant wholesalers are classified in terms of the number and the types of service they provide to the customer. The major division of the merchant wholesalers is termed as the Full-service merchant wholesaler and Limited -service merchant wholesaler.

The Full-service merchant wholesaler provides customers with a complete array of services in addition to the merchandise they offer. The service may include delivery, credit facility, advice and even assistance as accountant aid. These people are also called as full-function wholesalers. The full-service wholesalers are further classified into three types by the line of the goods they offer.

- General Merchandise: Wholesalers are those who sell large number of different product types or lines. It would be a one stop shop for the retailers to procure things from them at a much bargainable prices.
- General Line: Wholesalers are those who limit their offerings to one particular product line. They may hold all the products and variants in one particular product line.
- Speciality: Wholesaler reduce the line further, they may hold only select products in a particular product line. The traders of spices can be classified under this category.

The choice of being a more general merchant wholesaler or a much-specialized wholesaler depends on the choice of the target customers, whether their customers are speciality stores or a general stores.

The Limited-Service Merchant: Wholesaler is one who offers less than full service and charges lower prices. These types of wholesalers are also known as limited function wholesalers. This model comes to prominence when some customers may not want or may not be interested to pay for some of the services the Full-service merchant wholesaler offers. They may prefer to sacrifice the services offered to get lower prices. As a result of this particular category has emerged. This Limited-service merchant wholesaler is further divided into five types based on the various services they try to render and the on the basis of the payment for the goods they sell.

- ?Cash and Carry: Wholesalers are buyers who do not want certain specialized service such as delivery or credit. The wholesalers prefer the buyers to come to their warehouses and buy the products and pay for them at the same time. Metro, the German wholesaler refer exhibit 2.6.7 is a classic example for this type for this category
- Truck: Wholesalers are otherwise called the truck jobbers sell limited line of items. They operations are predominantly with the help of trucks and this helps in the immediate delivery offers. Some of the items used to be considered in this method are perishables and those which have great demand. Although this method is a expensive form of distribution this definitely a aggressive form of selling the offering
- ?Drop: Shippers are merchants who take title to the goods but not the possession of the goods. These merchants take orders form the buyers pass it to the manufacturers, which will, then ship the product directly to the buyer. As the product goes directly to the buyer, it minimizes in the loading and unloading of the product. This type is commonly used for commodities like cement, coal etc. The drop shippers are also called as the desk jobbers as they need minimum infrastructure. Since they do not handle the shipping, there is even no need for a warehouse to keep the products.
- Rack: Jobbers are another type of merchant wholesalers who contract with the retailers to set up display racks in the store and stock them with merchandise. This particular category of

wholesalers gained prominence after the emergence of departmental stores.

CLASSIFICATION OF AGENT WHOLESALERS

The agents are the next category of wholesalers, they take possession of the goods but at the same time they do not take title to them. The agents in no way provide warehouse facility or credits but provide facilities like arranging credit or delivery as a part of their service. The agents make business through commissions based on selling prices of the product. The percentage of the commission varies based on the industry as well on the perishable nature of the product. The agents can be classified as follows namely

- Brokers who are intermediaries who bring the sellers in touch with the buyers and also facilitate in the contractual negotiations and receive commissions based on the work. Brokers are considered to be neutral and are found in every field. The commissions they receive from both the parties will be relatively less and this requires minimum investment. Most organizations prefer brokers because they work on commissions and do not have long-term relationships with one particular organization.
- Commission Merchants are similar to brokers but are given certain powers by the sellers of the product. They perform majorly the pricing function and work closely with the producers of the products. The commission merchants are most common in the agricultural products. The commission merchants take possession of the goods so that the prospective buyers have a chance to inspect the products; once the deal is finalized the commission merchants deduct their commission past and return the balance to the producer.
- Manufacturer's Agents are those who are available for the producer who are not interested in performing the sales activity or who lack the expertise to have one. The manufacturer's agents work in limited geographical areas and in low priority zones. If a producer of electronic goods feels having a separate sales force for the rural areas is an expensive decision they may go in for a merchant's agent to do the job of selling their offering. The merchant's agents will be familiar with the area they operate and this is one reason why producers opt for the merchant's agents. One another benefit of these people is that they need not be paid till the deal is finalized.

- The Selling Agents are paid a commission and are expected to be familiar with the products and the markets. Unlike the manufacturer's agents they do not restrict themselves to one particular geographical area but rather to all places where the product has got a market. Since they concentrate on a much larger scale they are given more responsibility including the elements of promotions and pricing of the products. The organizations who utilize these people are otherwise called as external marketing department.

Note: The Timberland Company (Timberland) is one of the global leaders in designing, engineering and marketing of footwear, apparel and accessories for men, women and children. The company's key brands include Timberland, Timberland PRO, Mountain Athletics, SmartWool, Timberland Boot Company, Howies and IPATH. The company primarily operates in North America, Europe, and Asia. It is headquartered in Stratham, New Hampshire and employs approximately 6,000 people. For a case study visit company's www.timberland.com

8

Nature of Marketing Channels

One of the major purposes of marketing is to satisfy the human needs and wants by delivering products to buyers when and where they want them at a reasonable cost. One of the key aspects we find in this process is delivery. Over the past two decades, economic clout has shifted from the producers of goods to distributors of goods. The shift in economic power has been significant in the retail level of marketing channels, where mass merchandisers like Wal-Mart, Big Bazaar have become dominant players. As a strategic marketing tool, the distribution channels had for many years taken something of a backseat to the other three strategic areas of the marketing mix namely the product, price and promotion. Today there has been a shift in the emphasis and this has been credited to four developments, viz.

- Explosion of information technology and e-commerce.
- Greater difficulty of gaining a sustainable competitive advantage.
- Growing power of distributors especially retailers.
- The need to reduce distribution costs.

DISTRIBUTION CHANNELS

Different people perceive marketing channels in different ways, some see it as a route taken by a product as it moves from the producer to the consumer, and others describe it as a loose coalition of business firms that have come together for purpose of business. Customers may view marketing channels as simply 'a lot of middlemen' standing between the producer and the product. Given all these different perspectives it is not possible to have one single definition for marketing channels. Marketing channels can be defined as the external contractual organization that management operates to achieve its distribution objectives.

There are four terms in this definition that has to be given a special mention namely external, contractual organization, operates and distribution objectives. The term external means that the marketing channel exists outside the firm. Managing of the marketing channel therefore involves the use of interorganizational management (managing more than one firm) rather than intraorganizational management (managing one firm). The term contractual organization refers to those firms who are involved in the negotiatory function as the product moves from the producer to the end user. The function of these firms involves buying, selling and transferring of goods and services.

Transportation companies, public warehouses, banks ad agencies do not come under these and are referred to as facilitating agencies. The third term operates suggests the involvement of management in the channels and this may range from the initial development of the channel structure to the day-to-day management. Finally the distribution objectives explain the distribution goals the organization has in mind. When the objectives change, variations can be seen in the external contactual organizations and the way in which the management operates. In simpler terms a channel then consists of producer, consumer and any intermediary.

Marketing channel strategy is one of the major strategic areas of marketing. In most cases eliminating middlemen will not reduce prices, because the amount that goes to the intermediaries compensates them for the performance of tasks that must be accomplished regardless of whether or not an intermediary is present. In simple terms, a company can eliminate intermediaries but cannot eliminate the functions they perform.

FLOWS IN MARKETING CHANNELS

As discussed a conventional channel of distribution consist of a manufacturer, a wholesaler, a retailer and the ultimate consumer. Not all the channels include all these marketing institutions. At times the product passes directly from the manufacturer to consumer. When a marketing channel has been developed a series of flows emerge. These flows provide the links that tie channel members and other agencies together in the distribution of goods and services. There are five most important flows namely

- Product flow
- Negotiation flow
- Ownership flow

- Information flow
- Promotion flow

Product Flow

The Product flow refers to actual physical movement of the product from the manufacturers through all the parties who take physical possessions of the product from the point of production to the final consumer.

Negotiation Flow

In the negotiation flow, this represents the interplay of the buying and the selling functions associated with the transfer of title. If you note the diagram you find the transportation firm is not included in the flow because it does not participate in the negotiation function, also you can find the arrows flow in both the directions, indicating the negotiation is mutual at all levels of the channels.

Ownership Flow

The ownership flow shows the movement of the title to the product as it is passed along from the manufacturer to the consumer, here as well we find the transportation function missing since the transportation firm does not take title or is actively involved in the facilitating function. It merely involves in transporting physical products

Information Flow

In case of the Information flow, we can see that the transportation function has reappeared and all the arrows are two-directional. All the parties participate in the exchange of information. For example Coke may obtain information from the transportation company about its shipping schedules and the rates, while the transportation firm may seek information regarding when and in what quantities it plans to ship its products. Some times the information bypasses the transportation company directly to the wholesaler or the retailer when the information does not concern the transportation firm. If there is an offer, or a price reduction these information are not needed by the transportation firms.

Promotion Flow

Finally the Promotion flow refers to the persuasive communication in the form of advertising, personal selling, publicity. There is a new component that is added to the flow and that is the advertising agency and this actively provides and maintains the information flow. The organizations work closely with the promotional organizations so we find a two-directional arrow.

From the management view, the concept of channel flows provides a useful framework for understanding the scope and complexity of channel management. Changing scenario does make the role of the firms' complex, as a result of which innovative channel strategies and effective channel management are needed to make this happen.

FUNCTIONS OF DISTRIBUTION CHANNELS

Some of the major functions performed by the intermediaries are mainly physical distribution, communication and facilitating functions. When we talk about physical functions, they include braking bulk, accumulating bulk, creating assortments, reducing transactions and transporting and storing.

Breaking bulk: One of the important role intermediaries perform is bulk-breaking function. Here these organizations buy in large quantities and break them into smaller quantities and pass them to the retailers, wholesalers or even to the customers. By doing so, the intermediaries reduce the cost of distribution for the manufacturers as well as the consumers. This particular function is also termed as 'resolution of economic discrepancies'.

BULK-BREAKING FUNCTION

Accumulating Bulk: At times the intermediaries also do the task of accumulating the bulk. The intermediaries may buy bulk from different small producers accumulate them and offer to those buyers who prefer large quantities. The intermediaries in accumulating the bulk are mostly found in the agricultural businesses, whereby the intermediary will procure vegetables from local farmers and assemble them and sell it to the wholesalers. Once the marketers accumulate bulk they start to sort the products identifying differences in the quality, grades and classify them into different categories

BULK-ACCUMULATING FUNCTION

- Creating Assortments: The third important function of the intermediaries is creating assortment. When we take the case of magazines, on an average there are around thousands of magazines being published in a month and it is impossible for a particular newsstand to get it going, here big distributors and agents work in creating assortments and enable a speedy process. This needs a lot of teamwork and timing. Certain magazines become outdated within certain period of time.

- Reducing Transactions: One of the biggest reasons that keep the economy moving and the customer smiling is the presence of intermediaries, they reduce the number of transactions necessary to accomplish the exchange of goods.

Transaction without an intermediary

It becomes a complicated process for the manufacturers to work on with different retailers, when a intermediary comes in the form of a wholesaler we find the whole situation becomes different. Intermediaries do not only reduce the number of transactions but also help in the reduction of the geographical distances that both buyers and sellers have to cover. Channel intermediaries doing the roles of a buying agent for their customer and selling agents for the manufacturers does simplify the process of transaction considerably.

REDUCTION OF TRANSACTIONS BY AN INTERMEDIARY

Transporting and Storing: Apart from breaking, accumulating, creating assortments and reducing transactions they also perform two key marketing functions namely transporting and storing. The final product has to be moved from the point of production to the point of consumption. This means it involves storing the product along the way till it is delivered. Most of the big retailers hold enough of the product in order to cater to the consumers.

Credit Services: Apart from the function of physical distribution the intermediaries also help in offering credit services. Even though there are firms like Metro, which are predominantly cash and carry kind of intermediaries, most of the intermediaries provide credit facility or even paying in parts. Many intermediaries offer about 30 to 45 days to the retailers for paying back.

Risk Taking: One of the vital functions of the intermediaries is risk taking. Not every product finds favor in the eyes of the customer, much fallout within few months, as a result of which the intermediaries would be at risk. An uncontrollable factor like floods, earthquakes or even contamination or fire could pose a serious threat. The intermediaries have to bear these risks along with the market risks. These are some of the core functions intermediaries perform enabling goods and services to reach consumers at the right time.

Note: Republic Services is a service provider in the non-hazardous solid waste industry. The company operates in the US and Puerto Rico. It is headquartered in Phoenix, Arizona and employs about 35,000 people. For a detailed example in "Nature of Marketing Channels" visit www.republicservices.com

9

Structure and Design of Marketing Channels

CHANNEL STRUCTURE

Channel structure is distinguished on the basis of the number of intermediaries. There are different levels in a channel structure. The common levels are zero-level, one-level, two-level, three-level.

TYPICAL CHANNEL STRUCTURE FOR CONSUMER GOODS

Zero-level structure is one of the simplest forms of the channel structure. Here organizations like Avon, Eureka Forbes use direct selling mode to take the products from their production houses to the consumers directly. A lot of money has to be spent in order to make this channel structure effective, as there is no third party to take your product to the consumer. Even a bakery can come as a firm, which bakes cakes and sells it directly to the consumers. Marketers who use the mailing services, toll-free numbers are also using this service.

One-level structure is one in which we have one intermediary acting as a link between the manufacturer and the consumer. Here the retailers procure goods directly from the manufacturer and supply it to the consumers. Retailers like Viveks, Wal-Mart deal directly with the manufacturer. In some cases in order to retain profitable and reputed retailers the manufacturers act as wholesalers. One of the advantages for the intermediaries is the customization and the discounts they receive.

Two-level channel has two people interceding before the product reaches the consumer. Here there would be a wholesaler and a retailer who takes the efforts for a speedy delivery and this is one of the most commonly used structures for consumer goods. In the case of Metro, most of the small retail and Kirana stores buy all the merchandise from Metro and in urn sell them to the consumer. One of the advantages of the four-level structure is the benefit of using the wholesaler in the distribution of services. Three-level channel happens predominantly when the firms plans to go global. When a manufacturer enters another country, it always holds good when he uses the help of agents to operate in that environment. The agents are people who know the legal procedures and who can negotiate with the host country in case of a problem. Most of the airline firms that operate in different countries take the help of agents to penetrate the market.

When it comes for Business-to-Business operations, the channels differ from the consumer markets, in this structure, firms predominantly may use their existing sales force to sell the products to the customers, they may even use industrial distributors to take their products to the industrial customers.

B2B MARKETING CHANNELS

Mark Andy is one of the big names in the printing machines industry. In India Mark Andy supplies its printing machines to the industrial customers through Heidelberg, an industrial distributor. It also has its own representatives who pitch in when the customer needs information. In case of Industrial Channel, the zero-level, one-level and two-level are the most commonly used method. When it comes for Business-to-Business channels agents become the integral point of the whole process, since the characteristic of the business-to-business market is oligopolistic and are huge buyers.

In this digital economy, a shift has started in the channels on either side of the markets i.e. in both the consumer marketing channels and the business-to-business market channels. The web has created a platform whereby organizations can now directly communicate with the customers, as a result of which many of the channels are being disintermediated. This disintermediation does not necessarily mean that they completely eliminate the intermediaries, but rather when it comes to shipping the products it may outsource some of the distribution functions like the storage, transportation from third party firms.

DESIGNING DISTRIBUTION CHANNELS

Channel design refers to those decisions that involve in the development of new marketing channels or modifying the existent ones.

The channel design decision can be broken down into six steps namely:

1. Recognizing the need for channel design decision
2. Setting and coordinating distribution objectives
3. Specify the distribution tasks
4. Develop alternative channel structures
5. Evaluate relevant variables
6. Choose the best channel structure

Recognizing the need for a channel design decision

First and foremost task for the organization is to recognize the need for a channel design. An organization would go in for a new channel design for the following reasons namely:

- When a new product or product line is developed, mainly when the existing channels are not suitable for the new line.
- When the existing product is targeted to a different target market. This is common when an organization is used to catering the B2B, plans to enter the consumer market.
- When there is a change in the marketing mix elements, when an organization reduces its prices on certain offering the channel worked out will be based on the price points, they may look in for discounters
- When facing major environmental changes namely in economic or technological or in legal spheres.
- Finally when the organization opens up new geographic marketing areas.

The list by no means is comprehensive, but gives a picture about some of the most common conditions when channel design decisions are worked out.

Setting and Coordinating Distribution Objectives

Once a need for a design is recognized the next task for the channel manager is to work out to develop the channel structure, either form the scratch or by modifying the existing one. It is necessary for the channel manager to carefully evaluate the firm's distribution objectives. In order for the distribution objectives to be effective and well coordinated the channel manager need to perform three tasks namely:

- Become familiar with the objectives and strategies in other marketing mix areas and other relevant objectives and strategies of the firm. In most cases the person or the group that sets the objectives of the other marketing mix elements will also set the objectives for distribution as well.

- Set the objectives and state them explicitly. A good objective is one, which is clear, and explicit, and has a greater role in achieving the firm's overall objectives. Some examples of a good distribution objectives are as follows, at the start of the new millennium, Apple Computers set a distribution objective to reach more consumers with what it refers to as the 'Apple experience'. So, Apple reinvigorated and reestablished relationships with large retail chains, which it had neglected in recent years .In the same way Coca-Cola seeks to broaden its penetration in schools and college markets, as a result of which it has entered into contact with many schools and colleges, whereby these institutions would sell only Coca-Cola products on their campuses.
- Check and see if the distribution objectives set are congruent with marketing and other general objectives and strategies of the firm. This involves verifying if the distribution objectives do not conflict with the objectives in the other areas of marketing mix or even to the overall objectives of the company. In order to cross check, it is essential to examine the interrelationships and hierarchy of the objectives of the firms.

Specifying the Distribution Tasks

Once the objectives are formulated, a number of functions need to be performed in order for the distribution objectives to be met. The manager therefore has to specify the nature of the tasks that needs to be carried out in order to meet the objectives. The tasks need to be precisely stated so that it meets the specified distribution objectives. For e.g. a manufacturer of a consumer product, say a high quality cricket bats aimed at serious amateur cricket players would need to specify distribution tasks such as gathering info on target markets shopping patterns, promote product availability to the target, maintain inventory, and timely availability, compile info about the product features, provide hands on experience using the product, process and fill customers orders, transport the product, arrange for credit provisions, provide warranty, provide repair and service, establish product return to make the offering readily available. Sometimes these functions may appear to be production oriented rather than distribution tasks, but when we talking about meeting customers, they are indeed distribution tasks.

Developing Possible Alternative Channel Structures

Once the tasks have been specified by the channel manager he should find out alternate ways of allocating these tasks. In most cases the channel manager chooses from more than one channel to reach the consumer effectively. Britannia would sell their biscuits thorough wholesale food distributor, departmental stores, convenience stores and even in pharmacies. Whatever may be the channel structure, the allocation alternatives should be in terms of (a) the number of levels in the channel (b) the intensity at various levels, and (c) the types of intermediaries.

The number of levels can be from two level upto five levels. The channel manager can think of going for a direct way of meeting the customers to using two intermediaries as an appropriate way. Intensity refers to the number of intermediaries at each level. Generally the intensities can be classified into three categories namely intensive, selective and exclusive. Intensive saturation means as many outlets as possible are used at each level of the channel. Selective means that not all possible intermediaries at a particular level are used. Exclusive refers to a very selective pattern of distribution. A firm like Parle may use intensive distribution channel structure, while Rolex may use high degree of selectivity. The types of intermediaries, third component has to be carefully dealt. The firms should not overlook new types of intermediaries that have emerged in recent years particularly the auction firms such as baazee, bid or buy as possible sales outlet for their products.

Evaluating the Variables Affecting Channel Structure

Once the alternative structures have been outlined, each channel structure has to be evaluated on a number of variables. There are five basic categories namely, Market variables - marketing management is based on the philosophy of marketing concept, which stresses on the consumers needs and wants, the managers have to take the cues from the market. The subcategories that have a greater influence on the market structure are market geography, market size, market density and market behaviour Product variables - some of the most important product variables are bulk and weight, Perishability, unit value, degree of standardization, technical vs. non-technical and newness. Heavy and bulky products have a high handling and shipping costs relative to their value. The manufactures of such products have to keep in mind to ship in large lots to a fewer possible points. It would always be better if the channel structure remains short. Food products, flowers are considered to be highly perishable. When products are highly perishable, the channel structure should be designed to provide rapid delivery from producers to consumers. One important consideration is lower the unit value of a product, the longer the channels should be as low unit value leaves small margins for distribution costs. Exhibit 4.10 explains the relationship between the degree of standardization and channel length. If the product flows directly from manufacturer or producer to the user the degree of customization is more, but as the product becomes more standardized it passes through many channels. Mostly the B2B machinery has a great degree of customization as it passes from the manufacturer to the industrial user, while many consumer market is predominantly a standardized one. When it comes for the technical component, the industrial products are mostly distributed through direct channels because of the technical expertise and service while many technical consumer products do use shorter channel structure. When the product is new and is in the introductory stage in order to capitalize on the aggressive promotion, a shorter channel is preferred to gain awareness.

- Company Variables- the important variables that affect a good channel design are size, financial capacity, managerial expertise and objectives and strategies. Larger the firms in terms of size it enables them to exercise a substantial amount of power in the channel. The size does give flexibility for the firm in picking the channel structures. The same hold true when it comes for the financial capability. Greater capital available with a firm, less dependency is seen on the intermediaries. When a firm is into industrial marketing, it prefers to have its own sales force, warehousing, order processing capabilities and larger firms with good financial backing are better able to bear the high cost of these facilities. When a firm lacks quality managerial skills, a comprehensive channel structure ranging from wholesalers to brokers are needed to perform the distribution activity, once the firm gains experience it can change or reduce the number of intermediaries. The objectives and strategies a firm has may limit the use of intermediaries. These strategies may emphasis on aggressive promotion and may even alter the distribution tasks. Overall this is one of the prime variables used for evaluating.
- Intermediary Variables- the important intermediary variables are availability, costs and services offered. The availability is one of the key variables as this influences the channel structure. If we take the case of Dell Computers, due to lack of a proper

channel structure he designed a direct mail order channel, which provided a strong technical backup as well. The cost is another variable a channel manager considers. If the cost of using a particular intermediary is too high compared the services it offers the manager may consider in minimizing the use of intermediaries. The services performed by the intermediaries is another integral component, a good intermediary is one, which offers efficient services at the lowest cost.

- Environmental Variables- the uncontrollable or the macro environmental forces may affect the different aspects of channel development and management. Forces like the Sociocultural, economic, technological, legal forces have a significant impact on the channel structure. The other variables are those the organization can work upon or change to the situation but the environmental forces are those the organization has to cope up with.

Choosing the 'Best' Channel structure

In deciding the manager should choose an optimal channel structure that would offer desired level of effectiveness at the lowest possible cost. Even though there is not one set method to pick an optimal channel structure, it all depends on the orientation of the firm. If the goal of the firm were profit maximization, the channel structure would be in line with the goal. Most channel choices are still however made on the basis of managerial judgment and the data that is available.

MANAGING CHANNEL MEMBERS AND THEIR CONFLICTS

After a particular channel is selected, the marketer must manage or administer the channel members or intermediaries. Managing channel members include

- Selecting intermediaries
- Motivating channel members or middlemen
- Controlling or managing channel conflicts, and
- Evaluating performance of channel members
- Selecting Intermediaries: Selection of intermediaries or middlemen is a continuous process because some of them leave the channel or get terminated by the marketer. Hence it is not part of channel design. It is necessary for the marketer to

determine criteria or factors for selection of intermediaries. These criteria differ depending on the type of middlemen and the firm's particular product/market conditions. Some of the common factors considered are financial standing, location, prior experience and type of customers served.

- Motivating middlemen: The marketer must continuously motivate his intermediaries to achieve long-term success. Motivating the intermediaries to achieve top performance should start with understanding the middlemen's needs, perceptions and outlook. The quality of support from middlemen will depend on the motivational techniques used and incentives offered.
- Controlling channel conflicts: Even though a manufacturer's channel design is well done, there will be some conflict because of the differences in the objectives and perceptions of the channel members. The conflicts or tensions between the channel members can damage channel performance. Marketers should periodically undertake surveys of intermediaries or conduct formal/informal discussions with them to assess the areas or sources of conflicts.

Sources of Conflict Examples

1. Differences in objectives: Manufacturers want long term profitability but middlemen prefer short term
2. Dealings with customers: Middlemen feel cheated when the manufacturer deals with large customers and asks them to serve small customers
3. Differences in interests: The manufacturer feels that the middlemen are not giving attention to the firm's products. The middlemen are interested in products that are fast moving or have higher margins for them
4. Differences in perceptions: The manufacturer wants the middleman to carry a higher inventory due to the perception of good market conditions. The middleman does not share this optimism
5. Compensation: Manufacturer's representatives (agents) feel that the commission percentage offered by the manufacturer is not adequate. The manufacturer thinks otherwise
6. Unclear territory boundaries: The territory boundaries between middlemen are not clear, resulting in competition among the

firm's intermediaries to secure business from the same customers

The channel conflicts can be controlled or managed in several ways, including:

- Effective communication network
- Joint goal-setting
- Diplomacy
- Mediation
- Arbitration and
- Developing a vertical marketing system.

An effective communication network between the manufacturer and the intermediaries can be developed through periodic formal and informal meetings and cooptation of intermediaries in board of directors or advisory committees. In joint-goal setting, the channel members come to an agreement on the super-ordinate (or fundamental) goals they jointly seek. Such goals can be market share leadership, customer satisfaction or product/service quality in a highly competitive market where survival and success of channel members depend on their performance and cooperation.

The channel members may resort to diplomacy, mediation or arbitration, when conflicts are sharp. Diplomacy is used when the conflict is resolved through discussions between the persons from both the parties. In mediation a neutral third party tries to conciliate the interests of the two parties. In arbitration, both the parties present their arguments to a third party (i.e. the arbitrator) and agree to accept the arbitration decision.

Evaluating Channel Members

It is a good policy for the marketer to evaluate the performance of each channel member periodically. An evaluation is useful to know which intermediaries are achieving favourable results and which are not. The intermediaries not performing well need to be counseled, re-trained, re-motivated or terminated. An evaluation data can also be used while deciding which type of middlemen to be used.

The factors or criteria to be used for an evaluation of middlemen's performance can include sales achieved versus sales quota, average inventory levels, customer delivery performance, customer complaints, cooperation in market feedback, support for new products and new customers generated.

CHANNEL DYNAMICS

Like any other concept, channel systems do change according to the development and the need of the hour. With consumers becoming conscious of where they buy and how they want things to be delivered there has emerged different systems namely the vertical, horizontal and multichannel marketing systems. The conventional or the traditional marketing channel encompasses a producer, one or few wholesalers and one or few retailers.

The objective of theses different players is to see that they make enough profits, they are highly independent and don't have control over other channel members. In contrast, the Vertical Marketing System (VMS) has the three members acting as one unified team, there is one channel member who owns the other members or allows franchising but ensures a greater role in the execution. Many organizations have started to operate in this format as strong channel members try to dictate terms for the producer as well as when they found the objectives of different channel members differ from that of the producer.

There are three variants of vertical marketing system namely corporate, administered and contractual vertical marketing system. In case of corporate the organization combines the production and the distribution under one roof. Organizations like Asian paints, Amul are not only involved in the production of the products but they also own a considerable no of outlets. An administered vertical marketing system coordinates the production and distribution efficiencies but use their size as a dominant influence.

HLL commands a greater shelf space or Samsung gets better displays in retail outlets purely because of their size and the reputation they carry with them. The third variant namely contractual vertical marketing system coordinates the activities of individual firms at different levels integrating their programs at contractual levels. Firms like McDonalds, KFC use this type of vertical marketing systems for the integration of their businesses.

The Horizontal marketing systems is one where two or more unrelated businesses come together pull in resources to exploit the emerging opportunities. Many private players especially banks have got into the act of tie-ups with retail stores or even with fuel outlets in order to gain greater market. ICICI bank has got tied with Big Bazaar, and this has greatly enhanced the reputation of both these firms as well as increasing the customer base respectively.

The Multi-channel marketing systems as the term simplifies it is one in which a firm uses multiple channels to reach different customer segments. In the present scenario most organizations have started to use multiple channel method because it helps in the expansion of the market coverage, it costs little when the target segment is small instead of using a bigger channel and mainly helps in customizing the offering according the need of the segments.

When distribution when goes overseas they are bound to face a lot of restraints and problems like the host country laws, the laws of the country to which the goods are shipped, the laws of the nations through which the goods pass must be abided by the company. Apart from this, other environmental factors do play an active role when considered from a macro-marketing perspective. In the next lesson, we deal with the role of retailers, wholesalers and logistics in this value chain and how do they facilitate the process of performing the channel function effectively.

Note: Stryker is one of the world's leading medical technology companies engaged in the development, manufacture and marketing of medical devices and instrumentations in the orthopedic as well as other medical specialties. The company provides products such as implants used in joint replacement, trauma, craniomaxillofacial and spinal surgeries; biologics; surgical, neurologic, ear, nose and throat and interventional pain equipment; surgical equipment; surgical navigation systems; and patient handling and emergency. For detailed information related to this chapter reader can visit www.stryker.com

10

Product Decisions

This unit on the first P of marketing, namely the Product, will help you answer the following questions:

- What product should the company make?
- Where exactly are these products to be offered?
- What should be the width of the product mix?
- How many different product lines can the company accommodate?
- How should the products be positioned in the market?
- What should be the brand policy?

OVERVIEW

It is a fact that product/service is a 'mixer of ingredients' where in the manufacturer / service provider who blends various marketing activities in a manner that strengthen the business the interests of the firm. The crux of any marketing strategy is to bring about the desired operation in the light of prevailing circumstances. We also learned from the pervious lesson that the planned manipulated to get optimum results in limiting environments. This lesson narrates the important concepts like marketing mix, products, brand, trademark, packing and labeling with suitable example from Indian marketing environmental.

SIGNIFICANCE OF MARKETING MIX

The most popular 4 Ps' framework as suggested by McCarthy with the marketing mix variables- products, place, promotion and price had origination from the study of the manufacturers - i.e. the organization engaged in production and marketing of goods - it is more oriented to deal with goods marketing situations. However service characteristics are radically different fro goods; and so are the challenges in their marketing. It is wrong to imply that services are just like products except for intangibility. But such wax-like logic as "apples are just like oranges, except for their apple ness" does not stand the heat of nuts-and-bolts.

Marketing Product / service characteristics and add new dimensions to a marketing situation that is faced by the service manager. Given the product / service characteristics and activities in product/service firms, eight Ps' framework for services has been proposed. For the services, the additional prescribed Ps given below refer to activities that are service marketing mix can be summarized as follows:

- Product - service core, levels, additional services, branding.
- Price - price, discounts, terms of payment.
- Place - location, channels of distribution, coverage.
- Promotion - Advertising, sales promotion, personal selling and publicity.

For Service Additional 4 Ps were Added for Marketing Services. They are:

People - customer-provider relationship, training, culture, skills, and attitudes.

Physical- ambience, appearance, equipment, machines

Evidence - Buildings, physical facilities

Process - Activity sequence, quality management, customer participation and delivery process.

Productivity - Efficiency of human and non-human capitals in the production process. But our discussion limits only to the first four Ps.

CONCEPT OF A PRODUCT

The term 'product' is widely used to refer a market offering of any kind. In its broadest sense this may be anything from the physical to the abstract - an idea or a moral issue. Generally, however, most products are made up of a combination of physical elements and services. This is true in services marketing, where the service offering can include tangible features, such as food in a restaurant, or be a 'pure' service, intangible in nature.

A service product refers to an activity or activities that a marketer offers to perform, which results in satisfaction of a need or want of predetermined target customers. It is the offering of a firm in the form of activities that satisfies needs such as hair styling done by a barber.

Consumers will buy only what suits them. As customers, we buy different kinds of products and services to satisfy our various needs. We buy toothpaste, butter, shaving cream, pen, scooter, and ticket for the U.S.A and many other such items in our daily life. As we understand, our decision to buy an item is based not only on its tangible attributes but also on psychological attributes such as services, brand, package, warranty, image, and etc. discussions about the marketing of goods apply to services as well. Services have special characteristics that make them different than products.

According to Alderson, W., "Product is a bundle of utilities consisting of various product features and accompanying services" according to Schwarte, D.J., "A product is something a firm markets that ill satisfy a personal want or fill a business or commercial need".

At the time of product planning, the marketer has to think about FIVE types of benefits.

From Generic to Potential product - Most of you would be aware that a product has a personality of several components-like the physical products, the brand name, the package, the label etc. all of us know that most of the products are undergoing a constant change and the marketing man has been constantly engaged in enriching his product offer. In his attempt to score over competition, he has been bringing about refinement on his basic product offer, but managing the product was becoming more and more difficult.

Hence the product traveled various levels:

- The Core Product
- The Generic product
- The branded Product
- The Differentiated product
- The customised product
- The augmented product
- The potential product

The Core benefits: what does the product mean to the customer? For example, a car offers generic benefits of convenience in traveling.

The Generic product Is the unbranded and undifferentiated commodity like rice, bread, flour or cloth.

The Branded Product: The branded product gets an identity through a 'name'. Modern bread, Harvest are branded products. We would study in detail about brand name in the brand section.

The differentiated product: The differentiated product enjoys a distinction from other similar products/brands in the market. The differential claimed may be 'real', with a real distinction on ingredient, quality, utility, or service, or it may be 'psychological' brought about through subtle sales appeals.

The customised product - Customer specific requirements are taken into account while developing the product. Commonly practised in the industrial product marketing, where the manufacturer and the user are in direct contact and the product gets customised to the requirements of the customer.

The augmented product: The augmented product is the result of voluntary improvements brought about by the manufacturer in order to enhance the value of the product, which are neither suggested by the customer nor expected by them. The marketer on his own augments the product, by adding an extra facility or an extra feature to the product.

The potential product: The potential product is tomorrow's product carrying with it all the improvements and finesse possible under the given technological, economic and competitive condition. There are no limits to the 'potential product'. Only the technological and economic resources of the firm set the limit.

Product differentiation - Is the act of designing a set of meaningful differences to distinguish the companies offering from competitor's offerings? The number of differentiation opportunities varies with the type of industry. The Boston consulting group has distinguished four types of industries based on the number of available competitive advantages and their size.

- Volume industry: One in which companies can gain only a few, but rather large, competitive advantages.
- Stalemated industry: One in which there are a few potential competitive advantages and each is small.
- Fragmented industry: One in which companies face many opportunities for differentiation, but each opportunity for competitive advantage is small.

- Specialised industry: One in which companies face many differentiation opportunities, and each differentiation can have a high payoff.

Theodore Levitt in one of his books "Marketing Success, through differentiation of anything" explains that in a market place, there is no such thing as commodity .All goods and services are differentiable. In a market place differentiation is everywhere .All the companies try to distinguish their offer from that of their competitor. This is true of even those who produce and deal in primary metals, grains, chemicals, plastics and money. Starting from technology to plant location to post sale service firms to the personnel/procedures employed for various functions like sales, production etc., companies can differ their offers in many ways. Companies usually choose those functions, which give them greatest relative advantage.

STRATEGY STANCES

It is natural for different firms to take different strategy stances as the requirement; situational design of each is different from the other. One firm might find it appropriate to have direct confrontation with the market leader; another may find it appropriate to keep aloof for some time from the competition; and the third might may find it relevant to chalk out a strategy of sheer survival. No strategy stance is universally valid. Broadly strategy stances can be classified under three heads- Offensive/ confrontation strategy, Defensive and Niche strategy.

Offensive Strategy -Is the strategy of aggression usually employed by the firm that is not presently the leader, but aspires to leadership position in the industry. It acts as a challenger and the leader is mostly its target. It tries to expand its market share and utilises all the elements of the marketing mix in attacking the leader.

Defensive Strategy -Is usually employed by the leader who has the compulsion to defend his position against the confrontation of powerful existing competitors or strong new entrants trying to remove the leader from the topmost position. The leader has to maintain constant vigilance and defend its position against the attack of the challengers.

Niche Strategy - Is usually employed by firms, which neither confronts nor defend it. It cultivates a small market segment for itself with unique products/services; supported by a unique marketing mix. Small firms with distinctive capabilities adopt this stance. A market niche to be worthwhile must have characteristics such as reasonable size, profit potential and growth potential.

PRODUCT CLASSIFICATION

The nature of product is found to have considerable impact on the method of product positing. There are two classes of products consumer goods, and industrial goods, and this classification is useful in product positioning. The table given below shows the categories of consumer and industrial goods. Marketers have traditionally classified products on the basis of there characteristics: durability, tangibility and use.

DURABILITY AND TANGIBILITY

a. Non - durable goods: non-durable goods are tangible goods normally consumed In one or a few uses, for example, soap, salt and biscuits.

b. Durable goods: for example, colour TV, Refrigerator, washing machine and Vacuum cleaners.

c. Services: services rate intangible, inseparable, variable and perishable products, for example, airline and banking services

CONSUMER GOODS CLASSIFICATION

a. Convenience Goods: these are goods that the customer usually purchases frequently immediately and with a minimum of efforts, example includes soaps and newspapers.

   a. Convenience goods can be further classification into three categories:

      i. Stable goods: consumer purchase on regular basis.

      ii. Impulse goods: consumer purchase without any planning or search efforts.

      iii. Emergency goods: consumer purchase on urgent need.

b. Shopping Goods: these are goods that the customer, in the process of selection and purchase characteristically compare on such bases as suitability and quality. Example: furniture, electrical appliances etc.

c. Specialty goods: these are goods with unique characteristic or brand identification for which a sufficient number of buyers are willing to make a special purchasing effort. For example, cars.

Unsought goods: these are goods the consumer does not know about or does not normally think of buying. The classic example of known but unsought goods is life insurance.

INDUSTRIAL GOODS CLASSIFICATION

- Material and Parts: these are goods that enter the manufacturer's product completely. They fall into two classes. Raw material and manufactured material part.
- Capital Items: these are long lasting goods that facilitate developing or managing the finished products. They include two groups: installation and equipments.
- C. Supplies and Business Services: these are short-listing goods and services that facilitate developing or managing the finished products.

USEFUL DECISIONS FOR PRODUCTS MANAGEMENT

The search for competitive advantage - and escape from price-based competition - often centres on the value - creating supplementary services that surrounds this core and add differentiation. Managers should be aware of the important of selecting the right mix of supplementary service elements-no more and no less than needed -and creating synergy by ensuring that they are all internally consistent. Customer research, evaluation of competitive offering and feedback from employees can all provide important inputs to the decision making process. Three principal factors should be considered here are.

- The nature of the market and competition from the product.
- The nature of assistance needed by the product regarding production, engineering, financing, staffing and so on.
- Strategic requirement of a border nature, namely, those affecting the product line, the business or the whole corporation.

CONSIDERABLE FACTORS IN ORGANIZING FOR PRODUCT MANAGEMENT

- What do we want to out of product management?
- What do we want our product manager to do?
- How do we want our product manager to do their jobs?
- What operational guidelines will we established?
- What expectation do we have for the specific contribution of product manager and product management?
- What authorities will be assigned to product managers?
- What are the number and nature of products and managers?

- What are product objective?
- How will we measure the effectiveness of our product management?

ROLE OF PRODUCTS MANAGER

In assessing the product manager's performance the following checklist can be used:

- Product line control
- Product life cycle, analysis and capitalization
- Product development and success of new products recommended
- Improved communication
- Improved supplies and sourcing
- More and better market information
- Wider and better market information
- Centralized products planning
- Coordination of activities
- Achievement of planned profits
- Cost and profit control

SUMMARY

What is a Product

- What you but, that satisfied what you want to be able to do.
- It can be "good felling" causes you bought some cosmetic and someone said you looked pretty.
- It could be a happy stomach cause you bought a meal that tasted great.
- It could be easier homework cause you bought new software for your company.
- Most customer think about product in terms of the total satisfaction.
- This can lead t statements such as "we don't sell cars, we sell safety!"
- We don't sell houses, we sell homes.

Product Line

- A series of related products.
- A group of products that are physically similar in performance, use or feature and intended for a similar market.
- "A set of products that are closely related."
- Shoes Nike, Adidas, Rebook, file, new balance, British knight, books, converse, vans, sic, puma notebooks, Toshiba, NEC, TI, Compaq, IBM, DELL.
- Apple, HP, Hitachi, mitsubishi, matsushita.

Cannibalization

- Situation involving one products taking sales from another offering in a product line.
- Cannibalization occurs when sales of a new product cut into (reduce) the sales of a firm's existing products.

Product Mix Decisions

- What product should the company make?
- Where exactly are these products to be offered?
- What should be the width of the product mix?
- How many different product lines can the company accommodate?
- How should the products be positioned in the market?
- What should be the brand policy?

Basically the answers to these will constitute the product policy of a firm. It constitutes the following:

Appraisal of the product line and the individual products- No product line is perfect and also does not run for all times to come. Changes happen in the business environment, customer tastes and preferences, extent of competition that pressurise the product policy of the firm. New, changed, advanced products are introduced or even old products are withdrawn from the market by the companies to revive the lost market image, to overcome the treat of functional obsolescence due to new improved /substitute products introduced by competitors, to regain profitability or when the product has entered a stage of decline. Firm needs to constantly monitor the company's product policy. This topic of Product Mix & Product Line is very important so concentrate on it.

When we say a firm's product mix we are actually discussing about all product items it offers.

Hindustan Lever's product mix includes agro-chemical products, soaps, detergents, toothpaste, shampoos, Talcum powders, cosmetics and now, frozen foods. Just suppose any organization is marketing more than one product then it has a product mix.

- Product item-a single product
- Product line-all items of the same type
- Product mix-total group of products that an organization markets

Now if I say a product line what do you understand from this?

It is basically a group of products that are related because of customer, marketing and or production considerations. I hope all of you know that Rin, Wheel, Rin Solarox, Rin detergent powder, Surf, and Surf Ultra are part of Lever's detergents line and Le Sancy, Lux, Rexona, Lifebuoy, are part of its soaps line. When we are discussing about a typical large multi-product firm's product mix includes new, growing, maturing and declining products.

Reasons for limiting to one product.

1. To counteract the effects of the PLC on a one product firm.
2. To even out seasonal sales patterns.
3. To use company resources and capabilities more effectively.
4. To capitalize on middlemen and consumer acceptance of established products.
5. To spread production and marketing costs over a wider product mix.
6. To become better known and respected by middlemen and consumers.

Breadth & Depth

Now you have a fair idea on what is a product mix. In product you have to define the structural dimensions of breadth (or width) and depth. Breadth refers to the number of different product lines. Depth refers to the number of product items within each line. A firm can expand its product mix by increasing the number of product lines or the depth within one or more product lines. HLL expanded in breadth when it entered the agrochemical business. It expanded in depth when it bought TOMCO a soaps and detergents company.

You would have noticed that so many companies market just one or two product lines, and hence their product mix is narrow. Do you know in which all areas General Electric operates? It basically operates in diverse fields, and has broad product mix. As all of us know that pharmaceutical company has a product line of antibiotics. It has several dosage forms like it can be in the form of capsules, dispersible tablets for children, vaginal suppositories, injections, eardrops, eye drops and Syrups under the dosage form and then the size of the package can be different. The company has several brands of antibiotics, and each brand has several dosage forms and sizes. We can say, that its product mix has depth. On the contrary, a few products, in one size only as one brand is an example of a shallow product depth.

All the decisions related to product lines offers are from company's strategic plan and marketing plan. It considers the segmentation of the market and targeting. Just suppose an organization wishes to target young' children, it can add a whole new product line for it. New product lines are either a matter internal development or can be acquire. Each product line also can be expanded. The important idea is that the product line of a company reflects the objectives of the organization, the targeting decided upon and the buyer behaviour in a given market.

Modifying the existing Product lines:

We have a number of reasons to alter either an existing product or a product line. The reasons could be to support marketing strategy, to improve sales, to improve profits, to expand market share. We can also consider what the product as such contributes to the product portfolio. We can modify a product line by altering either one or more than one of the following attributes:

1. Composition of the product line
2. Expansion or contraction of product line
3. Value addition process
4. Brand
5. Packaging
6. Physical characteristics
7. Positioning

The first two attributes are relevant to a set of products in the product line. The rest are relevant to either individual products or product lines.

Expanding and Reducing the Product Line:

As you are aware that there are many models of TV available in the market. There is a large variety of radio sets from Sony. Underlines bras are available in a number of styles. Syrups and crushes are available in many flavours, e.g., Rasna concentrates and Mala's crushes. There are technical products with higher and lesser sophistication. We find many product categories where consumers prefer to have a great variety for their satisfaction. Marketers are adopting strategies of adding new versions with new specifications, while retaining the old versions for the less sophisticated consumers. Sometimes this addition of new products to existing line is done to include complementary products, e.g., a toothpaste marketer may add toothbrushes to the product line. Camel may introduce paintbrushes, which go welt with its watercolours. Sometimes, there are occasion to delete a product/products from the line. A product, which shows decline in terms of sales, may be abandoned. Non-contributing products may be eliminated. While doing so, it should be seen that other products in the product line are not affected.

Product line length:

Now you should ask a question what is the optimum size of a product line?

A line is too long if after eliminating a product is results into increased profits. A line is too short when any addition to it results into increased profits.

One thing should be clear to you that the Company's overall objectives do affect the length of its product line. For instance, a company may have the objective of expanding its market share. It will then have a longer product line. Contribution of individual products to profits may be ignored. However, a company whose objective is to have larger profits will have a shorter product line consisting of those items, which contribute to profits substantially Product lines have a tendency, to lengthen over a period of time. Many a time, a firm may, have extra capacity, which is used for developing new items. Sales people and trade put pressure on management to keep on adding items to a product line so as, to satisfy their customers.

Lengthening of the line shoot up costs. At some point, this must come to halt. Loss making items are then eliminated. The contribution of items to profits is studied. Thus in the life of an organization, there is a cycle of longer product line followed by a pruned product line. This cycle is repeated again arid again.

Line stretching: Most of the companies have range of products in its existing product lines, like Videocon has a range of TVs in its product line, right from budget TVs to premium TVs. Line stretching occurs when this range is lengthened. This stretching could be upward, downward or both ways.

Upward stretching: Here a company operates in the lower end of the market. By upward stretch, it proposes to enter the higher end. Perhaps, it is motivated by higher margin of profits, higher growth rate or a position of a full-range marketer. This decision has its own risks. A well-established high-end marketer might assault the stretcher by stretching downwards. Besides, it is a question of credibility of a lower-end marketer -whether he will be able to produce high quality products. There is one more risk. The existing infrastructure of a low-end marketer may not be competent to deal with the high-end market.

Downward stretch: Lets start with an example: like all of you know parker, parker started with pens only at high price but if we look at parker today we can see products available in the range of 50 Rupees which no one could have though of in older times. Many companies start with high-end products, but later stretch downwards by adding low-priced products. The down-end products are advertised heavily so as to pull customers to the whole line on the basis of price. Videocon advertises its budget line 14" inches TV at Rs. 8,000. Once the customer is pulled, he may decide to buy a higher priced model- he trades up. This strategy needs careful handling. The budget brand being promoted should not dilute the overall brand image. Besides, the budget brand must be available. Consumers should not get a feeling that they were hooked to a bait, for switching later. Downward stretch is practiced in the following situations:

- A competitor stretches upward and challenges the marketer. He counter-attacks him stretching downwards
- Most companies start at the upper end, and then roll downwards.
- The high-end market has a slow growth rate.
- By filling the gap at the low-end, new competition is avoided.

Downward stretch has its own risks. The down-end item might cannibalize the high-end items. Besides, our downward stretch might provoke a competitor to move upward. Down-end product may not be managed properly as the company may not have that capacity. It may dilute the brand image of the company's products. It is, however, needs careful consideration - a product line should not have a gap at the lower-end. It exposes the company to competition, e.g., American car companies faced the competition from small-sized, Japanese cars at the lower-end of the market.

Two way stretch: Beside upward and downward stretch you can even stretch in two ways like several companies serve the middle-end market. They can stretch their product line in both the directions. A hotel company operating hotels in the comfort category where each room has a tariff 2000-3000 a day might decide to have elite upper-end hotels with tariffs of Rs. 5000-7000 a lower-end budget hotels with tariffs of Rs. 600-1500 a day. Ashoka group of ITC has thus elite 5-Star hotels, at the upper-end comfort hotels at the middleend and budget hotels like Ashoka Yatri Niwas at lower end.

Application exercise: Go to the area of your town that has a number of restaurants. Compare the product mix of one with the other. Are there any differences in width or depth? How could they stretch their lines?

Cannibalization: When the sales of the firms new products are due mainly because of decreasing sales of its existing and established product then we say that cannibalization has occurs in brief we can say by this you are actually eating away your own market. A good example of it would be Hyundai Santro they have introduced Santro Xing as a new product in the market in other way they have cannibalized their own market, like a person who wanted to buy Santro old model will buy Xing as it latest so they are not capturing new customer but converting their own customers only if they are able to make a person buy their product where he was planning to buy some product of Maruti then it is not cannibalization.

If you want to avoid cannibalization, the new product should not be identified too closely with established products. Instead it should be targeted with new appeals to different market segments. Cannibalization is desirable when margins on new products are higher than those on established Products. In highly competitive industries, it is often desirable to induce target customers to trade up to the firm's newer products. This strategy is adopted by Videocon International, Which entered the market with a low priced color TV with basic features and then introduced more sophisticated models up the price scale in order to ensure that customers in all segments would buy only Videocon products.

Product Lines and Brands

Most service organization offers a line products rather than just a single product. Some of these products are distinctly different from one another. Again in response to changing market opportunities, companies may revise the mix of products that they offer.

Following example illustrate this concept.

British airways (BA), which explicitly reorganizes eight different air travel products - or brand - under the British airways umbrella. (The company also has equity shares in several other airlines). There are four intercontinental service brands - Concorde supersonic deluxe service), first class (deluxe subsonic service), club world (business class) and world (business class), and world traveler (economy class); two intra - European brands-club world (business class) and euro - traveler (economy class): and within the united kingdom, the super shuttle brand, offering a graduated economy seat and high - frequency service. In additional, six commuter airlines, flying in British airways colors, operate service in partnership with BA under the British airways express brand. As described by Douglas each British airways brand has a key brand proposition and a set of clearly stated product specifications for preflight, in-flight and on-arrival service element. To provide additional focus on product, pricing and marketing communications, responsibility for managing and developing each brand is assigned to a brand management team. Through internal training and external communication, staff and passengers alike are kept informed of the characteristic of each brand.

Brand Decision

Many consumers products their basic feature, need attractive packing and a 'brand name'. A brand is a symbol or a mark that helps customers in instant recall, differentiating it thereby roam the competing products of a similar nature.

What is the brand? too often even marketing professional don't have an answer and to many have their 'own' answer. Which makes life very confusing! We've trawled though our resources to find some of the best definitions: the dictionary of business and management defines a brand Asia name, sign or symbol used to identify items or services of the seller(s) and to differentiate the from goods of competitors.

Signs and symbols are parts of what a brand is, but to us this is a very incomplete definition. Walter Land or one of the greats of the advertising industry, said: " simply put, a brand is a promise. By identifying and authenticating a products or service it delivers a pledge f satisfaction and quality. In his book, 'building strong brand' David Aaker suggests the brand is a 'mental box' and gives s definition of brand equity as: 'a set of assets (or liabilities) linked to a brand's name and symbol that adds to (or subtracts from) the value provided by a product or service.

According to the American marketing association, "A brand name is a part consisting of a word, letter, groups of words or letters to identify the goods or services of a seller or a group of seller and to differentiate them from those of the competitors." David Ogilvy defined a brand are not necessarily positive! Building from this idea of a 'mental box' a more poetic definition might be: these are all great definitions, but we believe the best is this: "a brand is a collection of perceptions in the mind of the consumer. A brand is the most valuable real-state in the world, a corner of the consumer's mind". Why is the best? Well, first of all it is easy to remember, which is always useful! But it is also best because it works to remind us of some key point:

This definition make it absolutely clear that a brand is very different from a product' or service. A brand is intangible and exists in the mind of the consumer. This identification helps us understand the idea of brand loyalty and the 'loyalty ladder'. Different people have different perceptions of a product or service, which places then at different point of loyalty ladder. A brand mark is a symbol or a design used for the purpose of identification.

For example: Air India's MAHARAJA. The legal version of a brand mark is the 'trade mark' e.g., Ashok Masal and Good Health Atta. A brand is given legal protection from being used by others because it is capable of exclusive approbation. A brand distinguishes a product or service from similar offerings on the basis of names are: LUX, LIRIL, REXONA, EVITA, PROTEX, HAMAM AND LE SANSI in case of toilet soaps; SUR, ARIEL, and NIRMA in case of detergents and NIVEA, FEM, OIL OF OLEY, CHARMIS AND VASELINE in case of vanishing creams.

Building Brands in the New Economy

- Clarify the corporation's basic values and build the corporate brand.
- Use brand managers to carry out the tactical work.
- Develop a more comprehensive brand-building plan.
- Define the brand's basic essence to be delivered wherever it is sold.

- Use the brand-value proposition as the key driver of the company's strategy, operations, services, and product development.
- Measure their brand-building effectiveness, not by the old measures of awareness, recognition, and recall, but by a more comprehensive set of measures including customer-perceived value, customer satisfaction, customer share of wallet, customer retention, and customer advocacy

Brand preference

Aaker's five levels of customer attitude:

- The customer will change brands, especially for price reasons. No brand loyalty.
- Customer is satisfied. No reason to change brands.
- Customer is satisfied and would incur cost by changing brand.
- Customer values the brand and sees it as a friend.
- Customer is devoted to the brand.

Brands provide a strong competitive advantage to the companies owning them and hence they are increasingly becoming important tradable assests. In 1993, Coca-Cola paid about Rs.175 crore to buy Thums-up, Limca, Citra and Gold Spot brands. In 1994 Godrej soaps paid Rs.12 crore to acquire the Rs.67 crore translectra.

In 1995, Smithkline Beecham paid Rs.42 crore to acquire the Crocin brand from Duphar Interfan. In 1997, Knoll Pharma sold Coldarin and Burnol for Rs.34 crore Ranbaxy paid Rs.80 crore to Gufic Labs for Mox, Zole Excel and Suprimox. In 1997, Hindustan Lever paid Rs.110 crore for Lakme's basket of brands and only Rs.29 crore for Lakme's two plants.

In 1999, Marico industries bought parachute and Suffola brands from Bombay oil industries for Rs.30 crore. The Gramophone company of India acquired Sangeetha, a leading audio producer of classical and devotional songs in the South. Acquiring a brand is a better, superior option over purchasing the entire operations of the company owing them for 3 months. The buyer buys only the brand name. The brand name could be used to sell anything, which comes under the established brand personality. For example, the Burnol brand name could be used to sell an antiseptic like Dettol. Buying a brand provides a ready-made market. Apparently, Ranbaxy bought Mox because its own brand in the name family, Amoxycillin was not doing too well. Buying a brand saves a lot of brand building time and cost. Drug companies are known to recoup the cost of acquiring a brand in less than four years.

A name, term, sign, symbol, or design used to identify the products of one firm and to differentiate them from competitive offerings. Something used to show customers that one product is different then the products of another manufacturer. Worlds, letters, or symbols that make up a name used to identify and distinguish the firm's offerings from those of its competitors.

Generic Name Brand: A brand name over which the original owner has lost exclusive claim because all offerings in the associated class of products have become generally known by the brand name (usually that of the first or leading brand in that product class).

Trademark

- Brand that has been given legal protection and has been granted solely to its owner
- Originally helped trace the source of the guild producer
- In modern era, makes it easier to identify all the products from a particular company.
- Makes shopping easier
- Helps the companies launching new products
- Brand Recognition - awareness, loyalty, quality, emotion "customers remember the brand"
- Brand Preference / Loyalty - the degree to which customers are committed to further purchases e.g. "choose the brand over other brands"
- Brand Insistence - "willing to search for it." and if they don't find the brand they want, will not but a substitute
- Brand Equity - "... the values of a brand's overall strength in the market..."
- Brand Awareness - your product is the first that comes to mind in a certain product category e.g. Snapple ice tea, jeans - Levi's, Walkman - SONY
- Brand Awareness - your product is the first that comes to mind in a certain product category e.g., ice tea = Snapple, running shoes = Nike

- Trademark
- A brand that has been given exclusive legal protection - name and the design

Packaging

Earlier, packaging was considered a major expense in marketing. For some toiletries, packaging costs actually exceeded the costs of contents. Today, it is however, fully recognized that packaging helps in branding and promoting brand loyalty. It also enables the buyers to handle and carry their products with case. Moreover, packaging may cut marketing costs thus adding to profit.

Qualities of Good Packaging

- Attractive appearance
- Convenient for storage and display
- Shield against damage or spoiling
- Product description shown on the package

Function of Packaging Especially for Consumer Goods

- Protection and presentation are the basic functions of a packaging
- Modern marketing methods demand that, package be convenient to handle transport requirements.
- A package must be made to consistent and rigid quality standards. The consumer demands uniformity each time he purchases a product.
- Transport economics
- Every package must be recognizable and
- Every package must have eye appeal

Packing to be satisfactory should satisfy the following conditions:

- It should be capable of withstanding the hazards of handling and transport. The cargo may be handled manually and mechanically. The handling methods may differ between places. When manually handled, it may be tilted, draped, thrown, pulled, pushed, rolled etc. further it may also be subject to compression dude to stacking. The packing should, therefore, be capable of withstanding such hazards of handling and transportation.
- It should be easy to handle. To facilitate easy handling, bulk packs may be provided with handling facilities like books,

handles, gripper's etc. in case of products which shall not be turned upside down, the position should be clearly indicated like marking 'this side up'. In case of fragile articles, which shall not be subject to rough handling, the size, shape and weight of the pack should be amendable for smooth handling. Further, it should also be indicated on the pack.

- It should be amendable to quick examination of contents. It may be remembered that the customs authorities of the exporting and importing countries may want to examine the contents.
- It should be easy to identify.
- It should be adequately marked.
- Unless it is necessary, the contents shall not be disclosed.
- It should be easy to dispose of.
- Packing must confirm to the buyer's specifications. If any and the regulations in the exporting and importing countries, guidelines and regulation by the shipping company, etc. care should be taken to observe the established has prescribed packing standards for certain goods. The British standard packing code, published by the British standards institution and Exporters Encyclopedia, USA, give detailed packing instruction. Shipping companies also given certain packing instructions especially for highly dangerous products. According to the products he intends to export, the exporter has to choose the right type of packing 1 to send the goods in good condition to the destination. A right package always guarantees the right quality of the product at the time of delivery.

Labeling

Labeling is regarded as part of marketing because packaging decision making involves the consideration of the labeling requirements. In international trade, many countries insist that labeling should be done in the absence of such a statutory requirement. Statutory obligations are important aspects of labeling. Many countries have laid down labeling requirements in respect of a number for commodities. According to the regulations labeling of food items should disclose information about a number of aspects like date of manufacturing, expiry date or optimum storage period for good which do not have an indefinite storage period, composition, storage conditions, necessary method of use, if necessary etc.

Role of Packaging

- It helps increase sales
- It adds to the use of a product
- It helps promote a product
- It contributes to the safety of a product
- It helps in storage
- It helps in product differentiation

PACKAGING DECISIONS

Packaging Design

It is not easy to design a package for various items. For example, all shaving creams come in tubes, but different brands of shaving cream have different packaging. Because of the high cost of packaging some companies have resorted to refill packs.

Color

Color is an important factor for determining customer acceptance or rejection of a product. The use of right colors in packaging may help marketers reap huge advantage. Packaging color should be attractive so that it may help promote sales.

Packaging the Product Line

A company must decide whether to develop a family resemblance in the packaging of its several products. Families packaging involves the use of identical packages for all products or the use of packages with some common feature.

New Products Development Strategies

With advances in technology and intense competition, the creation of new products has become a way of life in India. However, begin a developing country, India is yet to face a situation of too many products chasing a handful of customers. Moreover, the sheer size of the Indian market and the continuing economic development has opened up new vistas for launching new products. This lesson discusses new products development process in detail and also analyses the new product launches in India in the new millennium.

New Products Launches

An analysis of new products development in the recent past shows that these products have been either offshoots of technological development in the west or improvement over the existing products in the areas of their, style, substance or packing. In the recent past, new product launches in India have shown that these launches can be broadly classified into three categories.

Marketing Innovations

Companies have been improvement on existing products and have launched these as new products in the market. For instance, magi noodles, soft drink in tetra pack, shrikh and pan parag. Etc. are basically slightly alternated version of existing or old products. Here, consumers did not require changing their consumption habits drastically to accommodate these new products. These are example of improvement in the products whose success was derived more from marketing innovation such as packing, branding and easy availability, rather than any significant change in the substance of the product itself.

Product Improvement

The launch of 100cc two-wheelers, radical types, instamatic cameras are basically slight innovations on the technology / design of existing products, although the products category as such already existed in its primitive form. Such new products are generally targeted for a new class of buyers. The success of such ventures depends upon the ability of the marketers to convince the consumer about the improvement in the performance over traditional brands(s) as well as over similar new extract. For example, in the 100cc two wheelers vehicle market, TVS Suzuki was the entrant and it had captured a sizable market. Subsequently, hero Honda became the market leader in this category of motorcycle by virtue of better performance and marketing techniques.

Technological Innovations

The Indian market has experienced a rapid induction of products like personal computers, photocopiers and colour television. Generally these products require some kind of assembling of improved kits. Although adaptation of such products calls for substantial change in the consumption pattern, yet these products have succeeded in view of their significant utility to the user. Such venture require an initial awareness building and persuasion to install the product. Initial resistance to change may delay any adoption of new technologies. However, a look at the track record of such new product shows that early entrants have reaped the benefits of leadership. Subsequent entrants have faced difficult in established themselves.

Overview of New Products Development Process

New products development consists of the certain of new ideas, their evaluation in terms of sales potentials and profitability, production facilities, resource available, designs and production testing and marketing of the products. The main task of the product planners is to identify specific customer needs and expectations and align company's capabilities with the changing market demands. In each of these stages, the management must decide: (a) whether to move on to the next stage, (b) to abandon the product, or (c) to seek additional informations.

Routes of New Products Development

Transfer of Technology

New Products have often been launched, based on new technology, either acquired from the parent company or with foreign collaboration. Launch of the personal computer or photocopying machine is a move in this direction.

Diversification

Sometimes companies have entered into new lines of business and catered to altogether new markets for the first time. DCM'S entry into the LCV market fits into this category. Similarly, ITC's decision to enter into hotels, paperboards, edible oil, and tissue paper is a diversification strategy. Likewise, Shaw Wallace diversified to real estate business. In general, diversification strategy tries to reduce the dependence of a company on a limited line of products. At times, companies find the new business more profitable than their former activities.

Additions to Existing Product Lines

New product lines and brand extensions have sometimes supplemented a company's existing business. Videocon's entry in to washing machines and music systems form color televisions is a case in point. Similarly, as a business group, Godrej's strategy to expand its product range from consumer non-durables like toiletries to durable such as refrigerators, cupboards and even office equipments is a classic example of product line extension.

Improvements / Revisions in Existing Products

New products that offer superior performance and replace existing products are another way of entering the market. For example, the launch of transistor sets and cassette players, though primitive by today's standards, were at one time new to the market. They eventually replaced radios and gramophones. More recently Bata has successfully launched many sportswear, fashion jeans and apparels.

Cost Reductions

New products that provide similar performance at lower cost e.g., Nirma detergent, Tata - 407 LCV.

Products Relaunch

Sometimes old products have been relaunched with minor improvements and targeted at completely new markets or consumer segments, e.g., the launch of many food products like Good day biscuits, Tata Tea, Pan Parag, et. Fall under this type of new product launches.

Significance of New Product Development

Whatever may be nature of operation of a concern, product planning and development is necessary for its survival and growth in the long run. Every product has a life cycle and t become obsolete after the completion of its life cycle. Therefore, it is essential to develop new products and alter or improve the existing ones to meet the requirements of customers.

One of the most common products - planning problems relates to the addition of new products to the existing product line. Addition of new products involves generation of new product ideas, appraisal of various possibilities, economic analysis, product development, product testing, test marketing and developing markets.

Another important problem of product planning is modification or elimination of existing products. The need for continuous of the product is great because society's needs are always changing and improved products must be introduced to fulfill them. All products have certain deficiencies, as they are the result of great many compromises. The perfect product has yet to be made. Research makes possible the reduction of these deficiencies and brings about improved products.

New Product Development Process

The developers must be conscious of the probabilistic nature of their endeavors. New product development endeavors are complex, strongly dependent on diversified human resources and significantly affected by factors and events beyond the developers control. Thus, the belief that the implementation of a mechanical methodology can assure success is an illusion and at times a delusion.

Sources of New Product Ideas

- Customers: Customers are sometimes able to discuss their requirements and offer ideas that will meet those problems.
- Competitors: Systematic comparison or bench marking with the competition may offer good source of new product ideas.
- Distributors: Suggestions from distributors and their problems in handling present products often thrown up new ideas.
- Creative techniques: Brainstorming, focused interviews and technological forecasting enable one to find out the latent capabilities of innovations.
- External world: The external world, especially the use of their technology, offers a good source of ideas for implementation in the home market.
- Research and development: Create new product ideas through R&D.

From initial generation of ideas to full commercialization and well into the mature age of a product, the developers should strive to control what is in their power to control a do to monitor what is beyond their control. No single facet of new product development can assure success. Few facets are so deter mental that they are cannot be at least alleviated. Because of the probabilistic nature of new product development, planning and assessments must consider long-term repercussions.

Organizational Structure and Staffing

Given a clear strategy it is necessary to build the organizational capability to meet the challenge. At times this is simply appointing a committee. Other times it is creating an entirely new team and physically separating it from the ongoing organization. Selecting the right persons for such a team is difficult.

Concept Creation and Development

Once the enabling conditions of strategy and organization are identified, actual ideation can begin. First, the team must focus on one area of interest or activity - specifically, a product category, a group of team may study floppy discs and try to improve them. Another team may try to find better ways to solve the problems of teachers. Or they may work to develop improved gold balls or golf balls or golf clubs. They may focus on their design capability and find new applications. Or they may focus on combinations of two or more of these areas.

Concept Development

Concept development involves asking question such as the following:

- Need: Do customers find a strong perceived need for the benefit offered?
- Trust: Do they believe that the new product has the benefits claimed?
- Communicability: Do customers easily understand the key benefits being offered?
- Usage: Does it offer easy adoption?
- Perceived Value: Do Customers see it as offering value at the price being considered?

After the working area is defined, concept generation begins, often at a hectic pace. Ideas flow fast and in most cases rejection is equality fast. The team looks for the few fast and inmost cases rejection is equally fast. The team looks for the few concepts the warrant concepts development - the evolving of an original ideation attempt into a specific statement of need, form and technology that can be evaluated.

Concept Evaluation

Often considered the heart of the new products process, the Evaluation State is long, involved, and difficult. Evaluation actually begins when the strategist evaluates the organization's abilities. And it continues long after a product is marketed since a product often needs revision to remain competitive. Concept testing and other prescreening marketing research prepare the team for the actual screening evaluation. This evaluation is a full, detailed analysis of the proposal. If the concept passes screening, technical development begins. The technical work produces prototypes, which can then be evaluated and if all goes well, the finished product can be prepared for use testing. Next, the team joins the new product to its marketing plan for a test of them combined - called market testing. All of the above data combine to permit a full financial analysis near the end of development.

Commercialization

Management's decision that the new item is worth marketing either in a test market situation or in a full - scale launch - is called the point of commercialization. Pilot processes are then converted to full-scale manufacturing. Final design specifications are written. Marketing strategy is finalized, including actual brand, packaging, service commitment etc.

The team gradually moves the company from tentative exploration of a concept into production and marketing of a new product.

Review and Evaluation

After launch the entire project must be reviewed to see how successful the team was, those problems they faced and what they can learn to facilitate the next project.

Analysis of New Product Launches in India

Empirical data suggests that in highly competitive markets such as in the US, the success rate of new launches, depending on the strictness of definition of success, varies from a low of two per cent to a high of 10 per cent. Markets in India are not as competitive as in the West and therefore, the success rate of new launches is likely to be healthier. A study by Abraham Koshy, revealed the following facts

On an overall basis, out of all the new launches, 53 per cent were successes and the remaining 47 per cent were failures. This implies that, cater is paribus, even at an optimistic level, new launches are likely to have a probability of success of around 50 per cent. In reality, this proportion may even at an optimistic level, new launches in the country today, given the level competitiveness in the market and professionalism of companies, is likely to be less than 30 per cent! This is worse than even the odds when an unbiased coin tosses; no company can invest huge resources for new launches if the probability of success is so unfavorable. The message from this insight is clear when the chances of survival are so low, the only way to beat the odds is through a systematic and professional approach to managing new launches. Other wise it is 50 - 50.

The mortality rates of new brands indeed tend to the high; only about 36 per cent of new products launched in the market with new brand names survived, the remaining 64 per cent were failures. This is indeed more unfavorable than the overall situation presented in the preceding paragraph it means that if you do not have a strong brand to leverage and therefore, there is a need to build brand awareness and create brand preferences afresh, then you should be even more thorough in your new launch efforts. Life extensions and brand extensions were significantly more successful than the launch of new brands. Thus, 71 per cent of new launches that were line extensions and 63 per cent of brand extensions were successful in the market place. From one perspective, this suggests that your chances of success in a new launch are far greater if you leverage. From a different perspective, it also means that a levering strategy will not automatically guarantee you success; the results show that nearly a third of line extensions as well as brand extensions were failure. These in other words imply that even if you have strong brands, you need to be systematic in configuring your offer in tune with market needs. Inappropriate leveraging of brand names, leveraging weak brands and improper alignment of marketing mix elements are certified formulae for failures.

Success of New Launches

A perplexing question that a practitioner is often confronted with is the reasons for product failures. Marketing literature suggests several reasons for product failures. These reasons are broadly classified under product (or offer) related factors, market by the research team (or consumer) related factors, market by the research team related factors and competition related factors. The latter two reasons, namely market related and competition related factors provide the context of a firm's marketing operations and hence these are factors on which the firms can exert little control. All that a firm can do is to understand these given conditions and then align the total market offer based on these realities. And this is given where many firms slip rather badly. Findings of the study conducted by IIM, Calcutta provided interesting insights into the ways in which firms manage their new product activities.

Failure in Utilizing / Adopting Marketing Research Technique

The fundamental condition to succeed in any market is a deep understanding of consumers and an excellent appreciation of competitors and their activities. This can come about only if your company has strong systems and methods, not only to collect and analyze market data, but also to disseminate the information thus obtained to relevant decision makers within the organization. Studies revealed that nearly 67 per cent of the executives noted that market research agencies are seldom utilized by their companies to collect market data in a formal and structured manner; only the remaining 33 per cent of companies either frequently or almost always used marketing research agencies. Granting that it may be somewhat costly to use market research agencies on a regular basis, the extent of utilization of internal mechanisms to collect market data also does not seem to be very high. Nearly half the companies do not have strong formal mechanisms to collect systematic data on a regular basis from their own sales people and about a third of the companies rarely collect data from their retailers. If this is the general trend, then it is not very surprising that the success of new brand launches is low. The message, therefore, is that you need to review your internal systems and processes for gathering and utilizing market data relating to your consumers and competitors to what your decisions become sharper and data based. Success otherwise will be elusive.

Failure in Identifying Market Opportunities for New Brand Launches

One of the weakest links in many organizations is the absence of any systematic approaches for identifying market opportunities, either for introducing new brands and products, or for relaunching and\or repositioning of existing products. A glimpse at the mindset of companies, obtained from the survey of executives suggests that in most companies, the major source of new products ideas is the top management. These efforts are supplemented with analysis of foreign technology/ products or competitors' products. Seldom do companies obtain idea for new product launches from consumers. This is not surprising since the extent of utilization of market research for new products development. The picture then becomes clearer for new product opportunities; companies depends either on the secondary technology available in some markets. There is hardly any serious and systematic effort to understand consumer's needs and requirement in the context of competing offers and naturally the market opportunities thus imagined to have existed turn out to be here mirages!

Failure in Integrating Customer's Choice / Ideas in New Product Offering

Consumers do not pay for mere ideas; they only buy tangible offers that satisfy their needs. Companies, therefore, need to translate their brilliant ideas for new brand sand products into tangible offers that spell out the specific benefits that the new offer will provide, the needs that they will satisfy and the cost that the consumers will have to bear. This phase of transforming new ideas into tangible and viable market offer is very critical stage and is perhaps the stage where the firms commit major resource. But then can any firm take such major decisions without an assessment of likely consumer acceptance of the proposed new offer? In reality, unfortunately, many firms do not seem to be marking sufficient efforts in assessing consumers' reaction abut the new proposal and thus estimating the risks involved before investing huge resource to develop new offers. Further findings of the study suggest that 44 per cent of the firms do not carry out a formal concept testing and another 30 percent do it only occasionally. Data further suggests that 53 percent of the companies never or seldom make as per assessment of the financial viability of the proposed new products/brand before proceeding further with introduction plans.

These indications suggest that many a firms let pass occasion's access consumer preference carefully and fine-tune their proposal to reflect the value propositions of consumers. They slides over issues like leverage strengths of brands and appropriateness of equity of the brand for the proposed new product. Many a time firms even underplay the question as to whether or not the whole scheme makes the commercial sense. Given such limited in sight in to the likely future potential of the new venture, companies end up courting disaster. In fact, many sad endings could have been averted if only companies showed little more diligence in assessing consumer reactions to the new proposal and estimating commercial viability before making major resource commitments.

Failure in Product Testing

If the core product that you are offering to consumers does not provide the functional benefits that it is intended to provide, then no amount of advertisement and publicity can salvage the situation. Therefore, it is extremely important to ensure that the basic product meets consumer requirement. Research data revealed that nearly 56 percent of companies do test their products either frequently or almost always. Out of the remaining, 44 percent either never or rarely test their products. In all probability, the proportion of your offer, you do not have much to worry. However, even a good product will not survive if it needs to be made either before the invest in manufacturing and/or later. Many new brand failures in India today are more failures of concept rather than failures of basic product.

This observation suggests that you not only need to test the product to ensure that the functional performance under the laboratory as well as field conditions is satisfactory, but also it does address the felt needs of consumers better than competitors. This is also an activity, which will provide valid inputs to assess the likely market acceptance of the proposed new brand by way of volume prediction. This input certainly helps in assessing commercial viability of the proposal. Research findings suggest that most of the firms carry out some financial analysis at this stage.

Creativity in New Product Development

Consider a recent transformation at Procter & Gamble. Once a hotbed of creativity, P & G had in recent years seen the number of its product innovations decline significantly. In response, the company established Corporate New Ventures, a small cross-functional team that embodies creativity - enhancing practices. In terms of challenge for instance, members of the CNV team were allowed to elect themselves. How better to make sure someone is intrinsically motivated for an assignment than to ask for volunteers? Building a team from volunteers, it should be noted, was a major departure from standard P & G procedures. Members of the CNV team also were given a clear, challenging strategic goal: to invent radical news products that would build the company's future. Again departing from typical P & G practices, the team was given enormous latitude around how, when and where they approached their work.

In the three years since its inception. CNV has handed off II projects to the business sectors for execution. And as of early 1998, those products were beginning to flow out of the pipeline. The first product, design to provide portable heat for several hours relief of minor pain, was already in test marketing. And six other products were slated to go to test market within a year. Not surprisingly, given CNV's success, P & G is beginning to expand both the size and the scope of its CNV venture.

Flexible Product Design for New Product Development

Product design is fast emerging as a force in the new ICE - age economy - for Internet devices, Websites, office equipment and even household gadgets. All these technological changes are reducing the product life cycle and bringing in more and more design innovation. The market that has taken most of the beating is an electronic gadget, be it computers pocket devices or phones. Trendier, more vibrant than the earlier versions, they are getting smaller too. The shift towards sleek devices has come from the need for physical mobility, something that is crucial with almost all these gadgets. Studies indicate that the shift has more to do with analysis on human interaction with the devices. Product designs, today, focus on aspects of functionality, unlike the time when designs were incorporated to have a product extension in the market. The best product example to describe this is the hands- free option that most third generation cellular phones carry. Whether it is as simple as a pen or as complicated as a keyboard that can be folded and carried in the pocket, design is changing the way products are looked at. Another field that is witnessing a lot of design change is pharmaceutical and medicine and medical equipment. With new technological improvements and design innovations, one gets to know his or her blood pressure with a guage attached to one's watch. The watch gives out danger signals each time the pressure varies beyond the specified standards. It is amazing how quickly designers are able to conceptualize designs that are then incorporated into products. With designs playing such an important role in product differentiation, design specifications will change beyond imagination - soon.

Product design, the painstaking process by which prototypes are developed and specifications are created and implemented in actual production, is an integral part of any business strategy. For the process to work effectively, every aspect of each activity related to the product and its life cycle must be taken into account. These include supplier involvement, customer involvement, manufacturability, cost, time, management, usability, marketability and disassembly or recyclability. With such wide-ranging elements coming to play, a well - thought out design can provide a company with the competitive edge needed for achieving greater profits and higher market share. Organizations are always looking for better ways to design products. Intel, for example, has emphasized design ethnography, which focuses on understanding the customer and the culture in which a product is used. The world wide web is increasingly used for product design activities such as finding information on parts and materials, sharing designs among people, automating design sign-off's and linking geographically dispersed designed teams.

Majority of Chief Executives believe that design issues will be of increasing competitive importance in the coming years. Many product failures - even those by otherwise successful companies - might have been avoided if better product design methods were used. Author Tom Peters coined the phrase "design mindfulness" to refer to the benefits of a committed creative, an energetic focus on great design.

Integrating Consumer and Designer Preferences

Improved product design can be achieved by taking the viewpoints of both designers and consumers into account. In conventional product design, the marketing department sends consumers preferences to the designer, who then creates a design to meet those preferences. A delicate balance must be struck between the struck between the consumer and the designer since plans based solely on consumer preferences may be unfeasible or unrealistic. Designers acting alone, on the other hand, may come up with a product that is a technological marvel, but that consumers see as silly and unusable. Consumer's decision-making processes are not perfect and may given an inaccurate picture of preferences. They often think in terms of abstract goals that are difficult to translate into product features. A lack of expertise or incomplete consideration of alternatives can also lead consumers to make choices based on vague preferences, rather than considering ways to realize concrete operation benefits that would realized with greater experience and exploration.

Designers can make up for some of the short-comings of consumer input, since they usually understand more about future technologically possibilities and look at a longer time line. They are also in a better position to know that competitors might offer. For example, consumers may desire a "user - friendly" personal computer that is easy to get started with, but the designer realizes the computer should also meet longer - term needs. Therefore, designers should have the freedom to create innovative product designs that not only meet current user requirements but are also up to the demands of future consumer expectations. This give and take requires a delicate balance between designers and consumers since research has shown a high correlation between inadequate feedback from users and the failure of a new product containing technical innovations.

Striking a Balance between Consumers and Designers

The way a consumer looks at product attributes is usually much different from the way a designer looks at product "characteristics". For example, a consumer may want a boat to be fast, but a designer looks at characteristics that affect the speed of the boar, such as engine size and full shape. A distinction can be made between product characteristics and attributes: Product characteristics physically define the product and influence the formation of product attributes; product attributes define consumer perceptions and are usually fewer in number and more abstract than product characteristics.

Past product design research has focused on optimization with respect to either consumer attributes or designer characteristics. However, both the consumer and the designer will benefit from a balanced design. Plans based solely on consumer attributes ignore the relationship between attributes and characteristics; using only designer characteristics inadequately accounts for the consumer's preferences. A better approach to product design would account for the relationship between the two. In other words, what design characteristics would bring about the desired consumer attributes? In short, translating consumer attributes into the appropriate and corresponding design characteristics can optimize product design. This is the great benefit of multi-source product design: it optimizes both sides of the equation simultaneously.

THE FUTURE OF NEW PRODUCTS MANAGEMENT

In the new millennium, we are seeing more segmentation there will be even more competition for almost everyone than there is today; and life cycles of products will continue to get shorter or stay short. Similarly, most of the forces acting to increase the costs of innovation will remain high or will increase. In most instances productivity will increase as all producers focus so intently on it as the path to lower costs and higherquality product. On the positive side, three forces acting to at least partially forces acting to at least partially offset the negative forces described above. All three of these positive forces will get stronger, not weaker. The first, technology, is the strongest of all it can and that there is little left to invent, we know that this simply not so. Computerization, automated manufacturing, molecular biology, fiber optics and surface ceramics are just a few of many fields that offer what almost certainly will be more technological opportunities in the next 25 years than in the past 50. Molecular biology has the potential for outstripping anything else done so far in this century. Moreover, there is an amazing move to invest large sums of money in older technologies, especially in the so-called mature industries. And as a final plus international opportunity continues to grow and contribute new markets, new skills and new concepts of management.

The second positive force is the general willingness of consumers to accept new items - otherwise there is absolutely no basis for forecasting. And third, management's general capability has been growing almost exponentially, particularly by taking advantage of the many MBAs entering the work force and the wide array of continuing education opportunities for managers today. The combined results of these negative and positive forces are mixed, of course, but the negatives had no perceived effect on the development and marketing of home video systems or on the development of new drugs in recent years.

The general environment of social, economic and other forces seems to favor the continued viability of new products activities. At present no environmental force on the horizon has the power to blunt the force of product innovation. The leading on is the attitude of firms and their managements toward new products. More companies will eagerly seek such products and their searches will be more vigorous. Due primarily to (1) the interest in strategic market planning, (2) the subsequent growth in portfolio analysis and (3) marketing planning by individual business segments, more and more managements have come to see the dangers. The second force that will act directly on the motivation of new products managers is customer lifecycles - both consumer and industrial.

1. There are many basic new needs - an ever-growing number of them, amid an ever-growing population, with ever more money to spend.
2. Technology is fully capable of meeting many of this needs- never have we had find had the immediate technology potential that exists today?
3. And never have we had such knowledge and sophisticated new products profession and such industrial capability. We do indeed know how to develop new products successfully. Given trained individual as working in corporate environments that provide the conditions known to be effective output, the only reason for a new product failure is deliberate circumvention of correct procedure.

In summary regarding the new product process, we should expect that failure rates would fall, that budgets will be up and that there will be better all-round performance as expertise is build up both inside and outside the firm.

Many products generally have a characteristic known as perishable distinctiveness'. This means that a products, which is distinct when new, degenerate over the year into a common commodity. The process by which the distinctiveness gradually disappears as the product merge with other competitive degeneration. The cycle begins with the invention of a new product and is often followed by patent projection and further development to make it salable. This is usually followed by a rapid expansion in its sales as the products grains market acceptance. Then competitors enter the field with imitation and rival product and the distinctiveness of the new products. While some products fail immediately on birth or a little later, other may live long enough BPL's picture in pictures TV was eliminated and the introduction stage itself. This lesson focuses exclusively on the PLC of various products and its implications for managers in detail.

The innovation of a new product and its degeneration into common products is termed as the life cycle of products is termed as the life cycle of products. There are five distinct stages in the life of products as shown below:

Introduction: Research or engineering skill leads to product development. The product is put on the market; awareness and acceptance are minimal. There are high promotional costs. Sometimes a product may generate a new demand, for example, Maggi, Volume of sales is low and there may be heavy losses.

Growth: The product begins to make rapid sales gains because of the cumulative effects of begins to make rapid sales gains because of the cumulative effects of introductory promotion, distribution, and word of mouth influence. High and sharply rising profits may be witnessed. But to sustain growth, consumer satisfaction must be ensured at this stage.

Maturity: Sales growth continues, but at a diminishing rate, because of the declining number of potential customers who remain unaware of the product or who have taken no action. Also, the last of the unsuccessful competing brands will probably withdraw from the market. For this reason, sales are likely to continue to rise while the customers for the withdrawn barads are mopped up by the survivors. There is no improvement in the product but changes in selling effort are common. Profit margins slip despite rising sales.

Decline: Sales start to fall, as your product loses its appeal. Profits drop as production is often cut, competition in the marketplace gets stiffer as advertising is cut and plans are made to shelve the product in the future.

The following table shows the product life cycle and its different stages and the various characteristics, which they reflect, in the varying stages:

PCL Elements	**Introduction**	**Growth**	**Maturity**	**Decline**
Characteristics				
1. Sales	Low	Fast Growth	Slow Growth	Declining
2. Profits	Negligible	Peak Level	Declining	Low
3. Cash inflow	Negative	Moderate	High	Low
4. Competitors	Few	Growing	Many	Declining
5. Customers	Innovative	Mass Market	Mass Market	Laggards

PATTERN OF GROWTH

Even then the existence of initiative products/services and the emphasis of management on such products cannot be ignored. This may be due to the recognized marketing gap hitherto unfilled by the existing producers, product deficiencies and identified consumer dissatisfaction with available products in the market.

The super cautious attitude of management towards innovation, which may be due to fear and high cost of product failures, may also be a reason for increased emphasis on imitative new products. Just like a human being pass through different stages of the life cycle, a product in the market should also different stages of the life cycle a product in the market should also pass through different stages from introduction to decline and possible abandonment.

The concept of the product lifecycle indiscriminately applies both to innovative and imitative products. The noted stages of a product's life cycle include introduction, growth, maturity and saturation, decline and possible abandonment. He challenges and characteristics for innovative product imitative new product in their respective product life cycle stages are analyzed here. The strategies for meeting these challenges, at each stage of the life cycle for the respective products are also discussed.

Different Strategies

Innovative and imitative products require different kinds of marketing strategies. Right from the embryonic stage of product development, these differences in dealing with innovative and imitative new products are noticeable. For instance, a new brand of soap, toothpaste, scooter or car is an imitative new product; on the other hand, a flying car or scooter is an innovative product. Imitative new products have to overcome the existing competition to establish them in the market. But in the case of innovative products prospective and not the present competition is a challenge.

a. Introduction and Growth Stage: The introduction stage of the product life cycle is the entry of the product in the market. Generally, in the earlier days of introduction, because of the product is known and its positive characteristics are less known to the consumer, sales or less. Even though there is increase in sales, it is at a slow place. The ease of introducing a product depends on the degree of its novelty, improvements over the existing products, distinctiveness and a host of other factors.

Innovative products can be introduced in the market with relative competitive ease because there is no competition to be broken. This is much easier if the product has with a highly technical or utilitarian aspect. But for imitative products it is difficult even to enter the market under competitive conditions. No doubt, the degree of this difficulty is much influenced by the extent of market satisfaction number of existing rival products and the marketing and product advantage they offer to the customer.

Generally, the prospective consumers for a newly introduced product is already selective in his nature. Therefore new imitative products should have some step-up features and marginal improvements so as to divert the attention, affiliation and loyalty of the consumer from the already existing alternative brands in the market. But in the case of innovative or really new products, convincing the consumer about the product's marketing advantage or utility is enough to find a place in market. However, the initial positioning of the products should be on sound lines with a long run competitive perspective, so as to be less vulnerable to the competitor's strategies.

The introduction stage of any product is generally charactersied by low sales volume, limited distribution and high costs of promotion. These may be common to a great extent for innovative and imitative products. But with respect to promotion strategy, for truly innovative products the main objective is primary demand creations, whereas it is secondary demand for imitative products. In other words, due to the real newness of the product appeal to the consumer rather than bran appeal as in the case of imitative products on the other hand, where the existing products dominate the market, imitative products as new entrants should try to snatch away the market of other products and thus establish their share of the market..

The success of innovative products in the introducing phase depends largely on the promotional efforts and their positioning. But the success of imitative products is conditioned by the extend of competition, the existing competitors, strength and quality of their products, offered to the consumers through promotion and the life stage of the exiting products. The duration of the introduction stage for innovation is generally less, provided the products are effectively and extensively promoted. Moreover, the number of possible product failures is also less with respect to an innovative product. Because the direct competitive forces are absent the internal marketing effort and efficiency is the major deciding factor for the product's success. On the other hand, the imitative products often fail because of the competition and counter market strategies by the existing competitors.

Therefore, imitative products, which enter the growth stage should try to counter the marketing efforts of the marketers and at the same time develop a good image and a competitive edge by capitalizing the weakness of the existing products. The intensity of competition will also differ in this stage for innovative and imitative products should plan for product improvement or finding new uses for the product. Thus the marketer can maintain his competitive edge and retain his distinction and market market share. The duration of this stage of product life cycle may also vary in both cases. Imitative products, unless they are highly distinctive, of better quality and exceptionally appealing to the consumers, have a short span of growth stage. On the other hand, ceteris paribus, innovative products are likely to stay in the growth stage for a longer period because they take considerable time for the imitators to come up with their own versions of innovative products.

b. Maturity and Saturation Stages: Once the product passes through the growth or market acceptance sage in due course, it enters the maturity stage followed by saturation. The former is characterized by increase in sales but at a low rate and the alter by stagnation in sales. The maturity stage in a product's life cycle is characterized by increasing sales and profit, but the rate of increase is less than that in the growth stage. This reduced growth rate is certainly due to imminent competition in the market. Here one should not forget that innovative products face competition from new and improved imitative market entrants from time to time, whereas imitative products have to content with existing products. When the question of guarding against the phenomena of maturity and saturation stages arises a clear forecast of the setting in of these phases is essentially required. Otherwise, designing of effective marketing strategies to prevent the early setting in of maturity and saturation is not possible. Sometimes, if the products sales are close to the break-even levels, losses become inevitable especially in the saturation stage.

Moreover, there may be a drop-out of the products at this stage if actual sales fall below the break-even levels. In order to prevent such as eventuality, strategies such as product improvements, price reductions, effective advertising and sales promotion activities should be intensified. When compared to imitative products, innovative products, generally experience a longer span of maturity and saturation stages. This may be due to the early life cycle or the introduction stage of competing products and consequent less competition; or the competing and newly emerging imitations of the innovative products may have a low level of consumer acceptance. Moreover, innovative products may have a scope to adopt improvements through planned obsolescence when their imitations try to emerge a strong product in the market.

The strategy of systematic and timely planned untouched, potential segments of the markets and a number of other such strategies are quite significant to prevent the early entry of the product in to the decline stage. Especially, innovative products should not go for planned obsolescence before the entry of vital competitors with their own imitative versions. And growth so as to reserve it for maturity and saturation to revitalize the life cycle curve.

Just like any human being enters into the life cycle phase of inevitable physical deterioration and death, products also do enter into the stage of decline and possible abandonment. How fast a product approaches this stage is dependent on the marketing environment, market forces, product characteristics, and competitive strengths of the product and extent of product differentiation. As the new products enter the market, from time to time, virtually all the products enter the market, from time to time, virtually all the products are certainly caught in the clutches of obsolescence.

When the competing products establish their firm footing and consolidate their position in the market, the earlier entrants to the market fall prey to the clutches of decline. If a product, either innovative or imitative, stays in the saturation stage competitors try to aggravate their promotional effort to establish their superiority and push the innovative product to decline and consequently to the wall. How far a product can withstand the threat of the decline and curse of obsolescence depends on the managerial efficiency, efficiency of the marketing management and product strategies. This stage of any product's life poses challenges to the management. In this stage, the competitive strategies of promotion, re-pricing and repositioning are warranted to inject a new lease of life to the product. No one should be left unturned to revitalize the product lifecycle. For a successful revitalization, every effort to maintain the morale and loyalty of middlemen to carry out the product on their shelves as against those competitors is highly significant.

Strategic Considerations in the PLC Concept

- Competition: At the introductory stage, competition is given no important the growth stage, it is given a little important while at the maturity stage, there are many in the market slowly, however, the number of competitors or rivals gets reduced with the declining stage.
- Over all Strategic Focus: At the first stage, emphasis is laid on market establishment. At the growth stage, market penetration and persuasion of mass market are emphasis. Creation of brand loyally and brand preferences is focused at the maturity stage. At the decline stage, the strategy aims at overall preparation for renewal.
- Profit: At the introductory stage, profit are negligible but all the growth stage, they reach the peak levels as a result of growing demand. At the maturity stage, they decline due to the increasing competition. At the last stage, the declining volume pushes costs up and eliminates profits.
- Distribution Strategies: At the introduction stage, distribution is selective. However growth and maturity stages, it is intensive. At the decline stage, it becomes selective and hence low-end strategies are used.
- Advertising Strategies: At the introduction stage, advertising strategies aim at the needs of early adopters; at the growth stage. An attempt is made to make the mass market aware of brand benefits. At maturity stage, advertising is used as a vehicle for differentiating among otherwise similar brands. At the last stage, however it emphasizes, on low price of the product and minimum advertising expenditure.

Note: Big Lots is a broad line closeout retailer. Being a closeout retailer, the company generally purchases most merchandise at lower costs and offers the same at lower prices than those paid and offered by traditional discount retailers. The company primarily operates in the US. It is headquartered in Columbus, Ohio and employs about 37,000 people; this figure includes part-time employees. Reader can visit their site www.biglots.com For a detailed study of connected to this chapter.

11

Promotion Decision

OVERVIEW

Marketing communications is one of the four major elements of the company's marketing mix. Marketers must know how to use advertising, sales promotion, direct marketing, public relations, and personal selling to communicate the product's existence and value to the target customers.

The communication process itself consists of nine elements: sender, receiver, encoding, decoding, message, media, response, feedback, and noise. Marketers must know how to get through to the target audience in the face of the audience's tendencies toward selective attention, distortion, and recall. Developing the promotion program involves eight steps. The communicator must first identify the target audience and its characteristics, including the image it carries of the product. Next the communicator has to define the communication objective, whether it is to create awareness, knowledge, liking, preference, conviction, or purchase. A message must be designed containing an effective content, structure, format, and source. Then communication channels both personal and non-personal must be selected. Next, the total promotion budget must be established. Four common methods are the affordable method, the percentage-of-sales method, the competitive-parity method, and the objective-and task method.

The promotion budget should be divided among the main promotional tools, as affected by such factors as push-versus-pull strategy, buyer readiness stage, product life-cycle stage and company market rank. The marketer should then monitor to see how much of the market becomes aware of the product, tries it, and is satisfied in the process. Finally, all of the communications effort must be managed and coordinated for consistency, good timing, and cost effectiveness.

Introduction-the five major modes of communication (advertising, sales promotion, public relations, personal selling, and direct marketing)

The communication process-communications as the management of customer buying processes over time, the nine elements of the communications model, reasons why message may not get through the receiver (selective attention, selective distortion, and selective recall)

Developing effective communications

A. Identify the target audience

Image analysis is a major part of audience analysis that entails assessing the audience's current image of the company, its products, and its competitors

First step is to measure target audience's knowledge of the subject using a familiarity scale

Second step is to determine feelings toward the product using a favorability scale

Specific content of a product's image is best determined with use of semantic differential (relevant dimensions, reducing set of relevant dimensions, administering to a sample, averaging the results, checking on the image variance)

B. Determine the communication objectives

1. Based on seeking of a cognitive, affective, or behavioural response
2. Assuming the buyer has high involvement with the product category and perceives high differentiation within the category, base objectives on the hierarchy-of-effects model (hierarchy: awareness, knowledge, liking, preference, conviction, purchase)

C. Design the message (AIDA model). AIDA - Stands for attention, interest, desire, and action (AIDA).

Message content-choosing an appeal (rational appeal to audience's self interest, emotional appeal attempt to stir up either positive or negative emotions, moral appeals are directed to the audience's sense of what is right and proper)

Message structure-one-sided presentation versus two-sided argument

Message format-must be strong, based on headline, copy, "sound," nonverbal clues, color, expression, dress, etc.

Message source -expertise, trustworthiness and liability

D. Select the communication channels
   1. Personal communication channels-direct (advocate, expert and social)
   2. Non-personal communication channels-indirect (media, atmospheres, events)

E. Establish the total marketing communications budget
   1. Affordable method
   2. Percentage-of-sales method
   3. Competitive-parity method
   4. Objective-and-task method

IV. Deciding on the marketing communications mix
   - Promotional tools-benefits of each tool (advertising, sales promotion, public relations and publicity, personal selling, direct marketing)
   - Factors in setting the marketing communications mix (type of product market, buyer-readiness stage, product-life-cycle stage)
   - Measure the communications' results

V. Managing the integrated marketing communications process
   A. A concept of marketing communications planning that recognizes the added value of a comprehensive plan
      - Evaluates the strategic roles of a variety of communications disciplines
      - Combines these disciplines to provide clarity, consistency and maximum communications impact through the seamless integration of discrete messages

PROMOTION MIX

Advertising-the use of paid media by a seller to communicate persuasive information about its products, services, or organization-is a potent promotional tool. Advertising takes on many forms (national, regional, local, consumer, industrial, retail, product, brand, institutional, etc.) designed to achieve a variety of objectives (awareness, interest, preference, brand recognition, brand insistence).

Advertising decision-making consists of objectives setting, budget decision, message decision, media decision, and ad effectiveness evaluation. Advertisers should establish clear goals as to whether the advertising is supposed to inform, persuade, or remind buyers. The factors to consider when setting the advertising budget are: stage in the product life cycle, market share, competition and clutter, needed frequency, and product substitutability.

The advertising budget can be established based on what is affordable, as a percentage budget of sales, based on competitors' expenditures, or based on objectives and tasks, and based on more advanced decision models that are available. The message decision calls for generating messages, evaluating and selecting between them, and executing them effectively and responsibly.

The media decision calls for defining the reach, frequency, and impact goals; choosing among major media types; selecting specific media vehicles; deciding on media timing; geographical allocation of media. Finally, campaign evaluation calls for evaluating the communication and sales effects of advertising, before, during, and after the advertising. Sales promotion and public relations are two tools of growing importance in marketing planning. Sales promotion covers a wide variety of short-term incentive tools designed to stimulate consumer markets, the trade, and the organization's own sales force. Sales promotion expenditures now exceed advertising expenditures and are growing at a faster rate.

Consumer promotion tools include samples, coupons, cash refund offers, price packs, premiums, prizes, patronage rewards, free trials, product warranties, tie-in promotions, and point-of-purchase displays and demonstrations. Trade promotion tools include price-off, advertising and display allowances, free goods, push money, and specialty-advertising items. Business promotion tools include conventions, trade shows, contests, sweepstakes, and games. Sales promotion planning calls for establishing the sales promotion objectives, selecting the tools, developing, pretesting, and implementing the sales promotion program, and evaluating the results.

Marketing public relations (MPR) is another important communication/promotion tool. Traditionally, it has been the least utilized tool but is now recognized for its ability in building awareness and preference in the marketplace, repositioning products, and defending them. Broadly, MPR is those activities that support the ultimate sale of a product or service. Some of the major marketing public relations tools are news, speeches, events, public service activities, written material, audio-visual material, corporate identity, and telephone information services. MPR planning involves establishing the MPR objectives, choosing the appropriate messages and vehicles, and evaluating the MPR results.

ADVERTISING DECISION

Modern marketing calls for more than developing a good product, pricing it attractively and making it accessible to the target consumer. Companies must also communicate with the present and potential customers. In this respect, advertising is a potent promotion tool of marketing communication mix, while the rest four are:

- Sales Promotion
- Direct Marketing
- Public Relations and Publicity
- Personal Selling

Various marketing Gurus have defined advertising according to their own views: "Advertising Consists of all the activities involved in presenting to a group a non - personal, oral or visual openly - sponsored, identified message regarding a product, service or idea. This message, called an advertisement, is disseminated through one or more media and paid for by the identified sponsor". — W.Z. Stanton

"To give public notice or to announce publicly".

"Advertising is mass communication of information intended to persuade buyers so as to maximize profits". — J.E. Littlefield

To summarise, advertising means any paid form of non - personal presentation and promotion or ideas, goods or services by an identified sponsor.

SIGNIFICANCE

It is just not enough to manufacture a product. People must be informed of its existence and should be given good reasons to buy it. This is a job which is sought to be done by advertising. Without advertising, people would not be aware of the attributes of the product nor of its price. Let us now discuss the role and importance of advertising.

i. Way of Informing: Advertising is a way of communicating information to the consumer -information which enables him to compare and choose from the products and services available. Advertising enables consumbers to exercise their right of free choice " Encyclopedia Bitannica" such diverse media as handbills, newspapers, magazines, billboards, letters, radio and television broadcasts and motion pictures.

ii. Manufacturer's concerns: Advertising is the most economical means by which a manufacturer or an institution can communicate to an audience either to sell a product or to promote a cause of social welfare, such as, civic drive, or an immunization programme. This includes the process of mass communication which is different from ordinary communication. Here a macro level mass communication is between manufacturer and his mass audience. This is also connected through new sources. Mass audience gives various reactions as responses. Here audience is interconnected as a group within groups.

iii. Fundamental Right of Freedom of Speech: Advertising being a necessary means of communication is an inseparable part of free speech. Any restriction on the right to recommend legitimate services or ideas in public will diminish the fundamental right of freedom of speech.

iv. Improving productivity: Advertising can help in improving the economies of developed and developing countries. There is ample evidence to support this view. Advertising stimulates production and consequently generates more employment. It can help stabilize prices and leads to wider distribution and greater availability of goods an services.

v. Economic Growth of Country: Advertising is an essential and integral part of the marketing system. It is sometimes maintained that the marketing system is nothing but requirement of a country's social and economic growth. Advertising stimulates sales and compels the firm to improve its productivity and contributes substantially to the growth of the economy. Thus marketing and advertising are key tools used to aid a country's growth. Even though advertising costs a lot of money, and the costs are increasing day by day, a skillfully used advertising campaign can be the cheapest means of reaching the market and commutating with the consumers effectively. Advertising is wasteful if it fails to produce sales.

Advertisement leads to an increase in sales and market share. Pepsi came to India with a zero market share. By December, 1995, it had captured 40 per cent of Indian market. Promise, a toothpaste manufactured by a small -scale unit, was able to snatch a 15 per cent share of the market by strong customer -oriented advertisement. People feel safe in purchasing products they know of. Advertising makes them aware of the products and their attributes. In promoting a product or a brand, the manufacturer/ advertiser stakes his reputation. No manufacturer/ Advertiser would be foolish enough to risk his reputation by making misleading claims in his advertisements. Hence advertised goods are trusted the world over and India is no exception.

ADVERTISEMENT AND SALES PROMOTION

Advertising is a message which promotes ideas, good or services communicated through one or more media by an identified sponsor while sales promotion consists of short - terms incentives provided by the identified sponsors to consumers and traders to persuade them to purchase and stock his products

DEVELOPING THE ADVERTISING PROGRAMME

It is difficult to make an all - embracing generalization about distinctive qualities of advertising mainly because of its many forms and uses. Various companies do their advertising in different ways. In a small company advertising is handled by someone in the sales or marketing department who coordinates with an advertising agency. On the other side, large companies setup their own advertising departments, where Marketing Manager reports to the Vice -President, Marketing. The advertising department's job is to develop the total budget, help and develop advertising strategy and approach an advertising agency for advertising and designing a campaign. Most of the companies use an outside agency to help them design an advertising campaign and to select the media and decide about the timings and booking space.

In developing an advertising programme, marketing managers must always start by identifying their target market and the buyers involved. Thereafter, they have to make five major decisions in the programme development process known as the five Ms.

ADVERTISING GOALS

If an organization is spending crores of rupees on advertisement, then as managers we must attempt and be able to measure its effectiveness and delivery to find out whether we are receiving the value for money. However, advertising is only one part of marketing mix and the final delivery in rupees terms would involve the various marketing variables. The tragedy of advertising is that if it does not lead to an increase in sales of the product, the entire blame is put on advertising. Hence a clear definition of advertising goals in required. A successful advertising campaign can be compared with a military campaign where goal is set as "capture the army post No. 11" and the goal is achieved. Advertising goal can be defined as a clear and concise description of exactly what advertising is intended to accomplish, i.e.,

- To increase sales,
- To establish brand equity, and
- To enter the target market.

Sometimes these objectives are considered as marketing objectives instead of advertising objectives.

Need to set Advertising Objectives

Some of the possible objectives that are stressed are:

- Return on Investment (R.O.I) Advertising involves an investment of funds. Hence, it should produce a measurable return on the said investment in order to assess the desirability and profitability of advertising.
- Selection of media. The most effective advertising tool should be chosen in order to get the most profitable result.
- Coordination An appropriate co-ordination and integration of marketing and advertising efforts is imperative. Otherwise objectives of advertising are superimposed on objectives of marketing.

Various Approaches for Setting Advertising Objectives

i. DAGMAR Approach

This is the most popular method of setting advertising goals and was proposed by Russel M. Colley. DAGMAR stands for - Defining advertising Goals for Measured Advertising Results.

Colley outlined this method for turning advertising objectives into specific measurable goals. He lists 52 possible advertising objectives under the same approach. The theory is based on the following: " The consumer passes through a hierarchy of stages between the time when the first ideas about the product comes to his mind and when he actually buys it" For example, an advertisement of a Generator should highlight fuel efficiency, easy start, after -sales service and ready availability of spares.

Initially it would inform us and we shall become aware of such a product. Then through product endorsement and trial we shall develop a favourable attitude and ultimately, we shall buy the product.

To set advertising objectives, we shall need to identify the stage in which the product is available and then we can set the objective.

Example:

A detergent manufacturing company wanted to position its product as the most powerful cloth cleaner and as a low cost detergent.

They worked out a campaign targeted to 3 crore households who own automatic washers.

Prior to the campaign release, they did an attitude survey on brand perception. After the campaign was over, they repeated the attitude survey.

The questions were focused on three areas:

i. Which brand is the most effective in removing the spots?

ii. Which brand will you buy when you go to the market next?

Specific advertising objectives could have been:

- Increase awareness from 38 per cent to 52 per cent
- Top image ranking to 24 per cent than 9 per cent
- Increase preference to 21 per cent.

ii. Product Life Cycle Approach

Advertising effectiveness varies according to the different stages of product life cycle.

iii. Primary and Selective Demand Theory

According to this approach the advertising objective is categorized into two ways Informative Advertising and Persuasive Advertising.

a. Informative Advertising. This advertising is important when the product is in the pioneering stage and the objective is to build Primary demand. Primary demand is sought to be created especially by concept selling for a category of products. Some particular conditions are required necessarily to advertise for creating a primary demand. The existence of a strong and basic consumer need is the most important prerequisite as advertising cannot create demand for a new product. It can only stimulate an existing demand. There must be strong buying motives in existence. Besides this, social trends, design, price, etc. also play a crucial rate at this stage. For example, the manufacturer of "VIM" initially had to inform potential consumers of VIM Bar's economic benefits and many other advantages.

b. Persuasive Advertising. This becomes important in the competitive stage, where a company's objective is to build selective demand for a particular brand. Most advertising falls in this category. Persuasive advertising is undertaken when a strong primary demand is in existence. The product should be distinctive, its benefits should be visible and also a strong brand consciousness must be generated.

Media Profile for Advertising

Role of Media. Media has a vital role in the process of advertising communication.

Effective advertising is possible only if suitable media are available.

The appropriateness of media used vis - a -vis the target audience and their reach are also of crucial importance. A substantial portion of the advertising budget allocation to the mass media is spent on buying space and time. Therefore media decisions assume a considerable importance when financial implications come to the force.

Media Planning. Advertisement becomes effective only when it reaches the desired audience. The value of the advertisement is determined by the number of persons seeing it, reading it and thus becoming aware of the product or the service.

Media Selection. Each media has a specific function to perform and its selection depends upon the requirements of the job. Media can be divided into two categories:

Main Media -- also called "above the line" media, e.g., newspapers, T.V. Radio, Magazines, etc.

Secondary Media- also called " below the line" media, e.g., hoarding, direct mail, point of purchase, etc. These are also known as reminder media.

Media Planning Process. The steps involved in media planning are:

i. Media planning and buying space is the financial side of advertising.

ii. It interacts with the creative process to form an important part of the overall marketing process.

iii. Whereas the creative process is a descriptive process, the media process is one of transforming their description to the public, i.e., a vehicle of communication.

iv. The primary responsibility of media practitioners is to ensure that the advertising message is seen, heard, read or recognized by the target audience. We believe this is a crucial role as there is no point in having the best advertising if nobody sees the advertisement.

Role of Media in the Advertising Process

The following points have to be considered while selecting the media for the rural markets:

- The total number of literates in the rural market and their reading habits.
- The extent and type of contribution of the product.
- The number of cinemas and video parlours, panchayat viewing and listening facilities and the type of audience.
- The number of publications which are circulated in the area concerned, the number of readers and their categories, whether casual, regular or headline readers.
- Whether the publications circulated in the area concerned are issued locally or are obtained fro the neighboring areas?

Media Selection Decisions

While selecting the advertising media the following factors should be borne in mind:

- Cost of advertisement,
- Nature of the product,
- Comparison of the medium selected with other media,
- Popularity of the media,
- Characteristics of customers, and
- Competition in the market.

Types of Media for Advertising

Print Media	Electronic Media	Outdoor Media	Direct Mail
Newspapers	TV	Billboards	Price Lists
Direct Mail	Video	Hoardings	Catalogues
Folders	Radio	Balloons	Personal letters
Product Literature	Voice mail	Advertising on transport means	Circulars
Journals	Cinema	Electric Display	

ADVERTISING AGENCY

An advertising agency acts as a consultant to the client, the advertiser, in formulating the advertising plans and translating them into an advertising campaign. Another role of the agency is placing the advertisement in the media, since it has a traditional association with the media. The placement aspect has assumed considerable importance owing to media boom and the resultant complexities.

An advertising agency can be defined as an independent organization of creative business people who develop, prepare and release the advertisements for the sellers seeking to find customers for their goods and services.

In India, there are about 7,000 advertising agencies out of which 700 ad agencies are recognized by the Indian Newspapers Society (INS). INS is a regulatory organization regulating ad agencies for:

- National Income Accounting
- Annual Billing
- Creditworthiness

The relationship between an advertiser and its advertising agency represents professionalism to the core. At the same time, capability in terms in culture and style of the two parties and the concerned persons is highly facilitatory for a fruitful relationship. Courage and candidness on the part of the agency can contribute much towards getting the client to appreciate the constructive use of a creative approach. It is in the interest of the client to provide the required reassurance to the agency so that communication is inhibited. The selection of an agency by a potential client has a degree of mutuality. A well considered and wise selection can pave the way for a productive relationship.

FUNCTIONS OF AD AGENCIES

Ad agency will be in a position to take an objective view of the advertiser's plan and proposals and thus venture to put forward its opinions and comments. Creativem qualified and trained personnel are required for an advertising agency. It may not be worthwhile for an advertiser to have on its permanent staff all the variety of skill required to produce appropriate advertisements. An agency provides an opportunity as well as flexibility for various combinations of agency personnel from different departments to form a team to work as per the specific requirements of their varied clients.

Advertising agency has regular contacts with various support systems required for the production of appropriate ad material. A major advantage of an agency is its regular dealing with the media and the expertise in developing advertisements to suit the requirements of its clients. The ad agency's skills can also be useful in the preparation of campaigns where the risks involved are high such as in the introduction of new products.

Clients' Expectations

Account Service: Responsive - prompt - accessible - listens - economical.

Creativity Review: Provide innovative proposals - ideas - visuals.

Production Review: Quality - timeliness - accuracy - economical.

Media Planning: Innovative media strategy - capable of coping with the budget changes - provide media trends update.

Buying Media Space: Explore cost effective alternatives - ability to negotiate attractive terms.

Market Research: Relate existing studies to the specific situation of the client - organize timely and meaningful research.

Retail Advertising and Sales Promotion: Innovative ideas - POP material, creative events - timeliness - economical.

Financial Control: Detailed estimates - accuracy in billing - reasonable rates - mutual trust.

Agency Education Parameters

- Knowledge of Client's Business
- Contribution to Market Planning
- Responsiveness to brief
- Listen, understand pro-act (be responsive)
- Develop Strategies and Plan Creativity
- Ability to involve Key Agency Resources
- Readily Accessible
- Cost Consciousness
- Effective Event Planning

MEASURING ADVERTISING EFFECTIVENESS

Good planning and control of advertising depend critically on measurement of advertising effectiveness. A lot of effort is, therefore, spent on fundamental research on advertising effectiveness. The most important measurement of advertising effectiveness is of an applied nature, dealing with specific ads and campaigns.

Most of the money is spent by ad agencies on pre-testing ads, and much less is spent on post-evaluation of their effects. Many companies develop an advertising campaign, put it on the national market and then evaluate its effectiveness. It would be better for them to limit their campaign to one or a few cities first and evaluate its impact before rolling the campaign throughout the country with a very large budget. Measuring advertising effectiveness could be of two types according to the objectives of the advertisers:

- Communication Effect Research.
- Sales Effect Research.

COMMUNICATION EFFECT RESEARCH

The study seeks to discover if advertising is achieving the intended communication effect. This method is also known as "Copy Testing". The objective of this research is an improvement in the present system.

- The testing can be categorized into two types:
- Pre-testing of advertising campaign, and
- Post-testing of advertising campaign.

Three major methods of ad pre-testing are:

- Direct Rating
- Portfolio Test
- Laboratory Test

DIRECT RATING

In this type, respondents are asked questions to rate the alternative ads. These ratings are used to evaluate an ad's attention, read through, cognitive, effective and behavioural strengths.

The following steps can be adopted.

Evaluate ad's

- Attention strength
- Read through strength
- Cognitive strength
- Effective strength
- Behavioural strength

Method of evaluation through rating scale.

Primarily helps in screening out poor ads rather than identifying great ads.

Note: PPG Industries (PPG) is engaged in providing coatings and specialty products. The company serves customers in industrial, transportation, consumer products and construction markets and aftermarkets. PPG primarily operates in the US and Europe. It is headquartered in Pittsburgh, Pennsylvania and employs about 44,900 people. For a very good study of "Promotion Decision" see www.ppg.com

12

Pricing Decisions

INTRODUCTION

A price is an expression of value. The value rests in the usefulness and quality of the product itself, in the image that is conveyed through advertising and promotion, in the availability of the product through wholesale and retail distribution systems, and in the service that goes with it. A price is the seller's estimate of what all of this is worth to potential buyers, recognizing the other options buyers will have for filling the need the product is intended to satisfy. To the extent that the product or service finds markets and is profitable at given price levels, it provides a viable economic base for building and maintaining a business.

In the competitive marketplace, pricing is a game. The struggle for market share focuses critically on price. Pricing strategies of competing firms, therefore, are highly interdependent. The price one competitor sets is a function not only of what the market will pay but also of what other firms charge. Prices set by individual firms respond to those of competitors; they also are intended often to influence competitors' pricing behaviour. All of marketing comes to focus in the pricing decision.

A way to think about making a pricing decision is that price should be set somewhere between what the product costs to make and sell and its value to the customer. If price exceeds the perceived value of the product to potential purchasers, it has no market. If the price is below what the product costs to produce, the business cannot survive for very long. Where a price should be set between cost and customer value is a strategic decision. Many factors can influence this decision, viz., competitors' product/price strategies, governmentally imposed constraints and the seller's and the buyer's sense of what is fair. Finally the most important determinant of price is the marketer's objectives - what is the firm trying to do.

PRODUCT COSTS

Costs may be classified as variable, fixed and semi-fixed. Take the case of an airline. It may consider the annual depreciation on an aircraft as a fixed cost. Taking the plane off the ground to fly from one city to another incurs certain semi-fixed costs like the fuel, the compensation of flight personnel, the airport fees and so on. These costs are approximately the same for any given flight whether the plane is empty, half-loaded or completely full of passengers. The variable costs of the flight would include primarily the costs of food and beverage. They vary directly with the number of passengers. If fixed and semi-fixed costs make up a larger portion of total costs, as in the airline example, pricing to get maximum capacity utilization is crucial. Until the seller covers fixed costs, money is lost. After fixed costs are covered, each incremental sale contributes proportionally large amounts to profits. If variable costs are a relatively high percentage of total costs (which is quite likely in many manufacturing firms), pricing to maximize unit contribution (i.e. the difference between the unit variable cost and price) will be critical to profitability. Under these cost conditions, the manufacturer would naturally work to maximize unit prices and to reduce variable costs. Above are two examples. In the first one, the objective of the airline's pricing strategy will be to generate enough total revenue to cover its fixed costs and above that to get maximum capacity utilization to make profits. In the second one, a manufacturer will price to cover its high variable costs per unit and get enough contribution to amortize fixed costs and make a profit.

Under certain conditions, firms may elect to price at less than full cost. In conditions of capacity underutilization, for instance, firms with high fixed costs may take business at prices that cover variable costs and make some incremental contribution to fixed costs (or overheads). The idea is to get through bad times, keep the factory running and hold some critical team of managers, skilled technicians and labour. Pricing temporarily at less than full cost may also be used as a strategy to get a particularly large order. The expectation is that by taking the business, the firm may be able to reduce its unit costs and/or later raise its prices so as to make a profit on subsequent orders. Taking business below cost with the hope of offsetting near-term losses with longer-term profits may be a risky tactic, since there is no assurance that the losses can be made up.

Pricing near or below cost may also be done to gain a large market share. Generally pricing low to preempt market share is predicted on the assumption that unit costs will come down significantly as volume increases. This may happen through gaining manufacturing experience.

In fact, in many firms, a so-called experience or learning curve is used to calculate what the effect will be of volume growth on unit costs. To a large extent, learning curve experience reduces the variable cost component of unit costs. Labour gains in efficiency and purchases of materials and parts in larger volumes all result in lower prices and manufacturing process improvements produce cost savings. Indeed, the fixed-cost component of unit costs may also come down with volume increases. Larger plants may be more cost efficient. Large-scale selling and advertising programs may also be more cost efficient. If product sales are particularly sensitive to heavy advertising, or the product requires widespread distribution or extensive field service support, fixed marketing expenditures for these purposes must usually be at a high level.

These so-called scale economies come in certain cost categories depending on the product, the processes used to manufacture it and the level of marketing spending required to be competitive. If significant scale economies are achievable, some competitors may be willing to price low enough to gain volume, thus preventing other competitors from going down the learning curve and hoping to emerge as low-cost producers with dominant market shares.

Product cost, then, is not a simple 'hard' number. How cost is calculated for pricing purposes is a matter of managerial judgment. It may be construed as full cost or as variable cost. It may be the cost levels being experienced or experience curve estimates of future costs. The interpretation of cost factors for pricing will depend greatly on product/ market objectives.

CUSTOMER VALUE

Some business managers set prices simply by adding a percentage over costs to provide an acceptable profit. That approach has two advantages. Price is simple to calculate and if a firm is a low-cost producer, relative to competitors, so-called 'cost-plus' pricing may seem to provide some protection from competitive attack. The trade-off for simplicity and security may be lost profits. In theory, the amount of profit that is sacrificed is the difference between what customers actually paid and what they would have been willing to pay. Compared with cost-plus pricing, pricing according to the value of the product to the customer is more difficult and speculative. The challenge is to determine what the value of the product is in the customer's mind.

First, it is useful to distinguish between perceived value and potential value. Perceived value is what the buyer now recognizes. Potential value is what the buyer can be educated to see in the product. That is the task of marketing. It may be accomplished through advertising, personal selling and getting the buyer to try the product.

Second, product value may be perceived differently by different customer groups or market segments. Different segments may place different values on the several elements that make up the set of product (which in the broadest sense, includes the product or service itself, its brand image, its availability, and the service that the seller provides) attributes. For example, a large firm may place little value on the technical service a supplier offers it (the large firm) has comparable or superior technical resources of its own. But a small company may be highly dependent on the supplier's technical services and place high value on them in making purchasing decisions.

A third factor to consider in establishing customer value is the options that a potential buyer may have. Clearly, if the buyer can purchase a product at a lower price from one source than another, the lower price sets the upper bound in the marketplace. But for the buyer to have such effective options, he/she must have knowledge of them. Another option the customer has may be not to buy the product at all but to makedo with what one has. Given this choice, the buy-not buy decision may be made by comparing the outcome of one course of action with the other. These actions are quantifiable. One may calculate the operative savings in either instance and relate this to the cost of buying new, as the case may be. The anticipated savings may be expressed as a percentage return on investment (ROI). This, the amount of realizable savings establishes the value of a product to the customer. Calculated for each of several possible uses for available funds, ROI measures may serve to establish the buyer's purchasing priorities. The choice between buy-not buy, of course, may not always be easily quantified with reference to expected savings. Nevertheless, it is a real and important consideration.

Finally, the price set by the seller is often taken by the potential customer as one measure of the value of the product. It is often interpreted by buyers as the supplier's estimate of the worth of the product it sells. If the seller does not value the product highly, it is not likely that the buyer will. Therefore, pricing a product significantly below what the buyer might pay for its functional equivalent can be self-defeating. The buyer may infer that value is, in fact, connoted by price and choose the higher-priced option.

Value, then, for a given product tends to be a function of (1) the utility of its several attributes to the prospective buyer, (2) the options the buyer has and is aware of (i.e. the offerings of competing suppliers and the option of not buying at all), and (3) the extent to which the buyer perceives price itself as a measure of product value. If the seller truly value-prices, then different prices would be charged for the product to different customer groups. It is referred as price discrimination. A relevant consideration in thinking about price as an expression of product value is how sensitive is the buyer to price. Price sensitivity will vary considerably among purchasers and, for the same purchaser, it will vary from one time and one set of circumstances to another. Buyers who can pass on the cost of the purchase are less sensitive to price than those who cannot. Price sensitivity also relates to the performance standards by which the purchaser measures. Viewed differently, performance measures effectively establish the relative worth of different product attributes for the manager who has to make the decision and be judged for it. Another factor in price sensitivity is the uncertainty that attends switching from one supplier to a lower-priced source. Modest price differences are often insufficient to overcome the purchaser's uncertainties about an untried supplier's product quality, reliability and service.

FACTORS AFFECTING PRICE DECISIONS

There are a number of factors which influence the pricing decisions of marketers. While some of these are external or environmental factors (such as competition, demand conditions and so on), others are internal factors (like marketing objectives, cost conditions and so on).

Internal factors: The internal factors, as the term implies, are mostly internal to the organization and therefore, largely controllable by the organization. They also have a direct bearing on the firm's pricing decision. The following are the important internal factors that must considered in pricing a firm's product/service.

- Marketing objectives - Before setting price, the firm must decide on its strategy for the product. This reiterates the idea that the corporate strategy must precede the marketing strategy and then marketing strategy must precede the pricing strategy. If the firm has selected its target market and positioning carefully, then its marketing-mix strategy (i.e. the 4 Ps) will be fairly straightforward. For example, if the Coimbatore-based Paramount Airways decides to target the corporate/business travelers with its single-class airplanes, this suggests charging a high price. Whereas, a no-frills, low cost carrier would charge a low price, as dictated by its targeting and positioning. Thus pricing strategy is largely determined by past decisions on marketing strategy. At the same time, the firm may seek additional objectives. The clearer a firm is about its marketing objectives, the easier it is to set price. Some of the common objectives include survival, current profit maximization, market-share leadership and product-quality leadership.

- Other objectives - Sometimes a firm might set prices so low as to prevent competition from entering the market as they might lead the competition to regard the market as less attractive. Non-profit organizations may adopt a number of other pricing objectives such as full cost recovery, partial cost recovery or set a social price geared to the distributed income situations of different clients.
- Marketing-mix strategy - Price is only one of the marketing-mix elements that a firm uses to achieve its marketing objectives. Therefore, logically pricing decisions must be coordinated with product design, distribution and promotion decisions to form a consistent and effective marketing program. Decisions made for other marketing-mix elements may affect pricing decisions. For instance, the decision to position the product on quality plank will imply that the seller must charge a higher price to cover higher costs and/or to match the price-quality perception in the mind of the customers. It is common for marketers to design a price position wherein a target cost is set, then met and the target price is set. However some marketers deemphasize price and use other marketing-mix elements to create non-price positions. The marketer must consider the total marketing mix when setting prices. If the product is positioned on non-price factors, then decisions about quality, promotion and distribution will strongly affect price. If price is a crucial positioning factor, then price will strongly affect decisions made about the others marketing-mix elements. In most cases, the company will consider all of the marketing-mix decisions together when developing the marketing program.
- Costs - Though this topic was dealt with earlier in this lesson, some finer aspects related to costs are described here. Costs set the floor for the price that the firm can charge for its product. A firm's costs may be an important element in its pricing strategy. The firm wants to charge a price that both

covers all its costs for producing, distributing and selling the product and delivers a fair rate of return for its effort and risk. The types of costs were explained earlier. To price wisely, managers need to know how costs vary with different levels of production. The concept of economies of scale comes into play here. Also, costs vary as a function of production experience. There is a drop in the average cost with accumulated production experience and this is attributed to the experience curve or the learning curve. Consider the semiconductor industry as an example. It has a strong experience curve effect. As a given chip is produced, manufacturing speeds go up, defect rates drop and costs plummet. These effects are seen dramatically in the PC market, where computing power increases and costs drop every year.

- Organization for pricing - Management must decide who within the organization should set prices. Firms handle pricing in a variety of ways. In small firms, prices are often set by top management rather than by the marketing or sales departments. In large firms, pricing typically is handled by product line managers. In industrial markets, salespeople may be allowed to negotiate with customers within certain price ranges. Even so, top management sets the pricing objectives and policies, and it often approves the prices proposed by lower-level management or salespeople. In industries where pricing is a key factor, companies will often have a pricing department to set the best prices or help others in setting them. Others who have an influence on pricing decisions include sales managers, production managers, finance managers and accountants.

External factors: The external factors, as the term implies, are external to the organization and therefore, treated as uncontrollable by the organization. They have an indirect, but definite bearing on the firm's pricing decision. The following are the important external factors that must considered in pricing a firm's product/service.

- Nature of the market and demand - While costs set the lower limit of prices, the market and demand set the upper limit. Buyers balance the price of a product or service against the benefits of owning it. Therefore, before setting prices, the marketer must understand the relationship between price and demand for his product. Price-demand relationship varies for different types of markets and how buyer perceptions of price affect the pricing decision. Economists recognize four types of markets, viz. pure competition, monopolistic competition, oligopolistic competition and pure monopoly. Each presents a different pricing challenge and pricing freedom.

- Under pure competition, the market consists of many buyers and sellers trading in a uniform commodity. A seller cannot charge more than the going price because buyers can obtain as much as they need at the going price. Nor would sellers charge less than the market price because they can sell all they want at this price.
- Under monopolistic competition, the market consists of many buyers and sellers who trade over a range of prices rather than a single market price. A range of prices occurs because sellers can differentiate their product/service offering to buyers. Buyers see differences in sellers' offerings and will pay different prices for them.
- Under oligopolistic competition, the market consists of a few sellers who are highly sensitive to each other's pricing and marketing strategies. The product may be uniform (as a commodity) or non-uniform. Each seller is alert to competitors' strategies and moves. An oligopolist is never sure that it will gain anything permanent through a price cut or a price hike.
- In a pure monopoly, the market consists of one seller. The seller may be a government monopoly (the Indian Postal service), a private regulated monopoly (a power company) or a private non-regulated monopoly (e.g. Sify, when it introduced Virtual Private Networks for corporate users). Pricing is handled differently in each case. A government monopoly can set the price below cost to make the product/service affordable, or set price to recover costs or set a high price to slow down consumption (an instance of demarketing). In a regulated monopoly, the government permits the firm to set rates that will yield a fair return. Non-regulated monopolies are free to price at what the market will bear. However, they will be careful not to attract competition nor invite government regulation.
- The price-demand relationship must also be studied before taking the price decision. Each price the firm might charge will lead to a different level of demand. The relation between

the price charged and the resulting demand level is described as the Demand curve. In the normal case, demand and price and inversely related. For 'prestige' goods, raising the price may result in more sales. In measuring the price-demand relationship, the marketer must not allow other factors affecting demand to vary. They also need to know price elasticity, that is, how responsive demand will be to a change in price. If demand hardly changes with a small change in price, the demand is said to be inelastic. If demand changes greatly, it is said to be elastic. Price elasticity of demand is determined by many situations. For example, buyers are less price sensitive when the product they are buying in unique or when it is high in quality, prestige or exclusiveness. They are also less price sensitive when substitute products are hard to find or when they cannot easily compare the quality of substitute products. Buyers are less price sensitive when the total expenditure for a product is low relative to their income or when the cost is shared by another party.

Competition - Another external factor affecting the company's pricing decisions is competitors' costs and prices and possible competitor reactions to the company's own pricing moves. For so-called commodities (i.e. virtually undifferentiated products), all competitors generally charge identical prices. If one goes above the market price, sales will drop off sharply; if one goes below, all others are likely to follow or risk significant reductions in market share. How much any individual firm is constrained by competitors' prices, therefore, depends largely on how differentiated its product is. A product that is set apart from other market offerings by its functional design, appearance, brand image and the supplier's reputation for service and availability in ways that have value to customers can command a price premium. There are circumstances, however, in which firms will price over competitive levels even though the price differences are not really justified by superior product quality and service. A company may consciously elect, for example, not to meet competitive prices in a strategy of 'milking' the business, that is, yielding market share and gradually withdrawing from the market. It may continue to sell profitably for some time to its loyal customers, in the mean time gradually cutting back on selling and promotional expenses until it eventually phases out of the market. Some companies may choose not to price competitively because to do so would mean selling below cost. These so-called marginal firms eventually go out of business. Some large companies may not elect to meet the low price of a smaller competitor because to do so might mean giving up unit profits on a large sales base. It may be less costly in the short run to hold prices and give up some small percentage of market share. In the long run, the smaller competitor encroaches increasingly on the market positions of its major competitors until it becomes, itself, a major factor. Under shortage conditions, some firms may price opportunistically above prevailing market levels, knowing that demand far exceeds available supply and that some buyers will pay the high price. Finally, some firms may unknowingly be underpriced by competitors on some of their products. These products may be part of a broad line and the reporting system may not allow for monitoring the sales-profit performance of each item on the list. Thus the company may be losing sales and market position because of price and never realize, until too late, that the business has gone to more aggressive competitors. Generally, pricing strategies must inevitably be shaped with regard for present and future competition. In this respect, there is significant pricing interdependency among firms in an industry with each being heavily influenced by others' strategies and tactics. Some firms follow price trends; others, the larger ones, seek to lead them. Accordingly, in contemplating price changes, the marketing manager will often seek to anticipate competitive responses.

- Other environmental factors - When setting prices, the firm also must consider other factors in its external environment. Economic conditions can have a strong impact on the firm's pricing strategies. Economic factors such as inflation, boom or recession, and interest rates affect pricing decisions because they affect both the costs of producing a product and consumer perceptions of the product's price and value. The firm also must consider what impact its prices will have on other parties in its environment. How will resellers react to various prices? The firm should set prices that give resellers a fair margin, encourage their support, and help them to sell the product effectively. The government is another important external influence on pricing decisions. In regulated industries such as utilities, transport and so on, the government has the authority to approve or reject price changes. Finally, social concerns may have to be taken into account. In setting prices, a firm's short-term sales, market share and profit goals may have to be tempered by broader societal considerations.

PRICING OBJECTIVES AND APPROACHES

Ancient philosophers recognized the importance of price in an economic system. Some early written accounts refer to attempts to determine fair and just prices. Price continues to serve as a means of regulating economic activity. All the four factors of production, viz. natural resources, capital, human resources and entrepreneurship, depends on the prices that those factors receive. An individual firm's prices and the resulting purchases by its customers determine how much revenue the firm receives. Prices, therefore, influence a firm's profits as well as its employment of the factors of production. Traditionally, price has operated as the major determinant of buyer choice. This is still the case in the poorer economies and with commodity-type products. Although non-price factors have become more important in recent decades, price still remains one of the most important elements determining market share and profitability. Pricing has come to occupy centre-stage in many marketing rivalries. Many reasons can be attributed to this. Some of them are outlined below:

- In some cases, product differentiation is getting blunted, thanks to the homogenization of technology. This is more relevant in the context of global business where the million dollar question is whether the firms should offer a standardized offering or a differentiated offering.
- There is intense inter-firm rivalry in some industries. It may be attributed to the removal of entry/exit barriers. Also the cost of fighting these marketing wars must be recovered and often, it is transferred to the customer.
- In certain industries, the products and the markets are mature. The only way to differentiate may be is through an augmented service or price cuts. Here again, pricing decisions are crucial to the survival of the firm.
- Customers' value perception correlates with the quoted price. To a customer, price always represents product's value. The

price-quality perception must be taken into account during the product decision and the price decision.

- Inflation in the economy may also contribute to the significance of pricing decision in a marketing program. It lowers customer's purchasing power and increases input costs. As a result, the marketer has to make the price decision after careful evaluation.

PRICING OBJECTIVES

Just as price is a component of the total marketing mix, pricing objectives also represent components of the organization's overall objectives. The objectives of the firm and its marketing organization guide the development of pricing objectives, which in turn lead to development and implementation of more specific pricing policies and procedures. For example, a firm might set a major overall objective of becoming the dominant producer in its domestic market. It might then develop a marketing objective of achieving maximum sales penetration in each region, followed by a related pricing objective to set prices at levels that maximize sales. These objectives might lead to adoption of a low-price policy implemented by offering substantial price discounts to channel members. While pricing objectives vary from firm to firm, they can be classified into four major groups:

- Profitability objectives
- Volume objectives
- Meeting competition objectives, and
- Prestige objectives

Profitability objectives include profit maximization and target-return goals. Volume objectives pursue either sales maximization or market-share goals.

Profitability objectives: Classical economic theory bases its conclusions on certain assumptions. It presumes that firms will behave rationally. Theorists expect that rational behaviour will result in an effort to maximize gains and minimize losses. Profits are a function of revenue and expenses.

- Profits = Revenue – Expenses

Revenue is determined by the product's selling price and number of units sold:

- Total revenue = Price Quantity sold

A profit maximizing price, therefore, rises to the point at which further increases will cause disproportionate decreases in the number of units sold. A 10% price increase that results in only an 8% cut in volume will add to the firm's revenue. However, a 10% price hike that results in an 11% sales decline will reduce revenue. Profit maximization is identified as the point at which the addition to total revenue is just balanced by the increase in total cost. Consequently, marketers set target return objectives - short-run or long-run goals usually stated as percentages of sales or investments. Target return objectives offer several benefits for marketers in addition to resolving pricing questions. For example, they serve as tools for evaluating performance. They also satisfy desires to generate 'fair' profits as judged by management, stockholders and the public.

Volume objectives: Many marketers argue that pricing behaviour actually seeks to maximize sales within a given profit constraint. They set a minimum acceptable profit level and then seek to maximize sales in the belief that the increased sales are more important than immediate high profits to the long-run competitive picture. Such a firm continues to expand sales as long as its total profits do not drop below the minimum return acceptable to management. Another volume-related pricing objective - the market share objective - sets a goal to control a portion of the market for a firm's good or service. The company's specific goal may target maintaining its present share of a particular market or increasing its share. Volume-related goals such as sales maximization and market share objectives play important roles in most firms' pricing decisions.

Meeting competition objectives: A third set of pricing objectives seeks simply to meet competitor's prices. In many lines of business, firms set their own prices to match those of established industry price leaders. These kinds of objectives de-emphasize the price element of the marketing mix and focus competitive rivalries more strongly on non-price variables. Pricing is a highly visible component of a firm's marketing mix and an easy and effective tool for obtaining a differential advantage over competitors; still other firms can easily duplicate a price reduction themselves. Because such price changes directly affect overall profitability in an industry, many firms attempt to promote stable prices by meeting competitors' prices and competing for market share by focusing on product strategies, promotional decisions and distribution - the non-price elements of the marketing mix. When price discounts become normal elements of a competitive marketplace, other marketing mix elements gain importance in purchase decisions. In such instances, overall product value, not just price, determines product choice. Value pricing emphasizes benefits a product provides in comparison to the price and quality levels of competing offerings. This strategy typically works best for relatively low-priced goods and services. Value-priced products generally cost less than premium brands, but marketers point out that value does not necessarily mean cheap. Value is not just price, but also is linked to the performance and meeting expectations and needs of consumers. The challenge for those who compete on value is to convince customers that low-priced brands offer quality comparable to that of a higher-priced product.

Prestige objectives: The final category of pricing objectives, unrelated to either profitability or sales volume, encompasses prestige objectives. Prestige pricing establishes a relatively high price to develop and maintain an image of quality and exclusiveness that appeals to status-conscious consumers. Such objectives reflect marketers' recognition of the role of price in creating an overall image for the firm and its goods and services.

GENERAL PRICING APPROACHES

The price the firm charges will be somewhere between on that is too low to produce a profit and one that is too high to produce any demand. Product costs set a floor to the price and consumer perceptions of the product's value set the ceiling. The firm must consider competitors' prices and other external and internal factors to find the best price between these two extremes. Firms set prices by selecting a general pricing approach that includes one or more of these three sets of factors. Let us examine the following approaches:

- Cost-based approach
- Buyer-based approach, and
- Competition-based approach

Cost-based approach

The simplest pricing method is cost-plus or markup pricing - adding a standard markup to the cost of the product. Markups vary greatly among different goods. Some common markups (on price, not cost) in supermarkets are 9% on baby foods, 14% on tobacco products, 27% on dried foods and vegetables and 50% on greeting cards. Markups are generally higher on seasonal items (to cover the risk of not selling) and on specialty items, slower moving items, items with high storage and handling costs and items with inelastic demand. It must be noted that any pricing method that ignores current demand and competition is not likely to lead to the best price. Hence markup pricing only works if that price actually brings in the expected level of sales.

Advantages:

- It covers all the costs
- It is designed to provide the target rate of margin
- It is generally a rational and widely accepted method
- It is an easy to comprehend and simple method

Disadvantages:

- The cost calculations are based on a predetermined level of activity. If the actual level of activity varies from this estimated level, the costs may vary, rendering this method unrealistic.
- If the costs of the firm are higher than its competitors, this method would render the firm passive in relation to price.
- Another drawback is that sometimes the opportunity to charge a high price is foregone.
- It ignores the price elasticity of demand.
- The cost-based pricing would not be helpful for some of the objectives or tasks like market penetration, fighting competition and so on.
- It imparts an in-built inflexibility to pricing decisions. Another cost-based pricing approach is break even pricing, or a variation called target profit pricing. The firm tries to determine the price at which it will break even or make the target profit it is seeking.

Buyer-based Approach

An increasing number of firms are basing their prices on the product's perceived value. Perceived-value pricing uses buyers' perceptions of value, not the seller's cost, as the key to pricing. The company uses the non-price variables in the marketing mix to build up perceived value in buyers' minds. Price is set to match the perceived value. A company using perceived-value pricing must find out what value buyers assign to different competitive offers. Sometimes consumers are asked how much they would pay for each benefit added to the offer. If the seller charges more than the buyers' perceived value, the firm's sales will suffer. Many firms overprice their products, and their products sell poorly. Other firms underprice. Under-priced products sell very well, but they produce less revenue than they would if prices were raised to the perceived-value level.

Competition-based Pricing

Many firms follow the dominant competitors, particularly the price leader, in setting the price. The main advantages of this method are:

- It is a very simple method
- It follows the main market trend
- It has relevance to the competitive standing of the firm
- Holding to the going price will prevent harmful price wars

The major disadvantages and limitations of following competitors are:

- If the competitors' price decisions are unrealistic, the follower will also be going wrong on the price
- The cost factors of the follower may not be similar to that of the competitors'
- The pricing objective of the firm could be different from that of the competitors'
- Sometimes the competitor may initiate price change for wrong reasons

Competition-based pricing approach may take the form of going-rate pricing or sealedbid pricing. In going-rate pricing, the firm bases its price largely on competitors' prices, with less attention paid to its own cost or to demand. In oligopolistic industries that sell commodities, firms normally charge the same price. It is a popular pricing method. When demand elasticity is hard to measure, firms feel the going price represents the collective wisdom of the industry concerning the price that will yield a fair return. Competitionbased pricing is also used when firms bid for jobs. Using sealed-bid pricing, a firm bases its price on how it thinks competitors will price rather than on its own costs or on the demand. The firm wants to win a contract and winning the contract requires pricing lower than other firms. Yet, the firm cannot set its price below a certain level. It cannot price below cost without hurting its position. In contrast, the higher the firm sets its price above its costs, the less its chance of getting the contract.

PRICING POLICIES AND CONSTRAINTS

Firms do their pricing in a variety of ways as discussed in the previous lesson. Executives complain that pricing is a big headache and one is wary of committing a go/drop error in the pricing decision. Pricing less than what the customer wants to pay and pricing more than what the customer wants to pay are both costly errors. 'There are two fools in every market: one asks too little, one asks too much', says a Russian Proverb. Many companies do not handle pricing well. Some common mistakes are:

- Price is not revised often enough to capitalize on market changes
- Price is set independently of the rest of the marketing mix rather than as an intrinsic element of market-positioning strategy
- Price is not varied enough for different product items, market segments, distribution channels and purchase occasions

The importance of pricing for profitability was demonstrated in a 1992 study by McKinsey & Company. Examining 2,400 companies, McKinsey concluded that a 1% improvement in price created an improvement in operating profit of 11.1%. By contrast, 1% improvements in variable cost, volume and fixed cost product profit improvements of only 7.8%, 3.3% and 2.3% respectively. Effectively designing and implementing pricing strategies requires a systematic approach to setting, adapting and changing prices.

PROCEDURE FOR A PRICING POLICY

A firm must set a price for the first time when it develops a new product, when it introduces its regular product into a new distribution channel or geographical area, and when it enters bids on new contract work. The firm has to consider several factors in setting its pricing policy. A useful 6-step procedure to develop the pricing policy is discussed below.

- Selecting the pricing objective: The firm first decides where it wants to position its market offering. The clearer a firm's objectives, the easier it is to set price. A firm can pursue any of the objectives classified under four major groups, viz. profitability objectives, volume objectives, meeting competition objectives and prestige objectives. This was discussed in the previous lesson.
- Determining demand: Each price will lead to a different level of demand and therefore have a different impact on a firm's marketing objectives. The relation between alternative prices and the resulting current demand is captured in a demand curve. In the normal case, demand and price are inversely related: the

higher the price, the lower the demand. In the case of prestige goods, the demand curve sometimes slopes upward. However, if the price is too high, the level of demand may fall. The demand curve sums the reactions of many individuals who have different price sensitivities. The first step is estimating demand is to understand what affects price sensitivity. Generally speaking, customers are most price sensitive to products that cost a lot or are bought frequently. They are less price sensitive to low cost items or items they buy infrequently. They are also less price sensitive when price is only a small part of the total cost of obtaining, operating and servicing the product over its lifetime. Firms, of course, prefer customers who are less price sensitive. The following is a list of factors leading to less price sensitivity, as identified by Nagle and Holden.

- The product is more distinctive
- Buyers are less aware of substitutes
- Buyers cannot easily compare the quality of substitutes
- The expenditure is a smaller part of the buyer's total income
- The expenditure is small compared to the total cost of the end product
- Part of the cost is borne by another party
- The product is used in conjunction with assets previously bought
- The product is assumed to have more quality, prestige or exclusiveness
- Buyers cannot store the product

Most firms make some attempt to measure their demand curves using methods like statistical analysis, price experiments and surveys. In measuring the pricedemand relationship, the marketer must control for various factors that will influence demand. The competitor's response will make a difference. Also, if the company changes other marketing mix factors besides price, the effect of the price change itself will be hard to isolate and measure.

- Estimating costs - In the earlier discussion on costs, it was noted that demand sets a ceiling on the price, whereas costs set the floor. Also, the types of costs and the impact of economies of scale and learning curve on pricing was explained. To price intelligently, management needs to know how its costs vary with different levels of production. It is important to be aware of the risks presented by pricing based on the experience/ learning curve. It assumes that competitors are weak followers. It leads the company into building more plants to meet the demand, while a competitor may be innovating a lower-cost technology. Then the market leader will be stuck with the old technology. Today's firms try to adapt their offers and terms to different buyers. A manufacturer may negotiate different terms with different retail chains. One retailer may want daily delivery (to keep inventory lower) while another may accept twice-a-week delivery in order to get a lower price.

The manufacturer's cost will differ with each chain and so will its profits. To estimate the real profitability of dealing with different customers with differing requirements, the manufacturer needs to use activity-based cost (ABC) accounting instead of standard cost accounting. ABC accounting tries to identify the real costs associated with serving each customer. It allocates indirect costs like clerical costs, office expenses, supplies and so on, to the activities that use them, rather than in some proportion to direct costs. Both variable and overhead costs are tagged back to each customer. Another interesting costing concept is target costing. Costs change with production scale and experience. They can also change as a result of a concentrated effort by designers, engineers and purchasing agents to reduce them through target costing. Market research is used to establish a new product's desired functions and the price at which the product will sell, given its appeal and competitors' prices. Deducting the desired profit margin from this price leaves the target cost that must be achieved. Each cost element - design, engineering, manufacturing, sales - must be examined and different ways to bring down costs must be considered. The objective is to bring the final cost projections into the target cost range. If this is not possible, it may be necessary to stop developing the product because it could not sell for the target price and make the target profit.

- Analysing competitors' costs, prices and offers - Within the range of possible prices determined by market demand and company costs, the firm must take competitors' costs, prices and possible price reactions into account. The firm should first consider the nearest competitor's price. If the firm's offer contains features not offered by the nearest competitor, their worth to the customer should be evaluated and added to the competitor's price.

If the competitor's offer contains some features not offered by the firm, their worth to the customer should be evaluated and subtracted from the firm's price. Now the firm can decide whether it can charge more, the same or less than the competitor. But competition can change their prices in reaction to the price set by the firm.

- Selecting a pricing approach - Given the three Cs - the Customer's demand schedule, the cost function and the competitors' prices - the firm is now ready to select a price. Costs set a floor to the price. Competitors' price and the price of substitutes provide an orienting point. Customers' assessment of unique features establishes the price ceiling. Firms select a pricing approach that includes one or more of these three considerations. The pricing approaches are cost-based or buyer-based or competition-based.
- Selecting the final price - Pricing methods narrow the range from which the company must select its final price. In selecting that price, the company must consider additional factors, including the impact of other marketing activities, company pricing guidelines, gain-and-risk-sharing pricing and the impact of price on other parties.

The final price must take into account the brand's quality and advertising relative to the competition. The price must be consistent with the firm's pricing guidelines. When a firm establishes pricing penalties, it must be done judiciously so as not to unnecessarily alienate customers. Sometimes, buyers may resist accepting a seller's proposal because of a high perceived level of risk. The seller has the option of offering to absorb part or all of the risk if it does not deliver the full promised value. Management must also consider the reactions of other parties to the contemplated price. For instance, the reaction of marketing intermediaries must be thought about. The reaction of the sales force must be taken note since they will be the ones to sell at that price in the marketplace. All these reactions might hold clues to fine tune the final price.

PRICING AND PRODUCT LIFE CYCLE

From a strategic point of view, the product life cycle provides a framework for thinking about pricing decisions.

Introduction phase: During the introduction phase, pricing can be a quandary, especially if you enjoy a temporary monopoly. In that situation, there may be no direct competitor and thus no benchmark for what buyers will tolerate or for their sensitivity to price differences. There may be indirect competitors (substitutes), however, and they can be used as starting points for the pricing decision. The total economic value equation becomes relevant, wherein the price of the best alternative is known but the value of the performance differential of the new product is unknown. Customers themselves may have difficulty in sizing up the value of something that is new and different. They too lack benchmarks of value. In such instances, any of the following strategies may be adopted:

Skimming: Some people will be happy to pay a high price for anything that is new and unique. This strategy, of course, is short term and contains dangers like attracting competition.

Penetration pricing: A low price may have the threefold benefits of (1) getting established as the market share champion, (2) discouraging market entry by competitors, and (3) creating broad-based demand for the product.

Cost-plus: In a monopoly, the producer can administer its own price and cost-plus is one way of determining that price. However, product monopolies are short-lived. Pricing decisions in this introductory phase are not only difficult but also deadly important. Putting too high a price on a newly introduced product may kill it in its infancy, undoing the work of many employees over a long period of development.

Growth phase: The growth phase is characterized by increasing unit sales and accelerating customer interest. If competitors have not yet surfaced (which is an unlikely event), skimming may be appropriate. All the deep-pocketed buyers who simply had to be the first in their neighbourhoods to own the product have already been skimmed in the introduction phase. So now, the price must be reduced gradually, skimming other market segments that are progressively more price sensitive.

A producer that enjoys prime position on the experience curve will also want to progressively reduce prices during this phase. Doing so will maintain its margins even as the strategy expands unit sales and punishes late-into-the-game rivals in the marketplace. Some of these rivals will either take a loss on every sale or simply wind up.

Mature phase: By the time a product enters this phase, growth in unit sales is leveling off and the remaining competitors are trying to find ways to differentiate their products. During this phase, one may see sellers offer different versions of the product, each version trying to colonize a targeted segment. Price is one of the factors used in this strategy (i.e. by developing and pricing good, better and best versions to expand the product line).

Decline phase: Competition gets ugly in this phase. Total demand for the product category is now visibly slipping, perhaps because of the appearance of superior substitutes or because of market saturation. Whatever the case, unit sales will continue to decline. Some companies will get out of the business entirely; those that remain will aggressively try to take business away from the rivals. Every player in the market is trying to harvest as much as possible from a contracting market. Price tactics include the following:

Beat a retreat on price, but work overtime to reduce production costs. Success in the latter will maintain a decent profit margin

Increase the price on the few remaining units in inventory.

This is because there may be a small number of customers who still rely on that particular product. This is particularly true of replacement parts. Here the seller hopes that the higher price will compensate for fewer sales. When the inventory is exhausted, the product line is terminated.

Pricing is one of the linchpins of marketing strategy and success. How is the company making its pricing decisions? Are these decisions appropriate for the current phase of the product life cycle? The most reliable method of pricing is to get inside the heads of customers, because how they value the firm's products relative to those of competitors and substitutes matters more than anything else.

PRICING IN INDUSTRIAL (B-2-B) MARKETS

The differences between consumer marketing and industrial marketing can be explained based on the distinguishing characteristics of industrial pricing. Some of those characteristics are listed below:

- The true price as industrial customer pays is often different from the list price because of factors like delivery and installation costs, discounts, training costs, trade-in allowance, financing costs and so on.

- Pricing is not an independent variable. It is highly intertwined with product, promotion and distribution strategies.
- Price for industrial products cannot be set out without considering other products that are compliments or substitutes sold by the firm. Cross elasticities exist, where the price of one item affects sales of other items.
- Prices can be changed in numerous ways such as changing the quantity of goods and services provided by the seller, changing the premiums and discounts that are offered, changing the time and place of payment, and so on. This implies that pricing is often a more flexible decision than product or distribution decisions.
- Industrial prices are established, in many cases, by competitive bidding on a project-by-project basis. In a number of cases, prices are resolved through negotiation.
- Industrial pricing is often characterized by an emphasis on fairness. Industrial buyers, who are experienced and able to estimate the vendors' approximate production costs expect the price increases to be justifiable on the basis of either the cost increases or product improvements.
- Industrial prices are affected by a host of economic factors such as inflation, interest rate changes, exchange rate fluctuations and so on. This problem is particularly critical for the marketer locked into a long term contract with no escalation cause.

PRICING ON THE INTERNET

E-Commerce has been arguably the Web's hottest application. Yet the Internet is more than simply a new 'marketspace'. Internet-based technologies are actually changing the rules of the market. Here is a short list of how the Internet allows sellers to discriminate between buyers and buyers to discriminate between sellers.

Buyers can ...

- Get instant price comparisons from thousands of vendors - Consumers now regularly check online prices, compare them with those in their local stores and may well take a peek at what customers in other places/countries are paying and order from overseas. Consumers also may unbundle product information from the transaction themselves. For instance, someone might use the Internet to research on a holiday destination, but visit a travel agency to get some procedural requirements done, go home to use a search engine to find the lowest airfare to that destination. Sites like PriceScan.com lure thousands of visitors a day, most of them corporate buyers. Intelligent shopping agents (known as 'bots') take price comparison a step further and seek out products, prices and reviews from as many as 2,000 merchants.

- Name their price and have it met - Taking the example of Priceline.com, the customer states the price he wants to pay for an airline ticket, hotel or car rental and Priceline checks whether any seller is willing to meet that price. Consumers can fix their own prices, and sellers can use it too. Airlines can fill in demand for empty seats and hotels welcome the chance to sell vacant rooms at near zero marginal cost. Volume-aggregating sites combine the orders of many customers and press the supplier for a deeper discount.
- Get products free - Open Source, the free software movement that started with Linux, will erode margins for just about any company doing software. Open Source software is popping up everywhere. The biggest challenge confronting major software producers is now: how to compete with programs that can be had free?

Sellers can ...

- Monitor customer behaviour and tailor offers to individuals - Although shopping agent software and price comparison web sites provide published prices, consumers may be missing out on the special deals they can get with the help of new technologies. GE Lighting, which gets 55,000 pricing requests a year, has Web programs that evaluate about 300 factors that go into a pricing quote, such as past sales and discounts, so that it can reduce processing time from up to 30 days to 6 hours.
- Give certain customers access to special prices - CDNOW, an online vendor of music albums, emails certain (loyal) buyers a special website address with lower prices. Unless you know

the secret address, you pay full price. Business marketers are already using extranets to get a precise handle on inventory, costs and demand at any given moment in order to dynamically adjust prices.

Bother buyers and sellers can …

Negotiate prices in online auctions and exchanges - Want to sell hundreds of excess and slightly worn widgets? Want to purchase air tickets at a bargain price? Go to air ticket auctions at Rediff.com. Thanks to the Internet, pricing is no longer a rigid entity of marketing. It is the era of dynamic pricing in many categories.

PRICING METHODS

Firms translate pricing objectives into pricing decisions in two major steps. First, someone must accept responsibility for making pricing decisions and administering the resulting pricing structure. Second, someone must set the overall pricing structure - that is, basic prices and appropriate discounts for channel members, quantity purchases, and geographic and promotional considerations. Hence a firm sets not a single price, but rather a pricing structure that covers different items in its line. This pricing structure changes over time as products move through their life cycles. The company adjusts product prices to reflect changes in costs and demand and to account for variation in buyers and situations.

NEW PRODUCT PRICING STRATEGIES

Pricing strategies usually change as the product passes through its life cycle as illustrated in the previous lesson. The introductory stage is especially challenging. Firms bringing out an innovative patent-protected product can choose between two options, viz. market skimming pricing and market-penetration pricing.

Market-skimming pricing: Many firms that invent new products initially set high prices to 'skim' revenues layer by layer from the market. At product introduction in the marketplace, the firm may charge the highest price it could given the benefits of its new product over competing products. The firm sets a price that made it just worthwhile for some affordable segments of the market to adopt the new product. After the initial sales slowdown, the firm may lower the price to draw in the next price sensitive layer of the customers. In this way, a firm skims a maximum amount of revenue from the various segments of the market. It is important to note that skimming works well only under certain conditions. The quality and image must support its higher price and enough buyers must want the product at that price. Also the cost of producing a small volume cannot be so high that they cancel the advantage of charging more. In the mean time, competitors should not be able to enter the market easily and undercut the price. A skimming strategy offers several benefits to the markets, as listed below:

- It allows a manufacturer to quickly recover its research and development costs.
- It also allows a firm to maximize revenue from a new product before competitors enter the field.
- A skimming strategy offers a useful tool for segmenting a product's overall market on a price basis.
- It permits marketers to control demand in the introductory stages of a product's life cycle and then adjust productive capacity to match demand.

The chief disadvantage of skimming strategy is: it attracts competition. Potential competitors see innovative firms reaping big financial gains and decide to enter the market. This new supply forces the price even lower than its eventual level under a sequential skimming procedure. However, if patent protection or other proprietary ability allows a firm to exude competitors from its market, it may continue a skimming strategy for a relatively long period.

Market-penetration pricing: Rather than setting a high initial price to skim off small but profitable market segments, some firms set a low initial price in order to penetrate the market quickly and deeply - to attract a large number of buyers quickly and win a large market share. A penetration pricing strategy may also extend over several stages of the product life cycle as the firm seeks to maintain a reputation as a low-price competitor. Since many firms begin penetration pricing with the intention of increasing prices in the future, success depends on generating many consumer trial purchases. Penetration pricing works well under the following conditions:

- A good or service experiences highly elastic demand
- The market is highly price sensitive and a low price stimulates market growth
- Production and distribution costs fall with accumulated production experience.
- A low price helps discourage actual and potential competition.

PRODUCT-MIX PRICING

The strategy for setting a product's price often has to be changed when the product is part of a product mix. In this case, the firm looks for a set of prices that maximizes the profits on the total product mix. This pricing is difficult because the various products have related demand and costs and face different degrees of competition.

- Product-line pricing: Since most firms market multiple product lines, an effective pricing strategy must consider the relationships among all of these products instead of viewing each is isolation. In product line pricing, management must decide on the price steps to set between the various products. The price steps should take into account cost differences between the products, customer evaluations of their different features and competitors' prices. In many industries, marketers use well-established price points for the products in their line. The customer will probably associate low, average and high quality with the price points. The marketers task is to establish perceived quality differences that support the price differences.
- Optional-product pricing: Many firms use this strategy by offering to sell optional or accessory products along with their main product. These firms have to decide which items to include in the base price and which to offer as options. Often the basic model which is stripped of many comforts and conveniences sought by the customers gets rejected.
- Captive-product pricing: Firms that make products that must be used along with a main product are using this pricing strategy. Producers of the main products often price them low and set high markups of the supplies. For a competitor who does not sell these supplies, he will have to price his product higher in order to make the same overall profit. In case of services, this strategy is called two-part pricing where the price of the service is broken into a fixed fee plus a variable usage rate. The service firm must decide how much to charge for the basic service and how much for the variable usage. The fixed amount should be low enough to induce usage of the service and profit can be made on the variable usage fees.
- By-product pricing: In producing certain products, there are by-products. If these by products have no value and if getting rid of them is costly, this will affect the pricing of the main

product. Using by-product pricing, the manufacturer will seek a market for these by-products and should accept any price that covers more than the cost of storing and delivering them. This practice allows the marketer to reduce the main product's price to make it more competitive.

- Product-bundle pricing: Using this strategy, marketers combine several of their products and offer the bundle at a reduced price. Price bundling can promote the sales of products consumers might not buy otherwise, but the combined price must be low enough to get them to buy the bundle. Firms usually adjust their basic prices to account for various customer differences and changing situations.
- Discount and allowance pricing: Most firms adjust their basic price to reward customers for certain responses, such as cash payment, early payment of bills, volume purchases and off-season buying. Some of those adjustments are described below:
  - — Cash discounts - A cash discount is a price reduction to buyers who pay their bills promptly. The discount must be granted to all buyers meeting these terms. Such discounts are customary in many industries and help to improve the sellers' cash situation and reduce bad debts and credit collection costs.
  - — Quantity discounts - A quantity discount is a price reduction to buyers who buy large volumes. It must be offered to all customers and must not exceed the seller's cost savings associated with selling large quantities. These savings include lower selling, inventory and transportation expenses. Discounts provide an incentive to the customer to buy more from one given seller, rather than from many different sources.
  - — Functional discounts - A functional discount (also called trade discount) is offered by the seller to trade channel members who perform certain functions, such as selling, storing and record keeping. Manufacturers may offer different functional discounts to different trade channels because of the varying services they perform, but manufacturers must offer the same functional discounts within each trade channel.
  - — Seasonal discounts - A seasonal discount is a price reduction to buyers who buy out of season. It allows

the seller to keep productions steady during the entire year.

— Allowances - They are another type of reductions from the list price. Trade-in allowances are price reductions given for turning in an old item when buying a new one. Promotional allowances are payments or price reductions to reward dealers for participating in advertising and sales-support programs.

- Discriminatory pricing: Firms will often adjust their basic prices to allow for differences in customers, products and locations. In discriminatory pricing, the firm sells a product or service at two or more prices, even though the difference in prices is not based on differences in costs. Discriminatory pricing takes many forms as indicated below:

  — Customer-segment pricing - Different customers pay different prices for the same product or service.

  — Product-form pricing - Different versions of the product are priced differently, but not according to differences in their costs.

  — Location pricing - Different locations are priced differently, even though the cost of offering in each location is the same.

  — Time pricing - Prices vary by the season, month, day and even hour.

- Psychological pricing: It applies the belief that certain prices or price ranges make products more appealing to buyers than others. In using psychological pricing, sellers consider the psychology of prices and not simply the economics.

  — Pricing based on perceptions - The relationship between price and quality perceptions indicate that consumers perceive higher-priced products as having higher quality. When consumers cannot judge quality because they lack the information or skill, prices becomes an important quality signal.

  — Reference pricing - Reference prices are those prices that buyers carry in their minds and refer to when looking at a given product. It might be formed by noting current prices, remembering past prices or assessing the buying situation. Sellers can influence or use these consumers' reference prices when setting price.

— Odd pricing - In odd pricing, marketers set prices at odd numbers just under round numbers. An odd ending conveys the notion of a discount or bargain to the customer.

- Value pricing: During slow-growth times, many firms adjust their prices to bring them into line with economic conditions and with the resulting fundamental shift in consumer attitudes toward quality and value. Value pricing is offering just the right combination of quality and good service at a fair price. In many cases, value pricing has involved redesigning existing brands in order to offer more quality for a given price or the same quality for less.
- Promotional pricing: In promotional pricing, a lower-than-normal price is used as a temporary ingredient in a firm's selling strategy. Some promotional pricing arrangements form part of recurrent marketing initiatives. Some may be to introduce a promotional model or brand with special pricing to begin competing in a new market. Promotional pricing takes several forms and some of them are described below.

— Loss-leader pricing - It happens when retailers drop price on well-known brands to stimulate store traffic in the hope that customers will buy other items also, at normal mark-ups

— Special-event pricing - Sellers use special-event pricing in certain seasons to draw in more customers. The seasonal need of the customers is capitalized on by the sellers using this pricing strategy.

— Cash rebates - Manufacturers will sometimes offer cash rebates to consumers who buy the product from dealers within a specified time.

— Low-interest financing, longer payment times, longer warranties - all these represent the promotional incentives offered by the sellers to the buyers. Since they provide some flexibility and also bring down the perceived risks (in case of longer warranties), buyers are motivated to make the buying decision.

— Psychological discounting - The seller may simply offer discounts from normal prices to increase sales and reduce inventories. For the buyer, the motivation to buy below normal prices may be compelling.

- Geographical pricing: Geographical considerations strongly influence prices when costs must cover shipping heavy, bulky, low-unit-cost materials. Buyers and sellers can distribute transportation expenses in several ways:
  - — The buyer pays all transportation charges;
  - — The seller pays all transportation charges; or
  - — The buyer and the seller share the charges.
  - — This choice has particularly important effects for a firm seeking to expand its geographic coverage to distant markets. The seller's pricing can implement several alternatives for handling transportation costs.
- FOB-origin pricing - It means that the goods are placed free on board (FOB) a carrier, at which point the title and responsibility pass to the customer, who pays the freight from the factory to the destination. Though it looks fair, the disadvantage is that the firm will be a high-cost firm to distant customers.
- Uniform delivered pricing - It is the exact opposite of FOB pricing. The company charges the same price plus freight to all customers, regardless of their location. An advantage is that it is fairly easy to administer and it lets the firm advertise its price nationally.
- Zone pricing - It falls between FOB-origin pricing and uniform delivered pricing. The company sets up two or more zones. All customers within a given zone pay a single total price; the more distant the zone, the higher the price.
- Basing-point pricing - The seller selects a given city as a 'basing point' and charges all customers the freight cost from that city to the customer location, regardless of the city from which the goods actually are shipped.
- Freight-absorption pricing - The seller who is anxious to do business with a certain customer or geographical area might use freight-absorption pricing. This strategy involves absorbing all or part of the actual freight charges in order to get the desired business. It is used for market penetration and to hold on to increasingly competitive markets.
- International pricing: A wide variety of internal and external conditions can affect a marketer's global pricing strategies.

Internal influences include the firm's goals and marketing strategies, the costs of developing, producing and marketing its products, the nature of the products and the firm's competitive strengths. External influences include general conditions in international markets, especially those in the firm's target markets, regulatory limitations, trade restrictions, competitors' actions, economic events, customer characteristics and the global status of the industry. In general, a firm can implement one of three export pricing strategies, as described below.

— Standard worldwide price - Exporters often set standard worldwide prices, regardless of their target markets. This strategy can succeed if foreign marketing costs remain low enough that they do not impact overall costs, or if their prices reflect average unit costs. A firm that implements a standard pricing program must monitor the international marketplace carefully, however, to make sure that domestic competitors do not undercut its prices.

— Dual pricing - It distinguishes prices for domestic and export sales. Some exporters practice cost-plus pricing to establish dual prices that fully allocate their true domestic and foreign costs to product sales in those markets. Others opt for flexible cost-plus pricing schemes that allow marketers to grant discounts or change prices according to shifts in the competitive environment or fluctuations in the international exchange rate.

— Market-differentiated pricing - It makes even more flexible arrangements to set prices according to local marketplace conditions. Effective market-differentiated pricing depends on access to quick, accurate market information.

Note: Kimberly-Clark Corporation (Kimberly-Clark) is a global health and hygiene company offering personal care and consumer tissue products. The company's products are sold under brands such as Kleenex, Scott, Huggies, Pull-Ups, Kotex and Depend. The company has manufacturing facilities in 38 countries and its products are sold in more than 150 countries across the world. The company primarily operates in North America. It is headquartered in Dallas, Texas and employs 53,000 people. For further knowledge regarding this chapter reader can visit www.kimberly-clark.com

13

Integrated Marketing Communication

INTRODUCTION

The purpose of communications is to directly or indirectly influence individual groups, and organizations to facilitate exchanges by informing and persuading one or more audiences to accept a company's products and/or services. In any communication there are three basic components: A source, a medium and a message.

MARKETING COMMUNICATION

Marketing communications is one of the four major elements of the company's marketing mix. Marketers must know how to use advertising, sales promotion, direct marketing, public relations, and personal selling to communicate the product's existence and value to the target customers.

The communication process itself consists of nine elements: sender, receiver, encoding, decoding, message, media, response, feedback, and noise. Marketers must know how to get through to the target audience in the face of the audience's tendencies toward selective attention, distortion, and recall. Developing the promotion program involves eight steps. The communicator must first identify the target audience and its characteristics, including the image it carries of the product. Next, the communicator has to define the communication objective, whether it is to create awareness, knowledge, liking, preference, conviction, or purchase. A message must be designed containing an effective content, structure, format, and source. Then communication channels both personal and non-personal must be selected. Next, the total promotion budget must be established. Four common methods are the affordable method, the percentage-of-sales method, the competitive-parity method, and the objective and- task method.

The promotion budget should be divided among the main promotional tools, as affected by such factors as push-versus-pull strategy, buyer readiness stage, product life-cycle stage and company market rank. The marketer should then monitor to see how much of the market becomes aware of the product, tries it, and is satisfied in the process. Finally, all of the communications effort must be managed and coordinated for consistency, good timing, and cost effectiveness.

MEANING

Modern marketing calls for more than just developing a good product, pricing it attractively, and making it available to target customers. Companies must also communicate with their customers, and what and how they communicate should not be left to chance. For most companies, the question is not whether to communicate, but how much to spend and in what ways.

"Promotion is the co-ordination of seller's aim to set up channels of information and persuasion to facilitate the sales of goods/services or acceptance of an idea". "It includes all those activities which are aimed at creating and stimulating demand" In our daily life we all are exposed to various tools of promotion aiming at communicating one thing or the other to us.

For our convenience, all those promotional tools can be categorised in five major components, constituting the promotional mix - advertising, sales promotion, public relations, personal selling and direct marketing.

Promotion serves three essential roles - it informs, persuades, and reminds prospective customers about the company and its products. Ultimately, using all these three in various ways, the company tries to modify the behaviour of the consumers to suit its objectives.

MARKETING COMMUNICATION MIX

A company's total marketing communications mix is called its promotional mix. The promotional mix is a specific mix of advertising, personal selling, sales promotion, public relations, and direct-marketing tools that a company uses to pursue its marketing objectives.

THE ELEMENTS OF THE PROMOTIONAL MIX

The five major tools are:

- Advertising: the first of these elements is described as being any paid form of non-personal presentation and promotion of ideas, goods, and services by an identified sponsor.

- Sales Promotion: the second element of communication tools, is a process of providing short-term incentives to encourage purchase or sales of a product or service. While advertising gives the buyer reasons to buy, sales promotion gives the buyer the incentive to buy now.
- Public Relations: the third communication tool, is an attempt to build good relations with the company's various publics by obtaining favourable publicity, building up a good "corporate image," and handling or heading off unfavourable rumours, stories, or events.
- Personal Selling: the fourth communication tool is face-to-face interaction with one or more prospective purchasers for the purpose of making presentations, handling objections and securing orders.
- Direct Marketing: the fifth communication tool is the process of using mail, telephone, fax, e-mail or internet to communicate directly with the customers and prospects. viz., to buy its products/services.

NATURE OF PROMOTIONAL TOOLS

Each promotional tool has unique characteristics and costs.

1. Advertising
   - Public presentation (public mode of communication).
   - Pervasiveness (permits seller to repeat the message many times. It also allows buyer to receive and compare the message with those of competitors).
   - Amplified expressiveness (provides opportunities for dramatizing the company and its product through the artful use of language, print, sound, colour, etc.)
   - Impersonality (it cannot be as compelling as a company's sales representatives).
2. Publicity
   - High credibility (news features and stories seem more authentic and credible to readers/viewers than ads do).
   - Off guard (can reach many prospects who might avoid sales people and ads. The message gets to the buyers as news).
   - Dramatization (like advertising, it also has a potential for dramatizing a company or its products).

3. Personal Selling
   - Personal confirmation (both way communication).
   - Cultivation (all kinds of relationship - short time or long time).
   - Response (makes the buyer feel under some obligation).
4. Sales Promotion
   - Communication (they grab the reader's attention and usually provide information that may lead the consumer to the product).
   - Incentives (give value to the consumer).
   - Invitation (to engage in the transaction now, without delay).
5. Direct Marketing
   - Non-public (message is addressed to specific person/ group).
   - Customised (to appeal to the addressed individual)
   - Up-to-date (message can be prepared very quickly for delivery to an individual).

PROMOTION IS AN ACT OF COMMUNICATION

- The word "communication" is based on the Latin word meaning "COMMON". Thus the term communication has come to mean sharing something of common use.
- Since marketing communications aim at influencing consumer behaviour in favour of the firm's offerings, these are persuasive in nature. These persuasive communications are more commonly called "PROMOTION" and constitute one of the 4 Ps of the marketing mix.
- Modern marketing calls for more than developing a good product, pricing it correctly and making it easily available to the customer. The company that wants more than 'walk in' sales must develop an effective program of communication and promotion.
- Persuasive communication is said to take place when a communicator very consciously develops his messages to have a calculated impact on the attitude and/ or behaviour of a target audience. A study of 'Marketing Communication' is a study of the promotion function of marketing.

OBJECTIVES OF PROMOTION

- To increase sales.
- To increase market share.
- To build brand loyalty.
- To build product differentiation in customers' mind.

THE COMMUNICATION PROCESS

Two parties in a communication process are sender and receiver; message and media are communication tools, whereas major communication functions are: encoding, decoding, response and feedback.

ELEMENTS OF THE COMMUNICATION PROCESS

- Source or sender or communicator
- Encoding (putting the thought or idea in symbolic form)
- Message (the set of symbols for transmission)
- Media (the path through which the message moves) from Sender to Receiver.
- Decoding (assigning meanings to the symbols transmitted by the sender).
- Receiver or audience or destination.
- Response (the set of reactions that the receiver has after having been exposed to the message).
- Feedback.

A BRIEF PROMOTIONAL DECISIONS INTEGRATED MARKETING COMMUNICATIONS

The sender's task is to get his or her message through to the receiver, but the target audience may not receive the intended message for any of three reasons:

- Selective attention.
- Selective distortion (people may twist the message to hear what they want to hear. Receivers have set attitudes; they will hear what fits into their belief system).
- Selective recall.

Fiske and Hartley have outlined some general factors that influence the effectiveness of a communication:

- The greater the monopoly of the communication source over the recipient, the greater the recipient's change, effected in favour of the source.
- Communication effects are greatest where the message is in line with the receiver's existing opinions, beliefs and disposition.
- Communication can produce the most effective shifts on unfamiliar, lightly felt, peripheral issues, that do not lie at the core of the recipient's value system.
- Communication is more likely to be effective where the source is believed to have expertise, high status, objectivity, or likability, but particularly where the source has power and can be identified with.
- The social context, group, or reference group will mediate the communication and influence whether or not the Communication is accepted.

PROMOTIONAL DECISIONS

- Who is the target audience? - 'Receiver'
- What responses are sought? - 'Responses & Decoding'.
- What message should be developed? - 'Message & Encoding'.
- What media should be selected? - 'Media'
- What source should be chosen? - 'Sender'
- What feedback should be collected? - 'Feedback'

1. Identify the target audience: The audience may be
   - Present users
   - Potential Users
   - Influencer
   - Decider

   After identifying the target audience, the Communicator should decide two important things

   - What is to be said to them?
   - When and where is it to be said?

   Given the target audience, the communicator has to ascertain several audience characteristics, such as:

   - Audiences' thinking towards the company and its product, and that of its competitors.

- Audiences' cognitive process (how the target audience processes the incoming information: "people differ in their cognitive complexity as a result of education and Intelligence")
- After identifying the target audience, communicator must decide very carefully exactly what responses are sought from the audience.

2. What messages should be sent:
   - The ultimate (sought after) response is purchase, the targeted change in the buyer's behaviour but this is the end result of a long process of consumer decision making.
   - Consumer goes through a series of stages before purchasing a product.
   - The marketing communicator should know the buyer's readiness stages and must assess where the target audience is at a particular point of time, since the communication may need slight modification from one stage to another.
3. How should messages be developed:

   Message content - "What has to be told"

   Communicator has to figure out what to say to the target audience in order to produce the desired response. This is called 'theme' or 'USP' (Unique Selling Proposition).

   There are three types of appeals which can be developed in the message:

   Rational Appeal, Emotional Appeal and Moral Appeal.

   - Message structure: "How to say it logically"

   The major issues in message structure are:

   — Conclusion drawing
   — One or two sided arguments
   — Order of persuasion (strongest point to be told first or last depends upon audience reaction and perception).

   Message format: " How to say it symbolically"

   - Print - Head Line, Illustration, colour, picture.
   - Radio - Voice, Music, Message, Source - Celebrities.
   - TV - In addition body language.

4. What media should be selected

   There are two choices available:

   - Personal communication
   - Non-Personal communication (Newspaper, Magazine, TV, radio, etc.)

   Advocate Channel - Company sales personal.

   Expert Channel - consists of independent persons with expertise making statements to target buyers.

   Social Channels or word of mouth - through friends, family members (product is costly and risky, product has got significant social status, etc.).

5. What source should be chosen

   - Source is the originator of the communication. The communicator has direct influence on the audience.
   - Messages delivered by highly credible sources will add to the persuasiveness of the image itself.

6. Collecting feedback

   - This generally involves creating a sample of members of the target audience and asking them relevant questions to check the effectiveness of promotional decisions.

INTEGRATED MARKETING COMMUNICATIONS

Not all product concepts are right for all individuals, which observation introduces the notion of market segmentation and targeting. The same holds true for marketing communications. One message does not fit all. Integrated marketing communications (IMC) focus on discrete customer segments. With IMC, the firm learns to understand that although mass-market promotion appears cost-effective on the front end, brand/ product messages are also offered to millions of people who are not interested… a waste of time, money and energy.

Mass media no longer serves the mass audiences sought by marketers. Individual audiences for each media have decreased, thus indicating a need to ensure that whenever and wherever the prospect is exposed to the message, he/she receives a consistent one. Customers typically do not differentiate between message sources; they only remember the message they received. Considering how many messages consumers are bombarded with on a regular basis, mixed messages from the same source are bound to cause confusion and, worse yet, they will be more quickly forgotten. Although understanding the importance of marketing communications is fairly simple, finding the best means through which to implement a marketing communications program is becomingly increasingly difficult. The buying public has been virtually buried alive in ads.

Consumers are bombarded with hundreds of ads and TV commercials, not to mention the thousands of billboards, packages, website pop-ups and other logo sightings every day. The IMC planning process is based on a longitudinal consumer purchase database. Ideally, this database would contain, by household, demographics, psychographics, purchase data, and perhaps some information regarding how the household feels about [or its experience with] the product category. In many cases, direct-marketing organizations already have this type of information at their disposal.

An IMC program is implemented according to the needs and lifestyles of the selected target markets, thus allowing for customised, yet consistent, message strategies to sell increasingly individualized products. Through integrated marketing communications, the company carefully integrates and coordinates its many communication channels to deliver a clear, consistent, and compelling message about the organization and its products. Integrated communications produce better communication consistency and greater sales impact. Integrated marketing communications is a way of looking at the whole marketing process from the viewpoint of the customer.

Marketing Philosophy: The successful salesperson cares first for the customer, second for the products.

- Integrated marketing communications is a concept of marketing communications planning that recognises the added value of a comprehensive plan that evaluates the strategic roles of a variety of communications disciplines - for example, general advertising, direct response, sales promotion, and public relations - and combines these disciplines to provide clarity, consistency, and maximum communications impact (through the seamless integration of discrete messages).
- IMC - combining and integrating different elements of the communication mix.
- The key idea behind IMC, however, is simply that advertising has various strengths and weaknesses and that it thus has to

be combined with other elements of the communication mix - in an integrated and consistent way.

- The different elements of the communication mix have to be used in a way that the strengths of one are used to offset the weakness of another.
- For instance, one of advertising's weaknesses is its frequent failure to induce immediate action. Very often, advertising can create high awareness and favourable attitudes, but it cannot create the final "push" needed to get the inquiry, trial or sale. When such a situation appears, a marketer must use direct marketing, or sales promotions, to get the necessary action, possibly after the advertising campaign.

THE CHANGING COMMUNICATIONS ENVIRONMENT

Two major factors are changing the face of today's marketing communications:

- Mass markets have fragmented, which is why marketers are shifting away from mass marketing and moving toward focused programs.
- Improvements in computer and information technology are speeding the movement toward segmented marketing. New technologies have provided means to reach smaller segments with tailored messages.

SUSTAINABLE COMPETITIVE ADVANTAGE BASED ON IMC

It has been said that integrated marketing communications will be the only sustainable competitive advantage for marketers in the near future. The other elements of the marketing mix, product development, pricing, and distribution, can be achieved at a very similar level, and in a similar way, among companies competing in a particular industry. In addition, we know the customer has taken on a completely new, powerful, role in the marketing process. Because it is largely through promotion that a company speaks most directly to its customers, it seems appropriate that a marketer's promotional strategy must change to reflect the dynamics of today's marketplace.

Some of these changes include:

- Changing technology, which has made it possible for media organizations to identify, segment, select, and attract smaller audiences for their respective vehicles.

- The trend toward de-regulation that has allowed for increased competition within many industries, such as air travel, banking, and utilities.
- Globalization of the marketplace, which causes promotional efforts, including advertising, sales promotion, public relations and personal selling, to be implemented throughout a worldwide market. Customisation for different cultures is key to competing successfully in this arena.
- Changes in the demographic and psychographic profiles of today's consumers, that have paved the way for new product category opportunities (such as healthcare for the aging "baby boomers" and health food/clubs for nutrition conscious consumers).
- Money-rich, time-poor consumers are seeking control of their purchases. Consumers have become adept at avoiding marketing communication, through the use of VCRs/ VCD/DVD players, remote controls, radio push buttons, etc., so when they are at all listening, the message should be simply stated and easy to understand. Today's generation is also more visually oriented than verbally, which means they rely more on images, symbols and graphics than any previous generation.

It is important also to note that a marketer can communicate with customers through means other than formal marketing communications. Every element of a product's marketing mix helps to position that product in the minds of consumers. The result is that the elements of the promotional mix should all present a consistent theme. The same is true of the other "Ps" of marketing, namely, product, price and place that also should support the theme:

- Products communicate through size, shape, name, packaging, and various features/benefits.
- Price communicates to the consumer that the product is high quality, low quality, prestigious, common, etc.
- Retail locations (place) where customers purchase the product will reflect upon the product's image as well. Stores are thought of as "high-class," exclusive, speciality, discount, etc.

OVERVIEW OF IMC

Advertising - the use of paid media by a seller to communicate persuasive information about its products, services, or organization - is a potent promotional tool. Advertising takes on many forms (national, regional, local, consumer, industrial, retail, product, brand, institutional, etc.) designed to achieve a variety of objectives (awareness, interest, preference, brand recognition, brand insistence).

Advertising decision-making consists of objectives setting, budget decision, message decision, media decision, and ad effectiveness evaluation. Advertisers should establish clear goals as to whether the advertising is supposed to inform, persuade, or remind buyers. The factors to consider when setting the advertising budget are: stage in the product life cycle, market share, competition and clutter, needed frequency, and product substitutability. The advertising budget can be established based on what is affordable, as a percentage budget of sales, based on competitors' expenditures, or based on objectives and tasks, and based on more advanced decision models that are available.

The message decision calls for generating messages, evaluating and selecting between them, and executing them effectively and responsibly. The media decision calls for defining the reach, frequency, and impact goals; choosing among major media types; selecting specific media vehicles; deciding on media timing; geographical allocation of media. Finally, campaign evaluation calls for evaluating the communication and sales effects of advertising, before, during, and after the advertising.

Sales promotion and public relations are two tools of growing importance in marketing planning. Sales promotion covers a wide variety of short-term incentive tools designed to stimulate consumer markets, the trade, and the organization's own sales force. Sales promotion expenditures now exceed advertising expenditures and are growing at a faster rate. Consumer promotion tools include samples, coupons, cash refund offers, price packs, premiums, prizes, patronage rewards, free trials, product warranties, tie-in promotions, and point-of-purchase displays and demonstrations. Trade promotion tools include price-off, advertising and display allowances, free goods, push money, and speciality-advertising items. Business promotion tools include conventions, trade shows, contests, sweepstakes, and games. Sales promotion planning calls for establishing the sales promotion objectives, selecting the tools, developing, pretesting, and implementing the sales promotion program, and evaluating the results.

Marketing Public Relations (MPR) is another important communication/promotion tool. Traditionally, it has been the least utilised tool but is now recognized for its ability in building awareness and preference in the market-place, repositioning products, and defending them. Broadly, MPR is those activities that support the ultimate sale of a product or service. Some of the major marketing public relations tools are news, speeches, events, public service activities, written material, audio-visual material, corporate identity, and telephone information services. MPR planning involves establishing the MPR objectives, choosing the appropriate messages and vehicles, and evaluating the MPR results.

SUMMARY

Marketing communications is one of the four major elements of the company's marketing mix. The communication process itself consists of nine elements: sender, receiver, encoding, decoding, message, media, response, feedback, and noise. The promotion budget should be divided among the main promotional tools, as affected by such factors as push-versus-pull strategy, buyer readiness stage, product life-cycle stage and company market rank.

"Promotion is the co-ordination of seller's aim to set up channels of information and persuasion to facilitate the sales of goods/services or acceptance of an idea". Promotion serves three essential roles - it informs, persuades, and reminds prospective customers about the company and its products. The promotional mix is a specific mix of advertising, personal selling, sales promotion, public relations, and direct-marketing tools that a company uses to pursue its marketing objectives.

Mass media no longer serves the mass audiences sought by marketers. Individual audiences for each media have decreased, thus indicating a need to ensure that whenever and wherever the prospect is exposed to the message, he/she receives a consistent one. The IMC planning process is based on a longitudinal consumer purchase database. Ideally, this database would contain, by household, demographics, psychographics, purchase data, and perhaps some information regarding how the household feels about [or its experience with] the product category. Every element of a product's marketing mix helps to position that product in the minds of consumers. The result is that the elements of the promotional mix should all present a consistent theme. Advertising decision-making consists of objectives setting, budget decision, message decision, media decision, and ad effectiveness evaluation. The message decision calls for generating messages, evaluating and selecting between them, and executing them effectively and responsibly. Sales promotion and public relations are two tools of growing importance in marketing planning. Sales promotion covers a wide variety of short-term incentive tools designed to stimulate consumer markets, the trade, and the organization's own sales force. Marketing Public Relations (MPR) is another important communication/promotion tool. Traditionally, it has been the least utilised tool but is now recognized for its ability in building awareness and preference in the market-place, repositioning products, and defending them.

Note: Cummins is engaged in the manufacturing of diesel and natural gas engines as well as power generation equipment in the world. The company primarily operates in the US. It is headquartered in Columbus, Indiana and employs 39,800 people. For a very good case study regarding this topic, reader can visit company's website www.cummins.com

14

Role of Advertising

Advertising is the structural and composed non-personal communication of information, usually paid for and usually persuasive nature, in about organization, products, services, ideas by identified sponsors through various media. An ad campaign includes a series of ads placed in different media based on an analysis of marketing and communications situations.

MEANING

Marketing management must make four important decisions when developing an advertising program:

- Setting advertising objectives
- Setting advertising budgets
- Developing advertising strategy
- Message decisions.
- Media decisions.

o Evaluating advertising campaigns

SETTING ADVERTISING OBJECTIVES

Setting objectives is the first step in developing an advertising program. These objectives should be based on past decisions about the target market, positioning, and marketing mix, which define the job that advertising must do in the total marketing program. An advertising objective is a specific communication task to be accomplished with a specific target audience during a specific period of time.

Advertising objectives can be classified by primary purpose as:

- Informative advertising, which is advertising used to inform consumers about a new product or feature and to build primary demand.

- Persuasive advertising, which is advertising used to build selective demand for a brand by persuading consumers that it offers the best quality for their money.
- Comparative advertising, which is advertising that compares one brand directly or indirectly to one or more other brands.
- Reminder advertising, which is advertising used to keep consumers thinking about a product.

FUNCTIONS OF ADVERTISING

The marketer can also be seeking a cognitive, effective or behavioural response from the consumer through the process of advertising. The marketer has to study the present state of the consumers' mind in terms of its knowledge about the organization and its products and also the attitude towards them. The advertisement works in the consumers mind in a Response Hierarchy Model. It is assumed that the buyer, after being exposed to the advertisement, passes through a cognitive, effective and behavioural state in that order.

We give a brief of the Hierarchy-of- Effects Model

- Awareness: if it is found that most of the target audience is unaware of the product/ brand, the advertiser's task is to build awareness, with simple messages repeating the product/brand name.
- Knowledge: in case the target audience have product/brand awareness but do not know more, the advertiser's task is to give them more information about the product/ brand by providing relevant information on product/brand attributes, consumer benefits, past records on reliability, price, availability, etc.
- Liking: the advertiser has to find out ways how to build favourable attitude about the product/brand. Here it should they take help of other promotional tools like public relations, etc.
- Preference: in case the target audience does not prefer the product/brand to other products/brands, even though they like it, the advertiser must try to build consumer preference by promoting quality, value, performance and other features.
- Conviction: a target audience might prefer a particular product/ brand but not develop a conviction - a firm decision - to buy it. Here the advertiser's task is to build conviction among the

interested consumers so that the particular product/brand is their best choice

- Purchase: finally members of the target audience should be induced to make the final purchase. This can be done again by the help of other tools such as sales promotion.

SETTING THE ADVERTISING BUDGET

- After determining its advertising objectives, the marketer must set the advertising budget for each product and market.
- There are four common methods used to set the total budget for advertising:
- The affordable method involves setting the promotion budget at the level management thinks the company can afford. This method is often used by small businesses. They start with total revenues, deduct operating expenses and capital outlays, and then devote some portion of the remaining funds to advertising. However, it completely ignores the effect of promotion on sales. It places promotional spending last and can lead to over- or under-spending.
- The percentage-of-sales method is setting the promotion budget at a certain percentage of current or forecasted sales or as a percentage of the sales price. This method is simple and it helps management to think about the relationships between promotion spending, selling price, and profit per unit. However, it wrongly views sales as the cause of promotion rather than the result. Yearly budget variations cause problems with this method and the method does not provide any basis for selecting the percentage to use.
- The competitive-parity method is setting the promotion budget to match competitor's outlay. Supporting this method are the arguments that competition knows the industry and parity helps to prevent promotion wars. Here, each organization tries to have equal share of their voice in the market place. However, neither of these arguments has proved to be reliable. Often, competitors do not have a justification for what they spend.
- The objective-and-task method involves developing the promotion budget by:
- Defining specific promotion objectives.

- Determining the tasks that must be performed to achieve these objectives.
- Estimating the costs of performing these tasks.
- The sum of the above costs is the proposed promotion budget.
- The objective and task method forces management to spell out its assumptions about the relationships between money spent and promotion results. It is a difficult method, but does produce good results if done correctly.

DEVELOPING ADVERTISING STRATEGY

Advertising Strategy consists of two elements and companies are realising the benefits of planning these two elements jointly, as depicted symbolically below:

Creating the Advertising Messages Selecting the Advertising Media

The first step in creating effective advertising messages is to decide what general message will be communicated to consumers (plan a message strategy).

- This begins with developing a message that focuses on benefits.
- Second, develop a creative concept (the big idea). This concept may emerge as Role of Advertising a visualization, a phrase, or a combination of the two.
- The creative concept guides the choice of specific advertising appeals to be used in an advertising campaign. The appeals should be:
  - — Meaningful.
  - — Believable.
  - — Distinctive.

The next major phase is to examine the impact of the message. Here, what is said is as important as how it is said. The creative people must find the best style, tone, words, and format for executing the message. Specific styles are:

- Slice of life: shows one or more people using the product in a normal setting.
- Lifestyle: shows how a product fits in with a particular lifestyle.
- Fantasy: creates a fantasy around the product or its use.
- Mood or image: builds a mood or image around the product.

- Musical: shows one or more people or cartoon characters singing a song about the product.
- Personality symbol: creates a character (animated or real) that represents the product.
- Technical expertise: highlights the company's expertise in making the product.
- Scientific evidence: trumpets the results of survey or scientific evidence that the brand is better or better liked than one or more other brands.
- Testimonial evidence: features a highly believable or likable source (celebrity or ordinary person) endorsing the product, e.g., Amitabh Bachchan for Maruti Versa.

MEDIA SELECTION

The major steps in selecting the media are:

- Deciding on reach, frequency, and impact.
- Reach is the percentage of people in the target market exposed to an ad campaign during a given period.
- Frequency is the number of times the average person in the target market is exposed to an advertising message during a given period.
- Media impact is the qualitative value of an exposure through a given medium.
- Each medium has different reach, frequency, and impact as well as advantages and limitations. Media planners consider the following factors when making their choice:
  - — The media habits of consumers.
  - — The nature of the product.
  - — The types of messages.
  - — Cost.
  - — The media planner must now choose the best media vehicles (specific media within a given type-magazines, radio, television, etc.). This choice is based on which vehicles give the best reach, frequency, and impact for the money.
  - — Deciding on the media timing is also an important decision. The advertiser must decide how to schedule the

advertising over the course of a year. They also have to examine the pattern of the ads (some advertisers only do seasonal advertising).

Forms to be considered are:

- Continuity: scheduling ads evenly within a year period.
- Pulsing: scheduling ads unevenly or in sporadic bursts over a certain time period.

EVALUATING ADVERTISING

- The advertising program should regularly evaluate both the communication effects and the sales effects of advertising regularly. This reveals whether or not an ad is communicating well. This involves copy testing (measuring the communication effect of an advertisement before or after it is printed or broadcast).
- The sales effect is often harder to measure than the communication effect since sales are affected by many factors besides advertising. Methods that can be used are:
  — Comparing past sales with past advertising expenditures.
  — Design experiments to examine different expenditure levels.

SALES PROMOTION

Sales promotion objectives vary widely.

- Sellers may use consumer promotions to increase short-term sales or help build long-term market share.
- Objectives for trade promotions include getting retailers to carry new items and more inventory, getting them to advertise the product and give more shelf space, and getting them to buy ahead.
- For sales force promotion, objectives include getting more sales force support for current or new products, or getting salespeople to sign up new accounts. In general, sales promotion should focus on consumer relationship building.

Sales Promotion Tools

The primary consumer promotion tools are:

- Samples: offer consumers a trial amount of a product or service.

- Coupons: certificates that give buyers a savings when they purchase a specified product.
- Cash refund offers (rebates): offers to refund part of the purchase price of a product to consumers who send a proof of purchase to the manufacturer.
- Price packs (cènts-off deals): reduced prices that are marked by the producer directly on the label or package. Quite a common feature used to promote FMCG sales.
- Premiums: goods offered either free or at low cost as an incentive to buy a product.
- Advertising specialities: useful articles imprinted with an advertiser's name that are given as gifts to consumers, e.g., Key chains, diaries, Wallets, etc.
- Patronage rewards: cash or other rewards for the regular use of a certain company's products or services, e.g., 'Frequent fliers' benefits given by airlines.
- Point-of-purchase (POP) promotions: displays and demonstrations that take place at the point of purchase or sale.
- Contests, sweepstakes, and games: promotional events that give consumers the chance to win something (such as cash, trips, or goods) by luck or through extra effort.

Trade-promotional tools include:

- Discount: a straight reduction in price on purchases during a stated period of time.
- Allowance: promotional money paid by manufacturers to retailers who agree to feature the manufacturer's products in some way.

Other forms include free goods, push money, and speciality advertising items.

PUBLIC RELATIONS

Public relations involves building good relations with the company's various publics by obtaining favourable publicity, building up a good "corporate image," and handling or heading off unfavourable rumours, stories, and events, e.g., Cadbury India's initiatives to tackle the infestation reported from a retail outlet, and which caused a major upheaval in their sales strategy, with even Amitabh Bachchan being called in as an our ombudsman.

Major functions are:

- Press relations or press agentry.
- Product publicity.
- Public affairs.
- Lobbying.
- Investor relations.
- Development.

Public Relations Departments may perform any or all of the following functions:

- Public relations is used to promote products, places, ideas, personalities, activities, organizations, and even nations.
- Public relations can have a strong impact on public awareness at a much lower cost than advertising.
- Despite its potential strengths, public relations often is described as a marketing stepchild because of its limited and desultory use. However, this may be changing. Many companies today are looking for public relations to take a more active role in marketing and promotion planning. Marketing public relations departments are being formed to lay greater emphasis on this important activity.

PUBLIC RELATIONS TOOLS

Major tools include:

- News.
- Speeches.
- Special events. Role of Advertising
- Written materials (such as annual reports, brochures, articles, company newsletters, and magazines).
- Audiovisual materials (such as films, slide-and-sound programs, video and audio cassettes).
- Corporate identity materials (such as logos, stationery, brochures, signs, business forms, business cards, buildings, uniforms, and company cars and trucks).

Companies also improve public relations by contributing time and money to public service and other Corporate Image Building activities.

SUMMARY

Setting objectives is the first step in developing an advertising program. These objectives should be based on past decisions about the target market, positioning, and marketing mix, which define the job that advertising must do in the total marketing program. The advertisement works in the consumers mind in a Response Hierarchy Model. It is assumed that the buyer, after being exposed to the advertisement, passes through a cognitive, effective and behavioural state in that order. Advertising Strategy consists of two elements and companies are realising the benefits of planning these two elements jointly. The advertising program should regularly evaluate both the communication effects and the sales effects of advertising regularly. This reveals whether or not an ad is communicating well.

Public relations is used to promote products, places, ideas, personalities, activities, organizations, and even nations. Despite its potential strengths, public relations often is described as a marketing stepchild because of its limited and desultory use.

Note: Google is one of the leading internet technology and advertising companies in the world. The company specializes in internet search engines and related advertising services. It maintains a large index of web sites and other online content, which are freely available through its search engine. The company generates revenue primarily by delivering relevant, online advertising. It also offers advertising in news papers, radio and television. The company primarily operates in the US, the UK and other countries. For a case study visit company's site www.google.com

15

Concept of Direct Marketing

INTRODUCTION

Some companies use direct marketing to inform and educate customers about product/ service in anticipation that it may precipitate future actions, reminding about offers, image building, maintain customer satisfaction, strengthen relationship, and reassure customers about purchases. Direct marketing is an interactive system of marketing and uses a set of all major direct- response media including print, TV, Internet and cellular phones as the tools to implement communications and accomplish its objectives.

DIRECT MARKETING

"Direct marketing is an interactive system of marketing which uses one or more advertising media to affect a measurable response and/or transaction at any location." A number of factors are promoting the attractiveness of direct marketing. The main factors are:

- Availability of consumer credit cards.
- Availability of professional agencies.
- Competitive Pressures, Rising Media Costs, and Market Fragmentation.
- Increasing family incomes, including dual-income families.
- Technological advances.

DIRECT MARKETING DECISIONS

For successful implementation of direct-marketing, marketers must establish objectives, specify target market, choice of strategies, and set evaluation criteria.

DIRECT-MARKETING OBJECTIVES

Objectives of direct marketing usually focus on seeking direct response in terms of behaviour. Order response rate varies across product categories and prices but in most cases, usually a two per cent order placement is viewed as good. Some organizations use direct marketing to inform and educate customers about product/service in anticipation that it may precipitate future actions, reminding about offers, image building, maintain customer satisfaction, strengthen relationship, and reassure customers about purchases.

MARKET SEGMENTATION

Market segmentation and targeting the right customers are critical to the success of promotional programme. Customers can be grouped on the basis of age, sex, income, education, lifestyle, and stage in family life cycle etc. Direct marketers use a database. It is much more than just names and addresses and is used to identify and profile the company's best customers and effectively target the customer segments.

Ongoing database updating helps companies identify trends and buying patterns. This information, can be used by the companies to strengthen relationship with its customers by satisfying their needs and wants more effectively. The database should provide the answers to the following questions:

- Where do they live?
- How did they make contact first time?
- What have they purchased?
- How often have they purchased?
- What is the monetary value of their purchases?
- How do they order or purchase, through the Internet, mail, phone, or in person?
- What is known about them and their families, occupation, education, children, interests, attitudes, and payment histories etc.?
- In case of B2B, who are the influencers, users, deciders, and purchasers?
- Location of corporate office and branch offices.

Well-managed companies usually develop and maintain their own database. Many independent research suppliers sell this kind of information.

Database helps in developing a mailing list that minimises waste coverage as much as possible. A good database is crucial to the effectiveness of direct marketing. If a direct marketing company buys database from outside sources, it is worthwhile to pay a little more for a good database that has been well researched and segregated than to pay for a list of names and addresses.

ADVANTAGES OF DIRECT MARKETING

- Direct marketing offers the advantage of reaching large number of well-defined target customers and almost eliminates waste coverage.
- Good quality databases are available from independent suppliers and the marketer can segment customer groups with considerable precision.
- Direct marketer can personalise the message.
- Direct marketing can deliver almost perfect offers to customers.
- Marketer can build desired frequency level based on media.
- Direct marketing offers creative flexibility in different media.
- Direct marketer can quickly develop a list of specific profiles for direct mail.
- Direct marketing is more effective in building customer relationship.
- It is very cost effective considering the sale generated per contact.
- The results can be measured most accurately.

DIRECT MARKETING OFFER AND MEDIA

According to Edward L. Nash, there are five important decision areas: Product, offer, medium, distribution method, and creative strategy. The marketer has to decide on each of these issues and develop the appropriate message to be conveyed. Direct marketers use all the available major media such as direct mail, telemarketing, direct-response broadcasting, print, the Internet, E-mail, and others.

- One-Step Approach: The marketer uses the medium to obtain an order. For example, exercise equipment and household items are presented through TV commercials, or many magazines insert subscription forms in their issues. The viewer or the reader places the order by calling a toll-free number. Magazine subscription forms can be filled and posted in postage-paid envelops.

- Two-Step Approach: This may involve the use of more than one medium. This may be done to first screen, or qualify prospects and then in the second step the marketer makes the effort to elicit a behavioural response. For example, many banks first use telemarketing to determine the potential based on interest, employment, and income and then follow-up by sending an agent with more information to close the sale.
- Direct Mail: Direct mail is unsolicited mail, most of us are familiar with. For some of us it is fairly irritating and we call it "Junk mail" and throw it or ignore without reading. Companies of all sizes and shape use direct mail. This mail is generally based on mailing lists the companies buy from independent sources, or in some cases is confined to customers who have made purchases earlier. Google, Yahoo, Hotmail, AOL, Amazon, Fabmart, Indiatimes, and many others have vast lists of home and e-mail addresses. Direct mails generally generate lower response rates from potential customers. The cost of direct mail as e-mail is practically nothing. John Goodman, CEO India and South Asia, Ogilvy & Mather believes the Internet is the perfect medium for direct marketing. HLL (Denim aftershave, Lux), Hyatt Regency, and several banks have effectively used direct mail for their credit cards.
- Catalogues: Both, consumer and B2B companies may send catalogues of their entire product lines, mostly in print form, sometimes also online, as CDs, or even videos. Considering the global scenario, many companies use catalogue to sell variety of merchandise including clothing, and cosmetics. According to Direct Marketing Association forecast, catalogue sales has reached $17.3 billion in 2006. Internet has particularly boosted the catalogue business and companies present their catalogues and accept orders over the Internet. Catalogues of marketers such as Fabmart, Amazon, McGraw-Hill, Prentice-Hall, Dell and others are available at their websites and anyone can place the order then and there. Some companies started as catalogue companies and subsequently also branched into retail outlets, such as First and second bookseller initially had a website that presented its catalogue but now also has a retail

outlet in New Delhi. Anjali Textiles, Otto-Burlingtons Mail Order (P) Ltd., Mothercare India, Charag Din and others use catalogues. Some authors make a distinction between manufacturer-originated and trading houseoriginated direct mail marketing by using either direct mail or catalogue. If the marketer is a manufacturer, it is called Direct Mail Marketing, and when the source is a trading house, it is called Mail Order Marketing or Mail Order Business.

- Broadcast Media: Direct marketer can use television and radio. Almost entire advertising with respect to direct marketing occurs on television. This type of advertising is either in the form of direct-response advertising, or support advertising. Direct-response advertising encourages customers to place orders by using a toll-free telephone number. Support advertising informs customers generally to take part in sweepstakes or expect something in mail. An interesting example of support advertising is on NDTV news channel. Airtel encourages customers to use its cellular service and make two calls then answer a simple question of the day. The winner gets Rs 100,000 for correct answer. The message is broadcast by NDTV and also the winner of the day is announced by NDTV in its news.

Some companies use a new form of direct-response advertising on cable and satellite called infomercials. These are lengthy commercials ranging between 30 to 60 minutes and resemble documentaries. Indian TV viewers are quite familiar with lengthy commercials about losing weight, and portable exercise equipments and satisfied users testifying the great benefits they derived and ease of use. Of course a toll-free number is included to place the order immediately. Infomercials have been reported to be quite effective, audience watch them and place orders. Widespread use of credit cards and availability of toll-free telephone numbers in more developed countries has promoted teleshopping. Some TV channels exclusively sell products and services 24 hours a day, such as Home Shopping Network. The programme host offers low prices on a variety of items including jewelry, kitchenware, fitness products, insurance, and CDs, etc. Customers sitting in their homes make their purchases by calling a toll-free number and the ordered item is delivered within 48 hours. QVC is a major shopping channel so far covering U. S., Germany, and Japan reaching 84 million households.

So far it seems there are no daylong teleshopping programmes in India. Some programmes being aired in India are actually infomercials.

Important names connected with such programmes include Dees' Home Shopping (DD, and C&S channels) offers home appliances, car accessories, fashion wear, footwear, beauty care products, air tickets, and groceries etc. Teleshopping Network (ATN, DD, Sun, local C&S), and United Teleshopping (DD National) are the other two names. So far the maximum time allotted in India to such programmes is limited to about 5-hours/day.

Print Media: Newspapers and magazines are not considered to be 'sound choice' for direct marketing. There are too many ads competing for attention. Specific interest newspapers focused on financial matters, or sports and hobby magazines are sometimes used.

TELEMARKETING

Direct marketing through telephone is called telemarketing. It gives the marketer a better chance of influencing the prospect and win a customer. As mentioned earlier, it is most often used in the screening process. Companies hire several telephone-callers, mostly girls, or operate through hired agents. Call centres have become a real arena of telemarketing activity. Several teams of 5 to 6 members are formed and for each team there is a supervisor. Individual team members sit in front of a computer terminal wearing a headset. They call different telephone numbers from a list and present the sales talk based on pre-tested script and update information on the computer screen. Unless handled carefully, telemarketing can irritate call recipients and actually harm the brand. According to Dr. C. R Sridhar, CEO, SRS-ICON Brand Navigation, instead of generating sales, telemarketing could damage your company's brand equity if not handled properly. We receive calls from well-known multinational banks, asking if Mr ... is home. The caller does not know that it's not a Mister but a lady. Then, they would call you at odd hours when you are engaged in some serious work requiring concentration. There is tragedy at home, and you receive a call greeting you with a good morning or good afternoon and would ask you to buy something. You keep on receiving bill after bill when you have not even used the credit card and the period expired and they renewed it without your consent. No one pays attention to your complaints and you still keep on receiving calls from different locations offering some additional benefit.

SUMMARY

"Direct marketing is an interactive system of marketing which uses one or more advertising media to affect a measurable response and/or transaction at any location." Direct marketers use a database. It is much more than just names and addresses and is used to identify and profile the company's best customers and effectively target the customer segments. A good database is crucial to the effectiveness of direct marketing. If a direct marketing company buys database from outside sources, it is worthwhile to pay a little more for a good database that has been well researched and segregated than to pay for a list of names and addresses. Direct mail is unsolicited mail, most of us are familiar with. For some of us it is fairly irritating and we call it "Junk mail" and throw it or ignore without reading. Companies of all sizes and shape use direct mail. Direct marketer can use television and radio. Almost entire advertising with respect to direct marketing occurs on television. This type of advertising is either in the form of direct-response advertising, or support advertising. Direct-response advertising encourages customers to place orders by using a toll-free telephone number. Support advertising informs customers generally to take part in sweepstakes or expect something in mail. An interesting example of support advertising is on NDTV news channel.

Note: Schering-Plough, which signed a $41.1 billion merger agreement with its Big Pharma rival Merck & Co. in March 2009, is engaged in the discovery, development and manufacture of human prescription, animal health and consumer health care products. The company markets its products in more than 140 countries worldwide. It primarily operates in the US, Canada, Europe, Latin America and Asia Pacific. The company is headquartered in Kenilworth, New Jersey and employed 51,000 people as of December 2008. For detailed information related to this chapter reader can visit www.schering-plough.com

16

Sales Management

INTRODUCTION

Most companies structure their sales force based on geography, customers, products or a combination of these factors. For a company marketing just a single product category and selling to different scattered customers in one industry, a territory-based structure would be suitable. If a company manufactures several different product categories and sells to different types of customers, it might find a customer type based sales force.

OBJECTIVES

Organization means the systematic coordination of the functions essential to achieving organizational objectives. The objective of a sales organization, therefore, is the performance of various activities necessary to promote sales. The functions of sales organization can be classified as follows

- Planning functions
- Sales forecasting
- Sales budgeting
- Selling policy
- Administrative functions
- Selecting salesmen
- Training salesmen
- Control of salesmen
- Remuneration of salesmen
- Executive functions

- Sales promotion
- Selling routine-execution of customers' orders.

PLANNING FUNCTIONS

SALES FORECASTING

Sales forecasting is the art that predicts the likelihood of economic activity on the basis of certain assumptions. The process of making certain estimates of future events is referred to as sales forecasting and the figure obtained from the process is known as a 'sales forecast'. Sales forecasting would be futile if the future were known. In order to determine the future course of events, aid is taken from an organized system of sales forecasting.

Different steps in sales forecasting are:

- Defining the objectives to be achieved
- Dividing the various groups into homogenous groups
- Analysing the importance of various factors to be studied for sales forecasting
- Selecting the method
- Collecting and analysing the related information
- Drawing conclusions from the analysis made
- Implementing the decision taken
- Reviewing and revising sales forecasting techniques from time to time.

SALES BUDGETING

The sales budget is the final point of a sales organization. All other budgets hinge on the basis of the sales budget. What then is a sales budget? It is a forecast of sales to be achieved in the stipulated period. The sales budget can be prepared on the basis of division, brand, products, dealers, territory and sales force. The following factors need to be kept in mind when preparing a sales budget:

- Past trends
- Sales force estimates
- Trade prospects
- Present position
- Potential consumers

- Government policies
- Changing business environment
- Sales promotion strategies.

SELLING POLICY

The object of a selling policy is to place the right type of goods in the hands of consumers at the right time and at the right place. Further, it should aim at attracting customers and rendering them satisfactory services. A selling policy includes:

- Method of distribution (sale)
- Terms of sale
- Guarantee and service

In case of products involving maintenance and repairs, the seller renders what is called after-sale-service. Technical representatives are sent to the user's place for repairing the machines/gadgets free of cost or at a nominal charge. Usually, free service is rendered during the "guarantee period". The after-sale-service policy is a strong selling point to push up the sales of industrial/durable goods. It enhances confidence in the buyers about the fitness of the product and impresses them with the seller's concern for the customer's convenience and satisfaction. It also helps in getting repeat sales orders.

ADMINISTRATIVE FUNCTIONS

SALESMEN

Once an organization has determined the number and kind of salesmen it requires, the next step is to get the right applicants, in sufficient number, for the positions. All the activities involved in securing applications for sales positions are referred to as recruitment.

There are various sources of recruitment:

- Advertisements
- Employment agencies
- Educational institutions
- Salesmen of non-competing companies
- Internal transfers
- Recommendations of present salesmen.

The basic objective of the selection process is to gather information about the applicants for the sales job. This information is then used to predict their success/failure probabilities.

TRAINING OF SALESMEN

The first step in designing a training programme is to assess the needs of the organization. A need assessment begins with training requirements that focus on the organization, the tasks and the personnel. Training methods can be very diverse and may include case studies, lectures, videos, behavioural simulations (role playing, computer simulations, interactive video, tele training) and absorption training. Basically, sales training is designed to change or reinforce behaviour that makes sales people achieve their sales goals more efficiently. Sales people are trained to perform activities they would not normally undertake. In addition, training is used to reinforce currently successful sales practices.

CONTROL OF SALESMEN

Controlling the sales force is a critical part of the marketing/sales management process. Outstanding planning and implementation are important, but control is essential for a firm to achieve its sales objectives. Controlling extends to a firm's selling methods, distributors, customers and sales force. An organization must analyse its selling methods to determine whether they are using the most efficient means possible to reach their customers. Selling methods are analysed using marketing effort analysis as it allows a firm to directly calculate the comparative performance of alternative selling methods.

REMUNERATION OF SALESMEN

A majority of compensation plans for sales force combine two or more payment methods.

The most widely used combinations are:

- Salary plus commission
- Salary plus bonus
- Salary plus commission plus bonus

The purpose of a combination plan is to eliminate the weaknesses of individual components and, at the same time, retain their strengths. The salary element is usually most popular in reputed, more experienced companies that enjoy stable sales. These days, more emphasis is put on the commission component by companies that are concentrating on expanding their business. There has been a recent trend by companies to emphasise incentive over salary. The salary/commission combination is extremely popular, especially when earnings are divided equally between the two. The sales staff has the benefit of security and the company can offer strong incentives to the staff to excel. In addition, if salary is an important part of the compensation package, the company can exert considerable control over the salesperson.

STRUCTURE OF SALES ORGANIZATION

Sales force consists of sales persons who work primarily with customers in person, although they may also use the telephone or assistance from computer links to expedite orders and provide customer service. The structure of a field sales force is usually based on some means of specialisation, such as geography, market, product, or activity/function, or a hybrid of these types. The following are the important field sales:

- Geographic sales specialisation organization
- Product-based sales specialisation organization
- Customer-based specialisation organization
- Activity/function-based specialisation
- Hybrid sales organization
- Team-based organization.

GEOGRAPHIC SALES ORGANIZATION

The most common means of specialisation of the sales force is by geographic region. In a geographically based sales force, a salesperson has to visit all current and potential customers in a given geographic territory.

Some advantages of geographic organizations are (a) Proper coverage of territory (b) Defining the responsibility (c) Familiarity with local economic and competitive conditions, making them better able to serve local customers.

The disadvantages of geographic specialisation is that the salespersons need to be responsible for the entire product line in their territory even though they may not be having uniform knowledge about all products. Further, within their territory, they may choose to concentrate on products and customers that are easy prospects.

PRODUCT-BASED SALES ORGANIZATION

Organizations that specialise their sales forces according to the product line create a product-based sales force. Product-based organizations are useful for complex products because they require the sales force to concentrate on a limited product line.

Product specialisation is generally combined with geographical specialisation at the higher levels, while at the level of field operators, different salesmen may be assigned to specific product lines. The disadvantages of product-based sales organization include duplication of calls and buyer frustration. This duplication of coverage can lead to increased selling costs.

CUSTOMER-BASED SALES ORGANIZATION

Organizations with several separate and distinct markets, accounting for major portions of their sales, often organize their markets on the basis of customers. Organizations such as Hewlett-Packard, Xerox and IBM are customer-based organizations. Customer specialisation enables the salespersons to become more knowledgeable about the unique problems and needs of each group of customers. A customer-oriented sales force is consistent with the marketing concept with its increased emphasis on consumer satisfaction. The main disadvantage of this form of specialisation is that geographical territories may typically overlap.

ACTIVITY/FUNCTION-BASED ORGANIZATION

An activity/function-based sales organization is able to focus on the use of high-cost selling methods, such as face-to-face sales calls, during a selling process. An activity/ function-based sales force can also be designed to meet the customer service issues that are most important at each stage of the selling process. A disadvantage of this type of organization may be the overlapping of accounts by using different techniques.

HYBRID SALES ORGANIZATION

A hybrid sales organization is formed when two or more organizational types are combined. This type of organization structure is designed to overcome the problems of individual sales organizations. Its main advantage is the ability to offer customers the service they need using the most efficient method. The primary disadvantage of hybrid sales organization is the difficulty of managing multiple sales forces, whether they are serving the same or different customers.

TEAM-BASED SALES ORGANIZATION

Many organizations are more responsive to their environment because they use team work as their basic building blocks making them team-based organizations. Teams are made up of people from different functional units, such as manufacturing, technical support, marketing and sales. These cross-functional teams are composed of a defined group of individuals bringing together expertise from different parts of the supplier organization to capture, retain and increase business with customers.

ORGANIZING AND MANAGING SIZE OF A SALES FORCE

Sales forces are regularly assigned particular sales territories. Various factors are taken into account when deciding the sales force for a particular territory. These include the physical size of the force for a particular territory, transportation links within a territory, purchasing power of consumers and their educational and living standards. Therefore, a sales force is deployed according to the geographical features of the territory and product or consumer requirements. A company should also devote considerable effort to the training and development of its sales force. There are two types of training which can be provided to sales force (a) In-house training, and (b) On-the-job training. It is also necessary for a company to arrange periodic meetings and discussions with its sales force. Finally, the performance of the sales force can be evaluated on the basis of targets and actuals.

COMPENSATION

Salesman's job involves a lot of hard work; he has to face many disappointments and still continue to do his job. So salesmen need a lot of motivation to do their normal job also. Consider an example. A normal person working in an office will take holiday and stay home and nothing will happen. Everyone will understand and the officer loses only one casual leave and everything is normal. But, in the same situation, the salesman will not stay home. He will try to reach the place of work, and then he will report that the work was not possible due to heavy rains. He will not want to lose the day as casual leaves are very precious for him. He also does not want to lose that day's daily allowance which becomes payable only if he has worked or tried to work. The daily allowance acts as a motivator to the salesman. There are many such situations when the salesman is found to be working only to avoid losing a casual leave and the daily allowance. Let us now look into various ways that are used to keep the salesman motivated and his compensation is a part of it.

If we look into the psychology of the salesman, we find that people accept salesman's job for the following reasons:

- Liking for meeting new people all the time.
- Liking for travelling to different places.
- Liking for understanding different cultures.
- Eating exotic foods.
- Staying in good hotels at company cost.
- Earning good money.
- Getting freedom from constant bossing.
- Avoiding routine life (9 to 5 schedule).
- Wearing smart dress to work.
- Travelling first class.

The novelty of all these pleasures lasts for only a few days, and then the people continue working only for the sake of good money and freedom of time. So it is very important for companies to keep paying good money to its sales staff. The salesman's compensation package should be made up of two parts (1) His salary which should be higher than people who are in the same cadre like him but work in sheltered conditions and with much lower or no responsibility (2) His compensation towards his lost opportunities to be with his family in the moments of joy and sorrow and towards keeping him motivated to accept hardships that he is required to face constantly.

The salesman's compensation is given in the following ways:

- Salary only (plus travelling expense, allowances for food and lodging).
- Salary + commission (plus travelling expenses and allowances of food and lodging).
- Commission only (plus travelling expenses and allowance for food and lodge).
- Commission only.

In the Indian economy and culture where a young man is looking for a job and its inherent security, getting people to work only for commission is very difficult. Eureka Forbes continued to operate on the same terms for the last many years as strategy but, thereafter its sales staff as well as support staff is working on salary. So commission only method works well where it is used to employ people as part time workers e.g. insurance sector, textiles, etc. The other reason why it is difficult to get people to work for commission only is the attitude of the companies. There are many companies who appoint people on commission only basis, the person works very hard to establish the product and when he is about to earn high returns on sales because of contacts that he has developed, the company terminates his contract and appoints another salesman on low salary or asks the same salesman to accept revised terms. Because of this, the commission only method is used only to get commission agents and not salesmen for consumer goods companies. The other methods - salary only and salary + commission-are very common and are acceptable to all. All the marketing oriented companies prefer salary only formula as they are assured of continued high volume sales generated by high volume advertisements and promotions. The responsibility of salesmen in such companies is not of selling but ensuring product availability at all possible outlets and creating and maintaining goodwill of the company in the minds of traders and consumers. The salary + commission formula is used by companies where efforts need to be made to make the trade accept the product and keep supporting it. The salary + commission formula is also popular in industrial and institutional sales areas.

It is important for any company to follow such a compensation formula which ensures that not only is the salesman compensated to his satisfaction but is also motivated if he is putting in reasonable efforts. No company is happy with the work it gets out of its salesmen. No salesman works to his maximum capacity without additional motivation/rewards. In tropical countries like India even to get normal work done, one is required to use motivating efforts. Let us now look at the motivational methods used by different companies. A sales manager should use various methods to keep his sales team happy and motivated and understand them well to use them effectively. Normally salesmen are above the basic needs level in Maslow's hierarchy of needs and fall in the safety, security level or the social needs level or in esteem needs level depending upon the size of the company and the level of salary that they are being paid. Depending upon the level of the salesmen's needs, a sales manager will decide what type of motivational methods should be used.

SUMMARY

Organization means the systematic coordination of the functions essential to achieving organizational objectives. The objective of a sales organization, therefore, is the performance of various activities necessary to promote sales. Sales forecasting is the art that predicts the likelihood of economic activity on the basis of certain assumptions. The process of making certain estimates of future events is referred to as sales forecasting and the figure obtained from the process is known as a 'sales forecast'. The object of a selling policy is to place the right type of goods in the hands of consumers at the right time and at the right place. The basic objective of the selection process is to gather information about the applicants for the sales job. This information is then used to predict their success/failure probabilities. Controlling the sales force is a critical part of the marketing/sales management process. A majority of compensation plans for sales force combine two or more payment methods. An activity/ function-based sales organization is able to focus on the use of high-cost selling methods, such as face-to-face sales calls, during a selling process. An activity/ function-based sales force can also be designed to meet the customer service issues that are most important at each stage of the selling process. A hybrid sales organization is formed when two or more organizational types are combined. There are many such situations when the salesman is found to be working only to avoid losing a casual leave and the daily allowance. Let us now look into various ways that are used to keep the salesman motivated and his compensation is a part of it.

Note: Hewlett-Packard (HP) is a global provider of personal systems, imaging and printing products, and technology solutions. The company is the largest player in the inkjet printer and laser printer market. HP is one of the major companies in the enterprise storage and servers markets. The company is also one of the market leaders in the global PC market. It operates in the US and other countries. It is headquartered in Palo Alto, California and employs 321,000 people. For further knowledge regarding this chapter reader can visit www.hp.com

17

Competition Analysis

INTRODUCTION

Marketers generally select product type as the basis of analysis for marketing planning because these products are viewed as close substitutes for one another. In reality, the range of a firm's actual and potential competitors is much broader and the chances are more that a company stands to get hurt by potential competitors or new technologies than the players already compelling.

IDENTIFYING AND ANALYSING COMPETITORS

In an industry there are likely to be several competitors, all with different profiles based on their size, resources, objectives, strategies, and areas of strengths and weaknesses. The competitor chosen might be basically either strong, or weak. Some of the these competitors might be categorised as "good" or "bad." Good ones follow industry rules, develop realistic assumptions about its future growth, they price their offers reasonably based on lower costs and advocate others to keep costs low, favour product differentiation, focus on a portion of the industry and favour a healthy industry. Bad ones ignore these healthy practices and adopt practices that upset the healthy balance in the industry.

Customer Perceptions of Value: It is believed that customers choose a brand from a set of available alternatives based on their perceptions of its value. This value is the sum total of quality, benefits (functional and image), costs, and service. It is believed that the brand that exceeds all others on the chosen criteria is purchased. The steps involved in assessing customers' value perception include:

- Identify major attributes and their relative importance from customers' point of view. Assess consumers' perceptions of the company's and competitors' performance on these attributes. Evaluate the company's one or two major competitors in a market on these attributes.

- Deliver customer value, and periodically conduct customers' value perception studies. The analysis will reveal four types of competitors in an industry, including the company itself. Some of the major characteristics of market leader, market follower, market challenger, and niche marketer are briefly discussed below:
  - Market Leader: The firm enjoys the largest market share and generally leads others in, new technology introduction or up-gradation, new product introduction, generally setting the changes in price, promotional practices, and level of distribution coverage. Such a firm is very likely to device offensive or defensive strategies to fight tooth-and-nail to maintain its position and stay the leader.
  - Market Challenger: Any other competing firms, whether second, third, or further down below in rank in the same product-market might decide to become the challenger. Much depends on the individual company's assessment of the leader's objectives, strategies, strengths and weaknesses, and also the firm's assessment of its own resources, strengths and weaknesses and objectives to challenge the leader. The strategies that a challenger may adopt is to go for head-on frontal attack, attacking in an area where the leader has a weakness, called a flank attack, or adopt guerrilla methods, that is, attacking in random corners in an attempt to weaken the competitor's market power.
  - Market Follower: Many companies in product industries that are capital-intensive and deal in products viewed as homogeneous such as cement, steel, and chemicals etc., prefer to stay follower. They usually copy the leader and present similar offers to customers in terms of quality, price, and service. Opportunities to create any meaningful differentiation of their offer are very little, and price sensitivity is considerable. Any attempt to pose a challenge to the leader requires huge investments. Those who try for challenging the leader, often take the route of expansion through acquisitions. For example, according

to a news item in Hindustan Times, Mittal Steel Co., became the largest steel producer in the world by acquiring some other steel businesses in the industry.

— Niche Marketer: A niche market is a very small sub-segment of a segment where customers seek a distinctive set of attributes resulting in certain most desired benefits. A niche marketer focuses on customer needs in this small sub-segment and customises its marketing effort to that group of target customers. These customers are prepared to pay a premium price to the niche marketer who best satisfies their needs. The niche usually does not attract competitors.

DESIGN COMPETITIVE STRATEGIES

MARKET LEADER

Market leader is either a pioneer or at least one of the first few entrants who first developed the product-market. Generally, the leader's objective is to maintain its leading share position despite the entry of new players. Maintaining early market share-lead in growing markets is challenging because of increasing number of competitors, fragmentation of market segments, and threat of product innovation from competitors. A company can maintain its market share in the presence of competitors only when its sales grow at a rate that is equal to overall market growth.

To gain and maintain leading market share a business needs to retain its existing customers by building brand loyalty to ensure they make repeat or replenishment purchases. The business should stimulate selective demand among later product adopter groups and makes sure of capturing larger product-market share of the growing market. With a view to speed up the expansion of product-market, the business may stimulate the primary demand, particularly when the product adoption process is slow because of complex product nature, or high product switching costs for customers. By expanding total market, it is the leader who gains maximum if it can maintain its high market-share position.

Market Share Expansion: One of the most attractive strategic options for a market leader is often to grow its market share. Coca Cola has managed to grow its volume at the rate of 7-8 per cent. In large industries, an increase of one share-point is often worth millions in monetary terms. For example, one share-point in soft drinks is in excess of US$ 120 million and for this reason the competition intensity among colas is of the highest order. David Zymanski, Sunder Bhardwaj, and Rajan Verdarajan report that many factors influence a company's ability to grow market-share and earn profits. For example, the cost of gaining share growth might far exceed the revenue gains. It is easy to get caught up in share wars without considering the unprofitable possibility of winning the battle of market share but losing the war for revenues. A business should consider four major factors:

1. Possibility of Competition Act 2002, or similar laws such as Anti-trust Action in U.S.A.: The merger of Jet Airways and Sahara Airlines drew investigation. Similarly, the protracted investigation of Microsoft is well-known. The risk reduces the attractiveness of increased share gain.
2. The cost involved in market share gain may rise and exceed the revenues: Robert D. Buzzell and Bradly T. Gale found that 31 per cent of the 877 marketshare leaders in the PIMS database experienced loses in relative share, and leaders were particularly likely to experience losses when their market share was very large. This may happen, for example, because of additional expenses involved in public relations exercise, existence of unattractive market segments, customers refusal to accept what is offered leading for disliking the business and their loyalty to competitors, and customers unique product feature preferences etc. Sometimes market leaders find it more appropriate to decrease their market share by taking it easy in less profitable segments and cutting down on maintaining market share.
3. Selecting and using an inappropriate marketing mix strategy: Apple computers introduced its Cube but could not sell much despite advertising and other communications. Avanti Garralli Moped did not sell because its advertising was addressing the wrong segment. Robert D. Buzzell and Frederick D. Wiersema identify three areas to excel in order to gain successfully, increased market share: New Product Development, (2) Product Quality, and (3) Marketing Expenditure.
4. Increased number of customers may put a strain on the company's resources and hurt service delivery and product value: Linda Hellofs and Robert Jacobson found that share growth might affect customer perceptions of product quality. A business leader can adopt defensive or offensive strategies to maintain share-position, increase market share, or expand

product-market. Depending on the situation a market leader faces, the strategic move options include:

- Position Defence Strategy
- Flanker Strategy
- Confrontation Strategy
- Pre-emptive Strategy
- Market Expansion Strategy
- Contraction or Withdrawal Strategy
- Position Defence Strategy: Almost always, the market share leader adopts position defence strategy. This strategy focuses on perpetually strengthening an existing position like a fortress and repulsing attacks by existing or future competitors. The share leader must take care not to leave any area exposed to a flank attacker, and determine which areas are most important to defend. By investing to support and maintain existing leadership position, the business can improve the feeling of satisfaction among present customers, and make the offer more attractive to new customers. Possibly the most important measure a market leader can adopt is to continue modifying its product and add innovative features. Hindustan Lever Limited introduced its top of the line Dove Gentle Exfoliating Bar that has pH range between 6.5 and 7.5, which is almost neutral unlike other toilet soaps that are alkaline with 9 pH or above. This can block moves by competitors to differentiate their offer by incorporating features or performance improvements not offered in leader's products. It would add to the competitive edge if the leader also reduces costs to discourage price-competition. In addition to adding new features, the market leader should take steps to improve customers' perceptions about the product. The focus of marketing communications should shift for building selective demand of company's brand. The sales promotion efforts should be directed to induce trial among late adopters, and repeat purchase among the existing customers. Another important aspect the leader must consider is to focus on increased pot-purchase service in case of durable products to strengthen its position. The leader should expand its distribution reach to ensure increased product availability and make efforts to minimise any possibility of 'out of stock situation' at retail level, or shorten product delivery time. It

makes good sense to build strong customer relationships right from the start in industrial and consumer durable product categories to build loyalty and ensure repeat or replenishment purchases. This relationship becomes very important during maturity stage of product-market life cycle when the competition becomes quite intense to win over established customers.

- Flanker Strategy: The market leader adopts this strategy to outsmart a challenger who simply decides to bypass the leader's fortress and attempts to capture a territory where the leader so far has not been able to develop a strong presence. This may happen when the product-market is fragmented with distinct segments and the leader's product-brand does not meet the needs and wants of some of those attractive segments. This may happen when a competitor with appropriate resources and strengths differentiates its offer that appeals to, one or more of these segments, where the leader so far is not established. In this situation, the challenger captures a big chunk of the share. To defend exposed flank against the challenger's attack, a leader might develop a fighting brand (also called Flanker brand) to compete against the challenger's brand. For example, this is what Hindustan Lever did when Nirma detergent made inroads in HLL Surf market share. Depending where the challenger focuses, the leader can introduce a higher quality brand at higher price, or lower-quality brand at lower than the challenger's price to appeal to the segment thus, protect the leader's main brand. A market leader first ensures position defence and simultaneously adopts flanker strategy. Obviously this requires investments and the company should have sufficient resources to fully commit to adopting both strategies at the same time.
- Confrontation Strategy: IBM was the leader in commercial PC market but in mid 1980s the company lost market share to competitors like Compaq. Compaq computers cost almost the same as IBM but offered customers more features or better performance levels. Later, Dell computers adopted direct distribution and offered customised machines at lower prices. The customers could choose components and place order online. When a market leader is attacked directly, it may have no recourse but to adopt confrontation strategy. A confrontation

strategy is often reactive in nature. It is not very common to gain reliable intelligence sufficiently well in time to become proactive and develop suitable marketing programme before the challenge occurs. The leader often decides to meet or beat the competition by offering more desirable product features of a competitor. The leader incorporates product improvements, increases promotional efforts, and sometimes lowers the prices. In case of products with high purchase rates or where the product diffusion process is long drawn, the leader should perhaps adopt a penetration pricing strategy right in the first place. This would pre-empt lower-price competitors from entering the market, and would also ensure competitive advantage of the leader and obviate the need to adopt confrontation strategy. This strategy requires investment to accomplish process improvements to reduce unit costs, improvements in product quality, customer service, or develop more advanced versions that offer greater value to customers. For example, Maruti was facing attacks from other manufacturers and share erosion in its hatchback car segment. The company has introduced a more advanced car in this segment, Maruti Swift that offers more value to customers.

- Market Expansion Strategy: The main objective of this strategy is to capture a large share of new customer groups who have different needs and preferences than the segment where company has been operating with initial offer. This is a proactive and more aggressive version of flanker strategy to defend leader's market share position by expanding the total market. This protects the company from future competitive threats. In case the company has abundant resources and competencies, market expansion strategy is particularly suitable where the market is fragmented. This strategy calls for product line extensions, new brands, or alternative products at different price-quality points. For example, Intel has processors at different price-quality points in its four brands: Pentium D, Xeon, Pentium, and Celeron for different market segments in a fragmented market with different set of needs and preferences and leads with the largest share in the global processor market. Similarly, Nike has sustained leading share of the athletic shoe market. It has developed a series of several line extensions that offer technical, design, and style features to satisfy customer preferences covering almost all the sports. Another approach, a market leader may adopt in certain product categories is to develop a specialised sales force to deal with different user groups. Yet another approach a leader can adopt is to retain several customer groups is to retain the basic product but vary other elements of marketing programme to make the offer attractive and appealing.

- Pre-emptive Strategy: This is an offensive strategy to defend leadership position before a competitor even starts attacking the market-share leader. A company can use preemptive strategy in several ways. A company can introduce several new products and announce it much in advance before the actual launch in the market. According to R. J. Calantone and K. E. Schatzel, a market leader's action of pre-announcing is deliberate to discourage competitors from attacking. Bayes, Jain, and Rao have called such newproduct pre-announcements by high-tech companies, much in advance of their actual introduction, as "Vapoware."
- Contraction or Withdrawal Strategy: If the market happens to be highly fragmented and new entrants have more resources than the leader, it might be difficult for a market leader to defend properly in all market segments. The firm may not have enough resources and have no options but to decrease or take no action in some market segments. The company focuses its efforts on segments where it has maximum competitive advantages or highest segment attractiveness and potential for growth.

MARKET CHALLENGER STRATEGIES

A challenger visualises capturing the market-share leadership in an industry. Many challengers have successfully overtaken the leader and some others have gained share points. There was a time when GM was the largest producers of cars but today Toyota leads the pack. Maruti Udyog was nowhere when Hindustan Motors and Premier Auto (Fiat) were the largest share companies. Today, Maruti produces and sells more cars than Hindustan Motors and Fiat in India.

A challenger has two basic strategic options to consider. In markets where the share leader and others have already cornered a very large portion of the potential market, there is no choice for a challenger but to capture some demand from other competitors' existing customers. A challenger could try head-on confrontation with chosen competitor by adopting various marketing activities aimed at giving it an advantage. Or a challenger can decide to leapfrog over the share leader by offering new generation products with more benefits to encourage existing customers to trade in their existing brand for a new one. This could also bring to fold a large share of late adopters in the mass market. In the early growth stage of product-market where no one has so far captured a clear leading share position of potential customers, the option for the challenger is to attract a substantial share of potential first-time customers. This could be a better choice in case overall market is heterogeneous and much fragmented, and the share leader has been successful in capturing a strong position in only one or few segments. The key would be successful differentiation of the offer from those of current competitors, and make it more attractive and appealing in underdeveloped segments. There are five major competitive strategies for a challenger that may be used singly or in combination and include frontal attack strategy, leapfrog strategy, flanking attack strategy, encirclement strategy, and guerrilla attack strategy. Most of these strategies seem similar to share maintenance strategies.

MARKET FOLLOWER STRATEGIES

Following pioneers in a product-market, there are late entrants. Of course, not all followers in a growth market dream of becoming the market-share leader leaving behind the pioneer. Many competing businesses enter the market, especially those with limited resources and competencies and may decide to enter a distinct segment of the larger market, overlooked by other entrants, and build a successful business. It resembles a kind of niche strategy that avoids head-on competition with larger players and may have some degree of success.

Most market structures have share leaders, followers, and niche marketers. A firm that has second largest share in a market and is a close follower has an interesting strategic choice whether to challenge the leader with an offensive strategy. Another strategy option is to protect its share position and maximise profitability. Much will depend on the competitive advantage of the leader and its pledge to defend its position, follower's resources, and the short-term profit needs of the follower. Many businesses prefer to stay followers rather than challenge the share leader. This is particularly true for more homogeneous industries such as food grains, fertilisers, chemicals, cement, and steel etc. Businesses in these industries have low opportunities to differentiate their offer; price sensitivity is high, and service quality is almost similar. Followers prefer to copy the leader and present similar offers to customers, and market shares remain stable. Market-share followers try to retain their customer base, try to acquire new customers but avoid any moves that might attract retaliation from competitors. Some commonly adopted strategies are:

- Counterfeit Strategy: This type of follower makes duplicates of leader products and sells at very low prices through grey market and dealers of doubtful integrity. For example, some operators in East Asian countries, duplicate/pirate software, music and movie CDs, Apple Computer, top selling novels, and some brands of expensive watches etc.
- Adapter Strategy: This business takes or copies a leader's product, improves it and sells in different markets. The differentiation is in terms of features, packaging, pricing, and distribution. Some firms pick up product ideas from established leaders and implement them in a different country with some modification. Research findings show that number one and two share-leaders earn the maximum ROI, and others may run into negative ROI. This is the reason that P&G aims to be either number one or two in a business otherwise the business is not worth being in.

MARKET NICHER STRATEGIES

Other competitors with small shares should avoid prolonged direct confrontation with large share firms. A small business can adopt niche strategy and focus on a smaller customer segment, with specialised needs and preferences. A niche strategy could be very favourable when a small sub-segment is less attractive to larger firms, or when the niche marketer can create a solid differential advantage, or brand preference among customers.

SUMMARY

The competitor chosen might be basically either strong, or weak. Some of the these competitors might be categorised as "good" or "bad." Good ones follow industry rules, develop realistic assumptions about its future growth, they price their offers reasonably based on lower costs and advocate others to keep costs low, favour product differentiation, focus on a portion of the industry and favour a healthy industry. Market leader is either a pioneer or at least one of the first few entrants who first developed the productmarket. Generally, the leader's objective is to maintain its leading share position despite the entry of new players.

One of the most attractive strategic options for a market leader is often to grow its market share. Coca Cola has managed to grow its volume at the rate of 7-8 per cent. In large industries, an increase of one share-point is often worth millions in monetary terms. Almost always, the market share leader adopts position defence strategy. This strategy focuses on perpetually strengthening an existing position like a fortress and repulsing attacks by existing or future competitors. Another important aspect the leader must consider is to focus on increased pot-purchase service in case of durable products to strengthen its position. A challenger visualises capturing the market-share leadership in an industry. Many challengers have successfully overtaken the leader and some others have gained share points. A challenger has two basic strategic options to consider. In markets where the share leader and others have already cornered a very large portion of the potential market, there is no choice for a challenger but to capture some demand from other competitors' existing customers. Many businesses prefer to stay followers rather than challenge the share leader. This is particularly true for more homogeneous industries such as food grains, fertilisers, chemicals, cement, and steel etc.

Note: Hewlett-Packard (HP) is a global provider of personal systems, imaging and printing products, and technology solutions. The company is the largest player in the inkjet printer and laser printer market. HP is one of the major companies in the enterprise storage and servers markets. The company is also one of the market leaders in the global PC market. It operates in the US and other countries. It is headquartered in Palo Alto, California and employs 321,000 people. For a very good case study regarding this topic, reader can visit company's website www.hp.com

18

Marketing Planning

Marketing management is a big job demanding a balanced approach and attention to detail. In this chapter reviews the key tasks. Marketing management is a generic skill. Its nature, importance and relationship with other activities are reviewed elsewhere in this work. Here the focus is on the day-to-day marketing management process, and this in turn relates to the nature of the marketing activity in a particular organization. In Marketing Force Management it is said:

"Marketing is important, not only because of the company's immediate need to generate revenue through t hemarketi ngof products and services, nor only because marketing is the largest marketing expense, but also because the future of the company depends on marketing people who can ...find more, win more, and keep more through carrying the voice of the customer throughout the firm."

"Managing the marketing function is one of the most important management functions in any firm, not just because marketing is so important, but also because managing marketing is unique."

Overlong sentences apart, this is fair comment. Marketing management is important, and it is unique amongst management tasks. While it is a process that must be applied differently in different organizations, industries and circumstances the key tasks are the same for all. These are:

- Planning
- Organizing
- Staffing
- Developing
- Motivating
- Control.

Each of these is reviewed in turn, with examples illustrating certain aspects of them and a link to current problems, issues or opportunities.

PLANNING

Planning is no academic nicety. Plans should drive the business, and the thinking that goes into planning is key to analysis and making sure that the activity reflects the real world. Essentially planning comes down to four key questions:

- Analysing the current situation;
- Demanding the setting of clear objectives;
- How will we get there? (this produces an action plan, setting out
- Who will do what and when); and
- The process of measurement and control).

These are no more than common sense, but they should prompt specific action by the manager in charge of the marketing team.

MARKETING OBJECTIVES

This process demands looking back and then forward. It is important that detailed and current information forms the basis of any extrapolation. Marketing revenue will no doubt be clear, but detailed statements are needed in terms of areas like:

- Marketing by product
- Marketing by customer category
- Marketing in different areas; and
- Marketing linked to price (at different discounts and levels of profitability, for example); and more.

With this in mind, marketing can be forecast, and this should be done in a way that recognizes and anticipates any changes that the forthcoming period will bring (it is not just a case of adding an attractive percentage increase). The next stage is to see how such a target can be met - this leads to the marketing plan.

THE MARKETING PLAN

The key questions here are as follows.

- What is to be marketed? (the detail, product by product as necessary): product mix is the key variable here. Depending on the product or service range, its positioning and design, direction may well be necessary for the marketing force - it may be that the items to which they give priority, perhaps because they are easiest to sell, are not the company's priority - with other lines having higher profitability. Clarity is needed here, and leaving the mix marketed just to "happen" should not be one of the options.

- To whom? (a statement that should reflect all categories of customer): here there may need to be plans for customers by category, or even by individual customer. Large customers may need to have strategies developed for them, especially where they have several different buying points (e.g. people, functions, geographic locations); this may be best thought of on a matrix basis.
- At what price? (recognizing the complexities of pricing policy): a logical pricing policy is necessary here, together with any discount structures that are necessary. Price is a marketing variable, but one of the places pricing policy must be implemented and work well is at the marketing interface with the customer. The marketing manager should be involved with decisions about pricing policy and must put the marketing people in a position to work with the details effectively. Factors such as what independent authority marketing people have to negotiate price and terms should be clearly understood by all.
- By what methods? (detailing how marketing will be organized): the plan must specify marketing actions very clearly. The mix of customers and the different levels and style of service they may want must be matched with the organization's intention to push for marketing. The system must categorize customers, assign call frequencies, allow time for any necessary activity such as prospecting or telephone contact (and administration) and prompt a practical array of activity. It is little good aiming for marketing results with no clear idea how they will be obtained or the scale of the effort required.
- At what cost? (and also with what cost-effectiveness): the marketing plan has a cost, so budgeting is one aspect here. Marketing productivity is the other concept that needs addressing here. Analysis of the ratio of marketing to marketing cost is just the starting point. Other measures may include: marketing per territory, number of customers managed by a

marketing person, number of calls made per person (and on average per day), time spent face to face, average order value, strike rate - orders to call ratio, most successful marketing person compared with the average (there can be a very significant gap here). There are details here worth constant vigilance and fine-tuning.

A significant part of many organizations' marketing plans is the development of individual customer strategies. These sub plans can include profitability analysis, and set out details of action over a period across a complex organization with multiple buying points, matching this to internal considerations including product mix. This then becomes the basis for prompting and checking action. An example relating to this appears in the In practice section).

With the foregoing methodology in mind certain key practical points are worth emphasizing:

IMPORTANT ISSUES

- Comprehensive marketing plans: plans must be activity as well as results based, and targets must link to both. Thus targets must be set not just for marketing figures but for the activities that potentially produce them, e.g. prospecting, calls, meetings, proposals etc. As business approaches change new activities may become important and need adding in to the planning process.
- Realistic targets: the link between forecasting and planning must be sound. Whatever objectives the organization sets, at the level of individual marketing person, targets must be achievable - they can, and perhaps should be challenging - but they should be achievable. Marketing managers must increasingly be involved at senior levels of marketing planning to get this right.
- Making the plan match real life: in years past marketing people had a territory, period. Now plans need to reflect a number of issues beyond geography, such include: product range, markets and different kinds of customer and buyer. A matrix approach is often the answer.

ORGANIZING

Organization addresses the basic design of the marketing resource. First, it must be decided how many marketing staff are needed. This is best done on a workload analysis basis, looking at the level of customer service required, the number of calls that will need to be made and relating that to the number of people able to undertake this amount of work; with costs albeit often demanding a compromise.

Secondly, marketing must be fitted into the organization structure. This too is dependent on size and activity. Questions such as: how many marketing people can one manager manage? How many different types of marketing people are necessary? How many territories or groups of customer have to be serviced? It may be that a marketing director heads up the function and is supported by a marketing manager with a number of area or regional managers reporting to them before the marketing people appear. It may be, in a small organization, that the general manager must cope with all of this. Two factors should primarily be born in mind.

- Customer categories: for example, in the way that a building materials company might need to relate to: building firms and contractors (large and small), architects, surveyors, builders' merchants, local authorities, government departments and maybe more. In this case they might have different people calling on specifiers (architects and others) and direct purchasers. The complexities here will dictate the scale and arrangement of the organization structure.
- Number of customers: obviously if the customer base is small less marketing people are needed to cover them and vice versa. Similarly if part of the job of marketing is done in some way separate from a field marketing operation: online or on the telephone, for instance.

In considering organization, remember:

- To review regularly: it is a variable. Many organizations hit problems because their marketing organization becomes regarded as fixed, and then - over time - ceases to match the market conditions. External changes can accelerate this;
- To link with marketing: sometimes marketing innovation necessitates change. For example, Usborne who sell books for children use normal channels and marketing organization, marketing to book shops etc. They also sell through party style events (like Tupperware) getting mothers with small children to organize gatherings at their homes to demonstrate and sell books. This works well, but represents a change that needs different people and organization to make this side of their operation work; and

- To prompt organization at individual territory level: the way individual marketing people manage their own "patch" is also vital. They need to link intentions for call frequency and the customer mix (large and small) to a map and ensure that the way they "work" the territory is efficient and productive (e.g. minimizing travel time and cost). Again this is something they need to be reminded to review regularly.

STAFFING

One of the key issues addressed in the final chapter is staffing. The rule here is simply stated. Assemble and maintain a team of good people. There is no room for passengers, and poor performers can end up monopolizing a marketing manager's time and this, in turn causes other problems as other things are delayed or neglected. Recruitment must be thorough and systematic. A systematic approach is recommended by many authorities. The following eight-stage approach is the basis of comment on this subject by Mike Wilson in his book Managing a Marketing Force.

1. Writing a job description: this is worth spending some time on. It should spell out the tasks in full (it is not enough just to say it is "to sell the product"). If prospecting is necessary say so. If a successful candidate must be able to give a technical demonstration of the product, work at the bottom of a mine shaft or carry out the marketing in five minutes while the buyer mans a busy cash till in a store of some sort, say so. Beyond duties and tasks this document can record such matters as reporting lines, evaluation procedures, and remuneration.
2. Writing a profile of the person: what kind of person is likely to be successful in the job? List basic characteristics (e.g. age, experience), character (e.g. persistent, self-reliant), motivations (e.g. attitudes to money, security etc.), emotional maturity (e.g. profile, capacity for self-discipline etc.). Past experience and what successes it has brought them are important here; so too are details (more than one marketing person has been appointed before it was discovered they could not drive a car!).
3. Recruiting candidates: review the options. You can advertise (in local or national papers, trade magazines etc.), but do not overlook other channels such as looking internally or asking existing staff for recommendations (and paying a reward if

successful candidates are produced this way). If you use an agency it may seem expensive - but so is your time! And try to get a personal recommendation, there are agencies and agencies (and currently a look on the Internet identifies more than 5000 agencies operating that way; take care - some will not be there tomorrow).

4. Assessing application forms: a good application form (which these days might be completed on line) is invaluable. Ask for comprehensive information, match it to the job description and profile and plan to interview only those who show well at this stage. The whole process works better with more forms and less interviews rather than the reverse.

5. Checking references: not always easy, but worth doing (telephoning those a candidate gives permission to contact may be best) - and worth doing up front. If it shows up any "nasties" then you save the time of the other stages.

6. Testing: similarly this is better done before interviewing. Some things are clear: you can test someone's fluency in French, numeracy or other straightforward skills precisely - and reject them if they are inadequate. Other tests need more care, though some swear by psychometric tests that profile candidates, they need careful choosing, add time and cost - and none can measure marketing ability as a specific factor.

7. Structured interviewing: this stage links your details of the job and the candidate with their personal showing. It is worth cross-checking what was said on an application form (there is a considerable temptation to lie on them) - indeed the form can provide the structure for the interview. One main interview, and perhaps a shorter second one for a shortlist works well; a second opinion might be obtained from a colleague on the second one.

8. Evaluating a shortlist and making a final decision: Check the facts, relate one candidate to another objectively - trust your judgment and experience - but beware of irrational hunches and pseudo-psychology.

This is a pivotal task and needs special care and attention.

- Assumptions: avoid making them. It is a common failing that people (especially men) believe they are a good, and worse, instant, judge of character - "I know the good candidates within five minutes of beginning the interview." Research does not bear this out. Recruitment needs a systematic approach to be successful - you skimp this process at your peril.

- Stereotypes: avoid using descriptions of marketing jobs that are totally clich´e - if you say nothing in an advertisement other than asking for someone - "dynamic, self-starting, highly motivated, persistent, personable and of exceptional character" - most people reading it will say - "That's me." Be factual about the job.
- Local difficulty: as has been made clear, this is not an area for compromise. Bad selection leads, almost inevitably, to bad performance and you very rarely hear marketing managers say that someone turned out better than they thought at interview stage. So if there is a particular problem (e.g. the difficulty of full employment in somewhere like Singapore) it must not be allowed to weaken resolve to make the right appointment.
- Legislation: make sure that all records, forms, contracts and processes are as they should be (check with your HR [human resources] department). In an increasingly litigious world you do not want to run foul of the law when candidates are rejected or unsuccessful people have contracts terminated.
- Experiment: and do not be hidebound by convention. For example, why do all prospective candidates have to have a degree, or have ten years experience in your industry? Maybe the place to fish is in new pools - in your own factory or amongst groups less obviously qualified. This is, without doubt, the most important element of the marketing manager's job. It starts as people are recruited.
- Induction training: even if you recruit experienced marketing people they need how to operate in your environment. They need to know about your organization and product, they need to understand the kind of people who will be their customers, and they need to know how - exactly how - marketing skills can be appropriately and effectively deployed for you. Time spent at this stage can pay dividends. Some things can be delegated, but beware. You do not want technical product knowledge put over by someone with no understanding of customers, and much - maybe most - of what must be done is best done by the manager.

- Field training: time must be spent regularly in the field, joint calling, with people - including experienced people. Marketing is dynamic and needs constant fine-tuning. A cycle of evaluation, counmarketing and action and advice to focus the marketing person's thinking on the quality of their approach and back to evaluation is a continuous process. The most important objective here relates to the numbers involved. Working with the marketing person (this is not, and must not be seen as, checking, control, or instruction) on a small, but regular and representative number of calls is a means of making all the many others they make alone go well. The most important aspect of the role is to establish the habit of self-evaluation and fine-tuning in people, making them better able to operate alone and making it more likely that they will always do so at the peak of performance. It is beyond the scope of this work to recommend specific evaluation systems on which to base this sort of process, but some formality of system may help. It must be tailor-made and seen to be clear, constructive, consistent, and fair - and above all practical, it must actually help review and improve performance.
- Group activities: field training allows the identification of common needs for development, which can then be better addressed on a group basis; one of the key reasons for having marketing meetings. These must be well planned and conducted, constructive in manner, content and approach - and must make a difference. Poor meetings quickly dilute motivation. Development activities here can involve people in, for example, leading projects and also allow other methods to be used such as role-playing, training exercises or training films.
- Formal training: sometimes development needs more formal solution. In a larger organization help may come from an HR department or there may be a training resource center (with a library and facilities to view videos or undertake e-learning of various sorts). Sometimes the answer may be an external or internal course, the latter can be tailored; sometimes the manager may be able to conduct short sessions themselves, alternatively there may be value in having assistance from a consultant.

The ongoing need for development should never be underestimated; equally any development activity should be practically based and genuinely likely to help maintain or improve performance. At the end of the day the person most likely to be able to do this on a regular basis is the marketing person themselves; but the manager should play a part and be an effective catalyst to more.

As has been made clear the development task is probably the single most important thing marketing managers can spend time on; indeed it must take up most of their time. A constructive view must always be taken of it, therefore, and thus the following need addressing.

- Time: in modern business, pressure on time seems to increase constantly. Managers must fight to spend an appropriate amount of time on this process. In a large organization different levels of marketing management may help spread the load (regional and area managers, for instance). For others the key task is to balance overall workload - and marketing managers seem inclined to have a wide range of responsibilities beyond actually managing the marketing team (getting involved in everything from promotion to pricing). If marketing approaches are to truly differentiate from competition, ways must be found to give this area priority.
- The personal touch: with more and more training provided through technology, and for marketing people in isolation (e.g. computer based training), there is a danger that actual face to face contact declines. By all means use technology or anything else that helps, but the key activity of individuals working creatively together may achieve most and this effect must not be diluted.
- Perception of the role: the days of marketing managers being regarded as primarily having a "police" role are, for the most part, long gone. Yet with control being part of the job, it is important that the relationship between marketing people and their manager is, and is seen to be, constructive. Too often one hears marketing people say something like "I never seem to see my manager unless there is something wrong." Managers must work with people, not just be seen as checking up on them or telling them what to do. Learning - certainly that prompts consistently different future practice - will only take place if lessons are made acceptable and people are involved in the process. New ideas, and thus new methods and approaches, will only be sparked or evolved if people work constructively and creatively together.

MOTIVATING

It is an inherent part of any manager's job to motivate. The motivational "climate," the net effect of many influences on people in their work, has a very real impact on the way they do their job. If development ensures that people are able to do what is required, then motivation ensures that they want to do so. For marketing people, faced with the attrition of customer attitudes, and often working largely on their own, the way they feel about their job is especially important. The theory of motivation that provides the most practical basis for a concept that links easily to action is that of Frederick Herzberg. His description of satisfiers and dissatisfiers, provides a good analogy for balancing motivational influences: actively creating positive feeling and acting also to minimize negative feelings. For example, most marketing people hate administration, but it needs to be done. It may always be an essentially negative aspect of the job, however explaining why it is necessary and creating the minimum straightforward system to get it done is appreciated, and that aspect becomes motivational.

Incentives are perhaps worth a special word. Research over the years seems to show consistently that the best performing marketing people have a reward system that includes some element of payment on results. This is not always possible. Results need to be readily linked to individual effort (team incentives are less powerful). Such schemes need to be straightforward (it is no good if an hour needs to be spent with a calculator just to see how things are going); they must pay out regularly (for some marketing people thinking about Friday-week is long-term planning); they must represent a significant proportion of total remuneration (and that means bearing in mind family income); and they should be interesting - fun - linking to published results, newsletters, and league tables all help.

Variety is important too. Incentives can be linked to all sort of things, overall marketing but also opening new accounts, marketing in a new product or profitability of marketing. Simple quarterly schemes, with regular changes work well, as do mixing financial reward with other incentives (travel is a favorite). But a simple "Well done" can be as powerful as anything - and costs nothing. Motivation is a key part of marketing management and managers who are, or make themselves, instinctive motivators have a real asset in their management armory.

- Time pressure: without a doubt low motivation is more often a result of less being done than should be, than of the wrong thing being done. Motivating does take time, but it is time well spent - it needs building in as a priority.

- Resisting magic formulae: the easiest trap to fall into is a belief that money is a panacea. Incentives, including financial incentives, have a role to play. But a mix of activities is best, and small influences are just as important in the total picture as large. To motivate successfully you must work at it; the effort is worthwhile, the process can quickly become a habit and it can be as pleasurable to motivate as to be motivated.
- Being censorious: what matters most is the people. It is easy to base motivational practice on what you would like, when marketing people may have different priorities.
- Caring: if there is anything like a magic formula in this area, then it is that the simpler things - just taking an interest in people, working constructively with them, giving them authority, and recognizing achievements are probably more important than anything. But they have to be real. The manager needs to care (and the old saying that - "if you can fake the sincerity, everything else is easy" - must never be allowed to become the basis for action).

CONTROL

The word control can have connotations of' policing. The essence of control is change. The knowledge of what is happening allows action to be taken either aiming to bring things back on track if there is a shortfall, or to build on success. This last point is key. Control is not simply to correct faults. It is to accentuate the positive. It is just as useful to see a positive variance, ask why this should be happening and build on the action that is creating it. While management has a duty to provide a framework and encourage discipline amongst marketing people, their prime job is to act as a catalyst to success. By viewing control as both focusing on positive and negative results and acting as a spur to change, its value will be maximized.

- A surfeit of information: the biggest problem these days may seem perverse. There is too much information. Certainly information is probably easier to collect and more up to date than was the case in the past, but key indicators can get buried. Management must focus on those factors (whatever they are from volume of marketing to the number of new accounts opened) that are key; and must know what they are.

- Optimizing information collection: however information is collected, and it may be filling in a form or inputting to a computer of some sort, the process must not be over-engineered. Making marketing people aware of how important it is, and making the system straightforward should get information flowing well; this must not be an area of constant hassle as this just wastes time and puts the veracity of information in doubt
- Fit internal aspects of control to the outside world: for example, if marketing people man an exhibition stand at a trade show at the beginning of the financial year, high marketing volume over this time may negate the effect of incentive schemes throughout the remainder of the year.

FUTURE

It has been mentioned several times in this work that marketing is a dynamic process. One of any marketing manager's key tasks is to ensure their team is marketing in just the right way. Indeed their job takes its shape from that of those they manage. So it is a prerequisite that they are not only able to define what is necessary now, but that they are ahead of the game in spotting, better still predicting, changes that will require changes to marketing practice. None of us can be sure what the future holds; however working to keep ahead can be approached systematically. The following questions flag the areas that need watching:

- What further changes will technology bring?
- How will the marketing function fit in future within the organization's total marketing mix?
- With whom precisely will responsibility for individual customers (especially large ones) lie?
- How is thc rolc of the marketing force changing?
- What range of tasks will the members of the marketing team need to perform in future?
- What skills - and new or changed skills - will they need to have at their command?
- What new pressures will competition bring to bear and how will that change what we need to do?
- How do we rate against competitors and on the broader stage (including international competition and market activity)? and

- What different expectations will customers have in future and what new demands will they make?

Overall, marketing managers have a multifaceted task. Each aspect of it is important. Some responsibilities are more occasional than others. For example, time spent on recruitment must be well organized and wisely spent, but it is not something that must be done every day (well, not in a good marketing organization!). Conversely, time spent on a variety of counmarketing and development tasks are literally day by day tasks.

Key to being a successful marketing manager is getting the balance right; and being equally effective in a disparate list of operational areas. The preceding section focused primarily on tasks, finally the following sets out a check list more in terms of the personal characteristics of the successful marketing manager, who must:

- Have knowledge of marketing and an involvement in it, because marketing is an inherent part of the marketing mix;
- Be an effective manager, able to direct, control and inspire a team of usually free-spirited people;
- Take the long view (directing activities, setting strategic objectives and defining a framework of targets, policies and priorities to drive towards them);
- Be a corporate team player, as liaison with many different parts of the business is mandatory and must be done effectively;
- Be productive - able to balance conflicting priorities and still spend sufficient time with the team, singly and as a group; this is something that demands problem solving and decision-making abilities;
- Sell effectively. They do not need to be the best on the team, but must understand and be able to practice the full gambit of techniques involved: marketing, negotiation, presentation, numeracy etc.;
- Stay close to the market, because achieving a customer focus in marketing activities is always key;
- Communicate effectively - with staff, colleagues and customers; and
- Achieve results. Managing the activity is not enough - it must work.

Perhaps in one way or another everything here comes back to customers. In the survey The Future of Marketing the future role is defined as follows:

"Tomorrow's marketing leaders will need to develop a clear view of the way ahead for the customers in their industries, and be able to provide their marketing people with the direction and competencies to take full advantage of the opportunities available. "

Planning is one of the first functions in the process of marketing management. Before you undertake any other managerial function, having a good plan is imperative. The reality is often that certain aspects of a plan are carried over from the prior quarter, half, year, and so on. As is true with many of the areas of management, you do not often have the chance to start with a clean slate. However, just as you likely already possess some star marketingpeople, your current plan likely has certain very useful aspects. This chapter is meant to complement what is already in place and possibly challenge what your company is currently doing with the intent of improving the plan so that everyone will benefit.

CORPORATE STRATEGY WITH THE MARKETING TEAM

Plans exist at all levels within an organization. Typically senior management deals with long-range plans, that is, where the organization is heading, what changes may be necessary to generate more profits, what new products will be introduced, and other strategic issues that may occur over the next three to five years or longer. On a departmental level, planning is just as crucial. While you will incorporate some long-term strategies, the majority of the plan deals with the short and medium term (up to one year and between one and three years).

MEDIUM-TERM PLANNING

This part of the marketing plan deals with the means by which longer-range objectives are to be met. The focus is on defining road-blocks to success and then planning solutions.

SHORT-TERM PLANNING

This is probably the most important focus for the marketing manager. Short-term plans concern goals that need to be met over a period of ninety days to one year. These are most often very tactical in nature, having specific objectives that exist within the framework of higher-level plans. Whatever the time period associated with each part of the plan, nothing can operate in a vacuum. Corporate planning needs to take into account departmental plans, and each plan needs to consider the period of time.

THE MARKETING PLAN

The marketing planning process deals with numerous constituents. However, the key ones to focus on are:

- Customers (industry and markets)
- Employees (the marketing team)
- Your products/services (R&D, finance, engineering, manufacturing, operations, suppliers, etc.)
- Competition

Of course, you will need to ask many questions when preparing the marketing plan that will fit into one of these four categories. Depending on your industry, the questions you will need to answer could be as follows:

- What is the length of a typical marketing cycle (one week, one month, one year, etc.)?
- How do you segment your customers (industry, regions, etc.)?
- Do you have major, key, or strategic accounts, and does a separate structure exist to manage different types of accounts?
- Do you have global customers?
- At what level will your marketing people be marketing (multilevel, senior level, team marketing , etc.)?
- Do you have many competitors or are you involved in hyper competition (a few major players controlling and competing in the market)?
- How do you match up to your competition in terms of products, reputation, etc.?
- How does the marketing team tie into the new product/service development process?
- How is research conducted on products, markets, competition, etc.?

Depending on your business, you will need to answer these and many other questions, sometimes in great detail. However, before taking a look at some of these questions in more depth, you should understand your corporate structure and how marketing fits into this structure, and also how marketing touches the customer.

MARKETING IN THE CORPORATE STRUCTURE

It is critical that your department's planning process ties in with the overall corporate plan. The corporate plan should also be one where you have some influence, meaning not only does the plan filter down to you from the top, but this bigger plan should also be developed taking into account your guidance in the marketing plan and marketing forecasting for the future. If not, the corporate expectations are out of touch with your part of the business. This could mean that your team is working toward something that does not match the goals and expectations of the overall business. As importantly, this can have a major effect on the resources and budget you are allocated to generate the desired results.

In order to be an integral player in the corporate-wide planning effort, you need to know the key areas that could affect your team both directly and indirectly. One way to look at the overall role that marketing plays in your organization is by looking at your corporate structure.

There has been a long-standing debate about the best fit and reporting structure for marketing. Some believe that it is a part of the marketing function, while others say it belongs as a stand-alone unit. The answer is that it really does not matter. What is key is that they collaborate well with one another. Below are a couple of sample corporate reporting structures, one with marketing reporting directly to a very senior officer and the other with a senior executive heading up both marketing and marketing. Of course, marketing not only needs to tie closely in to marketing but also needs to work in tandem with the entire organization. This includes R&D, finance, human resources, manufacturing, customer service, and so on. Most important, whatever corporate structure you are in, the goal is to serve the customer.

IMPORTANCE OF CUSTOMER

There are two critical questions that everyone involved in the organization should be able to answer:

- What does your company define as a successful customer?
- What is the desired customer experience?

There has been a great deal of talk over the past couple of decades on how to develop a structure whereby the entire organization is focused on the customer and the customer experience. This is in contrast to the old days, when marketing, marketing, and customer service's main focus was in creating demand, marketing to, and then satisfying the customers, and others had very little involvement in the process; the back office, with human resources and accounting, was merely there to help ensure that the daily activities and processes were functioning, and they did not readily see any direct or indirect link to the customer.

While this still has validity and does depict the customer as the central focus of the organization, today a truly customer-focused organization is that much more complex and intertwined with the customer, and all parts of the organization are thinking in terms of customer value. This would mean that there are many areas of the organization that do not necessarily have regular direct contact with the customer but are still developing strategies and processes that enhance the customer experience. For example, instead of accounts receivable concentrating on just billing and collections, they might be looking to integrate their information technology systems with that of their counterparts at the customer. organization).

Furthermore, since team is not likely marketing directly to the final end-user (business to consumer marketing), you could have any number of layers involved in the supply chain that ultimately delivers the final product/service to the consumer. This more stepped approach common to business-to-business marketing opens the door to an array of areas in which to integrate your processes. Some major companies, for example, have their processes so refined that everyone involved in the supply chain meets certain standards of quality, communications, technology, and so on. Some of the key benefits to these companies are everything from cost savings to higher profit margins, improved quality, and increased customer satisfaction. When you think of it in terms of your marketing team, there are many ways that a customer-centric organization will have a direct benefit:

- Better Efficiencies. Members of both the marketing and buying organizations are working in conjunction with one another, communicating and collaborating in the most efficient ways possible.
- Barriers to Entry. The better your company's processes are working with your customers, the more difficult it is for one of your competitors to come and take away that business.
- Competing on Overall Value (not just price). You are able to compete on many more levels than just price, which then

becomes just one factor in the marketing as opposed to the main driver.

- Benefits to End-Users. Whoever the final end users are of your product/service, they will benefit from better value, quality, and service from you and those in your supply chain. They will therefore remain more loyal and become long-term customers.
- Benefits to You and Your Staff. All of this will culminate in more marketing and profits for your team.

With this understanding of a customer-focused organization and departmental synergies, it is now time to see more definitely how other departments work, and their importance in the marketing planning process. Furthermore, you will realize the extent to which they affect your team and its ability to sell.

MARKETING'S RELATIONSHIP TO SALES

Marketing is one such department to understand more in depth. As you saw in the corporate structure, marketing has, or should have, a great deal of interaction with marketing. In fact, in order to get a clearer picture of the customer and how to best approach him, you will find that some understanding of marketing is essential. Marketing probably has a greater impact on how your marketing team performs and the ability to maximize your team's efforts than any other single department.

Today marketing is much more than just one-way messaging through advertising and direct marketing. In some companies the line between marketing and marketing is quite blurred. For example, business development is at times a marketing function and other times falls into marketing. Again, it is important to understand each other's roles because the information that you can provide one another is critical toward building each of your department's business plans. Here are some common similarities as well as differences between marketing and marketing (as adapted from AMA's Advanced Course in Strategic Marketing) along with some useful integration strategies that can enhance both departments.

The Role of Marketing

- Front line with customers.
- Generate orders.
- Short- and medium-range (primary focus).

- Identify and set up key accounts and other account management strategies.
- Build one-to-one business relationships.

The Role of Marketing

- Creates leads for the marketing team.
- Develops messaging and brand image.
- Short-, medium-, and long-range.
- Informational and educational.

Of course, this will vary, depending on the organization and types of products/services. For example, a company that sells credit cards will be largely marketing-focused and would probably rely not on field marketing representatives, but rather on inside marketing and customer service representatives. The marketing department is therefore set up primarily to generate leads for transactional marketing. On the other hand, a niche high-end supplier of business software might be very marketing-focused. The message might not be as impactful through marketing tools such as direct mail, TV and print ads, the radio, and so on, so the focus and higher departmental budgets would be with the direct marketing channels.

Another way to look at this is how some companies are considered either "marketing organizations" or "marketing organizations." This is typically due to how large the budget is for marketing versus the size of the budget for marketing. Some examples that commonly fall under each category are:

Marketing Organizations

- Pharmaceuticals
- Consulting
- Auto
- Financial services

Marketing Organizations

- Consumer products
- Travel and leisure
- Retailers
- Entertainment

No matter the structure and emphasis, the key again is that marketing and marketing must work collaboratively with one another. The information and capabilities that each possess are so important to the other that it's foolish for the two departments to act independently. In companies where the integration is weak, marketingpeople often find that marketing is sending out messages that do not tie in to what they have to sell, or the key benefits are not highlighted properly. At the same time, while marketing believes problems or issues exist within marketing, the marketing department likely has its own set of challenges and difficulties when working with marketing. For example, it is not uncommon for marketing to feel that many of the leads they acquire through their various campaigns are not properly followed up on.

Therefore, it is incumbent on you now as a manager to try to move everyone toward a more collaborative work environment. Again, most of this can be done by accomplishing one major task- sharing of information. This could mean having your marketing force report what customers are saying back to marketing as well as providing competitive information regarding what the marketing force is seeing or coming up against in the field. Marketing could also provide some of those customer "pain points," or what the customer is really looking for in a product/ service or overall buyer/vendor relationship that is not currently being addressed. Marketing could then more accurately focus its messaging and highlight certain key benefits more clearly. At the same time, marketing can try to engage the marketing force more and reach out to them for ideas for marketing campaigns, bringing them into the creative process early on in its development. Additionally, marketing can be sure to work with marketing on all special promotions and keep them apprised of all of the details on any new offerings. Without this information a marketingperson can be at a great disadvantage with a new or potential customer.

Furthermore, whether or not your department is structurally intertwined with marketing, you as a marketing manager can adapt some core tools from marketing for the planning process. One tool that you are likely familiar with in some form is a SWOT analysis. SWOT stands for Strengths, Weaknesses, Opportunities, and Threats. A SWOT analysis is a basic tool for planning that a marketing manager can utilize in many ways:

By filling in what falls into each of the four areas, you can gauge in broad terms where you stand in whatever category you choose to analyze. You can conduct this type of analysis on many areas that relate to both your company and marketing team.

Things to consider for a SWOT analysis include:

- Current products and services
- Potential new products and services
- Brand image
- Pricing strategy
- Competition
- Experience of marketing team members
- Reputation in the industry
- Market share
- Training needs
- Service/maintenance capabilities

It is also helpful when plotting the above to think of internal factors such as new products and services as either a strength or weakness, whereas external factors such as competition and regulation fit into the categories of either opportunities or threats. Furthermore, the phrase environmental scan is a concept similar to the external factors piece of a SWOT analysis (i.e., you scan the external environment and see what is affecting your business). This type of analysis can be as general or detailed as necessary. For example, you can look at the competition even more precisely through an analysis from the perspective of each of your competitors; or you can analyze the strengths and weaknesses of each individual team member at a very granular level.

Another tool you could adapt from marketing would relate to ways to more precisely look at your products and markets. For example, you would look at each of your product lines, and determine its relative strength in the industry. Then you can compare that to the markets you are currently in along with what markets it might pay to try to break into.

You can then analyze where you rank with each product against each competitor. For example, you are strong in Product A and weak in Product D. Here again you can get more detailed and might even wish to weight each product based on one or more factors (e.g., revenues, profits, core competency, etc.). Another result that could come out of these kinds of analyses is that you might find that there are certain markets not worth competing in or products that you do not wish to carry. This might be the case in product lines where you have almost no presence (Products C and D), and it would be too costly or out of your core compentency to truly compete. A better strategy might be to partner with certain competitors in order to stengthen both of your positions against other competition.

Another function that typically falls into marketing is market research. You likely have some familiarity with market research through surveys or questionnaires (at least from having taken them over the years). However, market research is much broader and is a responsibility of every marketing manager, whether you conduct the research directly or others provide you with this service.

Besides surveys; other typical market research techniques are focus groups and observational research. Focus groups are a group of participants that share a common element that will enable the marketing organization to gauge their interest in the company itself, an existing product, a new product idea, and so on. Observational research is just like it sounds-researchers observe a customer using a product or service and see how they react with it (e.g., how they open the product, how they use/interact with the product, etc.). These three techniques (surveys, focus groups, and observational research) are what many think of as the main tools to conduct research. But these techniques are only one form, called Primary Research. These three types of primary research involve collecting new information from the customer in some way. Secondary research is the other major form of market research. This type of research includes all of the information you already possess but that has not yet been formulated. Once it is, however, a great deal of analysis can be done. Some areas that fit into the category of secondary research are:

- Marketing growth (or decline)
- Customer geographic distribution
- Percentage of marketing of newly launched products versus core products
- Industry growth
- Product or service growth

This is information that you either can readily get or can utilize others to help put together. You can then interpret it and incorporate the findings as needed in your planning process. The range of resources for secondary research is anything from your own records to departmental and company (internal) records, as well as through external resources (e.g., D&B, industry trade associations, Department of Commerce, etc.). Of course the key is to get the information in such a way that it can be analyzed. Another useful research component is other researchers' reports or survey findings that you are able to purchase or get for free.

The next two areas to understand, which are very intertwined with marketing (as well as other departments), are new product/ service development and pricing strategies.

Depending on the organization, new product/service development could be closely tied to marketing, marketing, R&D, engineering, manufacturing, or any combination of these. The idea is to bring about new products/services or new features that will generate increased marketing and profits. Since you are a marketing manager, your input as well as that of your team is invaluable. After all, who has their ear closer to the customer than the marketing force? It is imperative that you have some processes in place to funnel this information. Whether it be a structured, rigorous one or more ad hoc, it needs to get done. This helps to avoid finger pointing later on as to why a product was developed in a certain way.

A typical new product development process encompasses everything from generating ideas for new products to the launching and postlaunch refining or changes. To put into perspective the process and how it further relates to your marketing department, your team's input will be not only important in the idea stage but also in the testing of the products. After all, before the launch the products will need to get tested, and who else are they tested on but your customers?

Pricing decisions are also tied in closely to new products and services, and can reside in any one or more department(s). Pricing strategies can therefore greatly vary from organization to organization and industry to industry. Of course, they should always keep in mind the end-user. As it relates to your marketing department process, the pricing strategy will be very instrumental in helping you achieve your goals. Pricing often includes very senior-level officers who help to set the big-picture pricing strategy (price structure), and then individual pricing decisions can be made to fit within the structure. Furthermore, a great number of factors, both internal and external, will impact how your company makes pricing decisions. Here are some key areas that will play a role in pricing decisions (adapted from AMA's Advanced Course in Strategic Marketing).

External

- The economy.
- Demand for your types of products and services.
- Competitions-are you the only game in town or do you have many competitors with similar products and services?

- Are you in a commodity or premium products type of business/ industry?
- Government and other regulations.

Internal

- Pricing structure-what is your cost of goods marketed, fixed costs, variable costs, etc.?
- Are you a public or private company (i.e., who are your shareholders, and what is your strategy for increasing their value)?
- What is your company's brand recognition and reputation?
- What are your channels of distribution (manufacturer, distributor or wholesaler, direct to consumer, etc.)?
- What is your mix of marketing vehicles (field marketing, inside marketing, telemarketing, on-line marketing, etc.)?
- What types of marketing do you do (transactional, long-term, reorder/ replenish)?
- Do you deal with government contracts and bidding, requests for proposals (RFPs), global marketing (letters of credit, foreign exchange risk, etc.)?

You will need to take into account many of the above questions when making pricing decisions. Here again the internal players and their input in the process will vary depending on many of the answers to these questions. For example, in the credit card example given previously, the pricing decisions might be primarily driven by the marketing department. However, in the niche high-end software example, pricing might be more determined by the marketing department, with others such as marketing, finance, and R&D giving their necessary contributions.

Now that you have some of the foundational elements and tools to consider when initiating the planning process as well as an understanding of the key players and departments involved, it is time to take a look at the structure of a plan.

PLANNING

A reassuring thought when beginning the process is that for every hour spent planning, many hours of inefficient activity can be avoided. Furthermore, taking this time and initiative to develop and implement a well-thought-out plan will have a great deal of other benefits for you as a marketing manager. It will allow you to:

Set priorities and allocate resources, ensuring that time and resources are spent on accomplishing goals that are agreed upon and shared by all necessary stakeholders. Develop strong internal and external partnerships for sharing information and resources, and promoting new and improved business practices. Have a predictable budgeting process, whereby expenses, revenues, and income are planned for in advance, and adjusted as necessary. Create team stability that allows for continuous and progressive growth of your staff.

CHARACTERISTICS OF A GOOD PLAN

A good plan requires the following elements:

- Vision
- Mission
- Goals and objectives
- Strategies and tactics

This is a very common-type structure that is used in strategic planning. Your company is likely already involved at the higher levels in planning and therefore utilizes this type of planning framework or something similar. Other types of building blocks for strategic planning include issues-based planning, by which the planning process begins by looking at issues that the organization faces and then develops strategies to resolve these issues and ways to improve the organization. Whatever the specific planning model looks like, the key is that you work with all the necessary stakeholders to build from the corporate plan a marketing plan, with the end result being improved corporate, departmental, and individual performance.

Also, your company likely has a schedule for their strategic planning and some sort of process, be it formal or more ad hoc, in place. Typically it is a historical practice and one that is often determined by the industry you are in. For example, in some slower-growth, mature industries the corporate planning process can take place annually. However, with fast-moving high-growth industries, corporate planning can take place two times a year. Your marketing department will need to tie into this large plan as well, but keep in mind that you might have many more specifics that relate to much shorter time periods, such as quarterly, monthly, and so on.

VISION

Long-range corporate plans require a target called a vision statement. In most cases, you will find that your company has a thoughtout vision and might even communicate this internally and possibly externally through any number of vehicles (intranet, Web site, newsletters, press releases, annual reports, etc.). A vision statement answers the question, "How is the company's mission [to be looked at in a moment] to be served in the future?" A vision statement should both inspire and guide. It must balance aspiration with realistic insights into future potential. In order to guide, the vision statement must capture what is unique about the company and what will continue to be unique about it in the future.

Some like to look at the vision as the "stretch" goal for the organization. For example, what is possible if all aspects of the corporate plan come together consistently and all goals are reached over a sustained period of time (e.g., at least three years)? If this happens would you be satisfied achieving the vision you have in place? If so, then your vision is likely on target. If not, you likely have not aspired enough in your vision. One very simple way to think of it is "No pain, no gain!"

The irony is that despite all its importance, the vision should be summed up in only a very short statement-usually one quick succinct sentence.

The mission is the main purpose for conducting business activities. It is a compass that gives the direction to stay the course. Like the vision statement, it is likely already communicated to various stakeholders through any number of methods. It is a tool frequently used for corporate, departmental, and individual motivation. The mission statement, more so even than the vision statement, is written not only for employees, but also for customers and often stockholders. Since it is a core, rallying cry used to unite a company, it is often printed on business cards, posted about the offices, and used in marketing literature.

Also, while the mission statement should carry a great deal of weight, and receive buy-in across the organization, like the vision statement, it is also a short precise statement, typically one sentence in length. The company's mission statement can then be broken down by department. The mission statement for each department within the corporate structure needs to be personalized by the manager for that area of responsibility. By reframing the definition of a mission statement, the process becomes definable.

CORPORATE-LEVEL MISSION

A corporate mission statement should answer the following types of broader questions:

- Why does this entity exist?
- What is the company's impact on society (local, national, international)?

As a marketing manager, you will not likely play a large role in developing a corporate mission. In fact, it is probably already in place and only changes if there is a major corporate directional shift. Most companies, for example, have the same mission for ten years are more. However, on a departmental and team level, you can have some or even a great deal of input.

DEPARTMENT-LEVEL MISSION

Of course the mission for a division or department needs to align with the larger corporate mission. This more specific mission is what others would ideally say about the people in the division and the manner in which business is conducted.

It would answer the following types of questions:

- Why does this department exist?
- What is the department's impact on the company?
- What is the department's impact on customers?
- Who (in general terms) are its customers?
- What (in general terms) are the products/services it provides?

It is also a good idea to include something about the employees, answering the question, how does the department take its employees into account? After all, it is the employees who need to buy into the mission.

You should find that everything in the plan needs to tie back into the corporate and departmental mission statements.

GOALS

The mission statement is the overall direction. Goals are the mandatory, shorter-term direction to move toward the mission. In its most basic sense, the goals are what needs to be accomplished. A plan should take into account three main types of goals. Some goals are corporate goals, which will be driven by the corporate mandate such as the dollar volume.

A departmental goal, on the other hand, might deal with targeting a new market or introducing a new product/service to specific accounts. The third type of goal is a personal business goal. Personal goals include activities that go beyond the corporate and departmental dictates. A personal business goal might have to do with learning a new computer program for making presentations. Some would even include a fourth type of goal, personal goals. When thinking of this in business terms, it might include working toward an advanced degree or a certification that might not tie in directly to your business responsibilities but is still something that you value, and at the same time, your company sees as something that helps you to build your character. Regardless of the types of goals you are establishing, the goals must always be SMART:

- Specific
- Measurable
- Attainable
- Relevant
- Timely

While this is a very common acronym, it is a very important one. In some descriptions, some of the letters represent different words, but the meaning is still similar. (Achievable is sometimes used instead of Attainable, or Realistic instead of Relevant.) Specific goals are definable. There are no gray areas or room for interpretation. All words used are concrete in nature; for example, a specific goal is a 25 percent increase in telemarketing calls this quarter over the same quarter last year. Relative terminology cannot be used in goal setting; "make more productive prospecting calls" is a goal that uses relative terms. What is more productive to you is not necessarily more productive to someone else.

Measurable goals have a beginning and an end. Therefore, at the end of a specific time, it will be obvious whether the goal has been reached. If the goal was missed, you will know the shortfall. If the goal was exceeded, the measurement will indicate the exact overage.

Attainable goals are real-world goals that push the comfort zone outward. Some people set goals too high and actually set themselves up for failure. Other people set goals too low because they do not want to overextend or necessarily push themselves. Attainable goals are balanced and meant to be challenging.

Relevant goals are directly related to the mission and have meaning. If the goal does not mean anything, the intensity may be low and the dedication to the goal lacking. Also, if certain goals are relevant and others are not, the associated work will be scattered and not necessarily benefit the company as a whole.

Timely goals could be measured at checkpoints along the way (say every thirty or sixty days) or have one fixed time for completion (by the end of the third quarter). This will vary depending on many factors, including the fact that "importance" should greatly affect timeliness. For example, if a project needs to be done in the next ninety days in order to secure a contract that will increase profitability by 6 percent, then the timeline should reflect this. What priorities you have set up will be key to making the plan effective.

Objectives in many cases are a subset of goals-your goals broken down into more specifics. Some like to use goals as something that all departments are working toward, whereas objectives are more department-specific. Like goals, objectives need to have the SMART elements. Also, certain objectives can apply to more than one goal. Typically they work in tandem with outcomes-those results, or lack of, that tell you whether or not you achieved your objective(s). For example, after you list a goal and then the associated objectives for the goal, at some point in time you need to verify the outcome that was either obtained or not and when.

STRATEGIES AND TACTICS

In order to achieve your goals and objectives a plan must incorporate the necessary strategies and tactics. Specific activities will always be necessary to move you forward. In this section you identify the strategies necessary and then the specific tactics or tasks for which to accomplish your identified SMART goals and objectives.

The specifics areas to include in this part of the plan are:

- Action Items: This is your road map for how you are going to get something achieved.
- List the actions that need to happen. By listing every action item, focus can be maintained, and productive communications can be established. Keeping a list also allows you the opportunity to have a log that you can see and check items off as they are completed.
- Responsibilities: This should answer the question of who is required to carry out a certain part of the plan. After overall responsibilities have been identified, determine who needs to do which task. Think about what assistance is required from others within the company to fulfill the necessary steps. Make sure the people in the other departments involved are fully aware of their part in the plan. Once people have committed to

certain responsibilities, follow up to make sure they have the resources needed to accomplish their part.

- Tracking: This tells you when parts of the plan are to be completed. Establish a realistic forecast. Think of a time frame that allows all involved parties enough time to complete their responsibilities. Keep company deadlines in mind. Set scheduled start and completion dates. Define checkpoints that will determine progress. Make sure the plan stays on track. If the schedule gets off track, the plan may also.
- Flexibility: Allowing for some flexibility will better your chances of not getting caught off guard when there are minor changes or challenges to the set plan. It is important to allow your plan to be flexible. Allow for juggling people or responsibilities if necessary. Try to stay on track as best as possible, but don't be surprised when unexpected things happen.

CONTINUOUS PLANNING

Continuous planning takes into account not only the need for day-to-day flexibility but the fact that in today's extremely competitive and fast-moving environment, trying to adhere too strictly to a plan, whether short-, medium-, or long-term, can often lead to dissappointment. For example, no matter how much competitive research and intelligence you have conducted, there is always the unknown. Who would have guessed ten years ago that the Internet and e-mail would have been what they are today? Only a few of the pioneers in this category, and not even they could have foreseen the explosive growth.

It is therefore imperative that, whether your planning process takes place one or more times a year, your team (and hopefully others in your organization) recognize that planning is meant to focus and give direction and should not be so rigid as to hold you back.

In essence, what you should really be asking during the planning process is the following:

- Who?
- What?
- When?
- Where?
- Why?
- How?

If you are able to answer these, you will have a successful plan that takes into account the realities of your business and the environment in which it operates.

EVALUATING THE BUSINESS

The planning process described above still needs a starting point. You can't just start off planning without having a baseline. This is where assessing the business, again bridging corporate and departmental areas, comes into play. In other words, what is the business environment today in which your company and your team are operating? While you are not involved in all aspects of the corporate assessment, certain key information undoubtedly will affect your department, and the knowledge of this will be helpful in developing your own strategies.

For example:

- If it is a public company, how is it faring in the markets?
- Are you meeting the numbers projected for the shareholders and other stakeholders?
- Is your company in a hiring mode, hiring freeze, or downsizing?
- Are you and/or any of your competitors involved in a merger or acquisition?
- What types of information is your company sharing with you regarding future planning?

In the absence of strict facts you might also need to make certain assumptions. For example:

- A defective product line has created a media frenzy and will continue to challenge your company's reputation for an unspecified period of time.
- X competitor just announced a new CEO, and, judging by her prior track record, she will likely initiate a pricing war.
- Interest rate hikes could likely benefit your overall business in the coming months.

As we mentioned earlier, planning can be initiated in various ways. Before you are able to fully conduct an assessment of your business, you should also understand the basics of decision making. Decision making typically follows a logical model or sequence of events. This includes:

- Defining the problem(s)
- Gathering and analyzing the pertinent facts

- Looking at the options available and weighing those options against one another
- Selecting the appropriate option based on the information at hand
- Implementing that option
- Evaluating the results (a final step would be to use that feedback as input for subsequent decisions).

Brainstorming is one way to get discussions going and gather information for decision making. There are many types of brainstorming, some more formal and others more ad hoc. Some of the keys to productive brainstorming sessions include these:

- Let all voices be heard.
- Don't get bogged down in minor details.
- Use a facilitator if necessary.
- Make sure all necessary stakeholders are present.

Most important in decision making is to have an atmosphere whereby you arrive at a true consensus. This means that the highest-ranking officer in the room does not make the decision for everyone. Of course, it is often the responsibility of the most senior-level person to have the final say, but it should be based on information that has been carefully analyzed first. In some group settings a voting process can help to eliminate this concern.

Thus far you have seen tools like the SWOT analysis, product/market analysis, competitive product/service analysis, and market research. These are all tools that could give you needed input for your plan. Also, as you saw, these are often cross-functional tools or ones that reside in another department altogether. It is therefore important to identify all of these other stakeholders and departments to be sure the necessary players are involved to help make accurate business assessments.

Some of the key categories of stakeholders are:

- Your company management-CEO, president, SVP, COO, VP of marketing and marketing, etc.
- Other marketing managers (your peers)
- Your marketing team-those you manage such as marketing representatives (in-house and/or independent), field and/or telemarketing people, customer service representatives, marketing coordinators, etc.

- Other department managers and key personnel-marketers, engineers, call center managers, accountants, human resources professionals, etc.
- Customers at all levels, including the senior managers, buyers, purchasing agents, buying assistants, etc.

BENCHMARKING

Another useful tool in assessing your business is benchmarking. Benchmarking is really a tool for making comparisons of any sort. Benchmarking can be conducted on anything from internal processes to the competition or the industry. It is a great tool for looking at current or past results and being able to compare them with the future. Benchmarking allows you to measure and then analyze the appropriate data to make decisions for improvements going forward. The areas you can benchmark are endless.

Internal benchmarking is used to measure against other departments or to get a baseline to then compare progress. It could include:

- Product and/or service satisfaction levels
- Number of complaints
- Number of defects
- Employee satisfaction

External benchmarking would look at similar processes or departments within your competitors' organizations as well as best practices in the industry. Some examples are:

- Customer service levels
- Market share
- Return on investment
- The marketing process
- New product development process

Each of these could of course be broken down in smaller parts. For example, employee satisfaction could break down into morale, job security, and opportunities for advancement. Once again, many of these categories for which you can engage in benchmarking will not reside fully in your department. However, they could be of enormous benefit to you and your marketing team as you set strategies going forward. For example, your marketing team could be out marketing a new product that offers first-of-its-kind features, yet production is way behind.

Benchmarking can help you and your organization see what processes internally are working best and to then transfer that knowledge to other departments. You can also look to the outside for best practices in different industries as well as processes within companies in such areas as new product development or supply chain management.

This knowledge would help to give direction to those involved so that production times can improve and customer satisfaction increases. Conducting business planning is a complex area. The types of tools that are used and the process it can follow vary greatly. By utilizing your enhanced communication skills you can more effectively work with your team, others in the organization, and outside stakeholders to gather the necessary information in order to plan for today and tomorrow. In the next chapter, you will look at one of the most challenging areas for the new and veteran marketing manager alike. It is also a key factor in the success of you and your team. While in many respects it is a specific piece of marketing planning, it also has many more implications and carries with it other long- and short-term implications. It is the area of territory planning and marketing forecasting. However, before delving into this critical topic, you will first need to fully grasp the importance of managing your time.

Note: Brunswick Corporation (Brunswick) manufactures marine and indoor recreation equipment. The company is engaged in manufacturing and marketing of boats, marine engines, fitness equipment, and bowling and billiards equipment. Brunswick primarily operates in the US. It is headquartered in Lake Forest, Illinois and employs 19,760 people. For a case study visit company's site www.brunswick.com

Bibliography

A. A. Luchak, "What Kind of Voice Do Loyal Employees Use?" *British Journal of Industrial Relations*, March 2003.

A. Bryman, "Leadership in Organizations," in *Handbook of Organization Studies,* ed. S.R. Clegg, C. Hardy, and W.R. Nord, Thousand Oaks, CA: Sage, 1996.

A. D' Innocenzio, "Wal-Mart's Town Becomes New Address for Corporate America," *Associated Press,* September, 2003.

A. Holeck, "Griffith, Ind., Native Takes Over as Steel Plant Manager," *The Times*, Munster, IN, May, 2003.

A. Klein, "A Merger Taken AO-111," *Washington Post,* October, 2002

A. Maitland and K. Rollins, "The Two-in-a-Box World of Dell," *Financial Times*, London, March, 2003.

A. Park and P. Burrows, "What You Don't Know about Dell," *Business-Week,* November, 2003.

A. Sinclair, "Approaches to Organizational Culture and Ethics," *Journal of Business Ethics*, 1993.

A.D. Galinsky, J. Stone, and J. Cooper, "The Reinstatement of Dissonance and Psychological Discomfort Following Failed Affirmation," *European Journal of Social Psychology*, 2000.

A.J. Slywotzky, *Value Migration: How to Think Several Moves Ahead of the Competition*, Boston: Harvard Business School Press, 1996.

A.M. Eagly and S. Chaiken, *The Psychology of Attitudes*, Orlando, FL: Harcourt Brace Jovanovich, 1993.

A.R. Damasio, *Descartes'Error: Emotion. Reason, and the Human Brain*, New York: Putnam Sons, 1994.

A.R. Malekazedeh and A. Nahavandi, "Making Mergers Work by Managing Cultures," *Journal of Business Strategy,* May-June 1990.

B. Darrow, "James Goodnight, Founder and CEO, SAS Institute," *Computer Reseller News,* December, 2005.

B. Kabanoff and J. Daly, "Espoused Values in Organisations," *Australian Journal of Managemen,* 2002.

B. Miller, "Brann Baltimore Marketing Finn's Office Gets a Fun Make-over," *Daily Record,* October, 2002.

B. Morris, "The Accidental CEO," *Fortune,* June, 2003.

B. Motion, "Positive Work Environment Keeps Them Happy, Staffers Say," *Vancouver Sun,* October, 2004.

B.K. Hunnicutt, *Kellogg's Six-Hour Day*, Philadelphia: Temple University Press, 1996.

B.M. Bass, "From Transactional to Transformational Leadership," *Organizational Dynamics,* Winter 1990.

C. Daniels, "Does This Man Need a Shrink?" *Fortune,* February, 2001.

C.A. Schorg, C.A. Raiborn, and M.F. Massoud, "Using a 'Cultural Audit' to Pick M&A Winners," *Journal of Corporate Accounting & Finance,* May-June 2004.

C.D. Fisher, "Mood and Emotions While Working: Missing Pieces of Job Satisfaction?" *Journal of Organizational Behavior*, 2000.

C.K. Prahalad and R.A. Bettis, "The Dominant Logic: A New Linkage between Diversity and Performance," *Strategic Management Journal*, 1986.

C.M. Christensen, *The Innovator's Dilemma*, Boston: Harvard Business School Press, 1997.

Christensen, *The Innovator's Dilemma;* C.W.L. Hill and F.T. Rothearmel, "The Performance of Incumbent Firms in the Face of Radical Technological Change," *Academy of Management Review*, 2003.

CJ. Fombrum, *Leading Corporate Change*, New York: McGraw-Hill, 1992.

D. Henry, "A Tense Moment at Kodak," *Business Week,* October, 2005.

D. Miller, *The Icarus Paradox*, New York Harper Business, 1990.

D. Roth, "My Job at The Container Store," *Fortune,* January, 2000.

D. Rynecki, "Putting the Muscle Back into the Bull," *Fortune,* April, 2004.

D.C. McClelland, *Power: The Inner Experience*, New York: Irvington, 1975.

D.M. Rousseau et al., "Not So Different after All: A Cross-Discipline View of Trust," *Academy of Management Review*, 1998.

D.V Day and R.G. Lord, "Executive Leadership and Organizational Performance: Suggestions for a New Theory and Methodology," *Journal of Management*, 1988.

E.A. Locke, "Why Emotional Intelligence Is an Invalid Concept," *Journal of Organizational Behavior,* 2005.

E.H. Schein, "The Role of the Founder in Creating Organizational Culture," *Organizational Dynamics*, , Summer, 1983.

E.J. Zajac and M.H. Bazerman, "Blind Spots in Industry and Competitor Analysis," *Academy of Management Review*, 1991.

E.M. Heffes, "Follow These Leaders," *Financial Executive,* April 2005.

E.W. Morrison and S.L. Robinson, "When Employees Feel Betrayed: A Model of How Psychological Contract Violation Develops," *Academy of Management Review,* 1997.

F.F. Reichheld, *The Loyalty Effect*, Boston: Harvard Business School Press, 1996.

G. Bethune, "From Worst to First," *Fortune,* May, 1998.

G. Morgan, *Images of Organization*, Beverly Hills: Sage, 1986.

G. Stalk and T.M. Hout, *Competing against Time*, New York: Free Press, 1990.

G. Yukl and R. Lepsinger, "Why Integrating the Leading and Managing Roles Is Essential for Organizational Effectiveness," *Organizational Dynamics*, 2005.

G.D. Gottfredson and J.L. Holland, "A Longitudinal Test of the Influence of Congruence: Job Satisfaction, Competency Utilization, and Counter-productive Behavior," *Journal of Counseling Psychology*, 1990.

G.D. Gottfredson, "John L. Holland's Contributions to Vocational Psychology: A Review and Evaluation," *Journal of Vocational Behavior*, 1999.

G.N. Powell, "One More Time: Do Female and Male Managers Differ?" *Academy of Management Executive,* 1990.

G.P. Pisano and S.C. Wheelwright, "The New Logic of High-Tech R&D," *Harvard Business Review,* September-October, 1995.

G.R. Salancik, "Commitment and the Control of Organizational Behavior and Belief," in *New Directions in Organizational Behavior,* ed. B. M. Staw and G.R. Salancik, Chicago: St. Clair, 1977.

H. Selye, *Stress without Distress*, Philadelphia: J.B. Lippincott, 1974.

H. Smith, *The Power Game: How Washington Works*, New York: Ballantine, 1988.

H.M. Weiss and R. Cropanzano, "Affective Events Theory: A Theoreti-cal Discussion of the Structure, Causes, and Consequences of Affective Experiences at Work," *Research in Organizational Behavior*, 1996.

J. Barling, T. Weber, and E.K. Kelloway, "Effects of Transformational Leadership Training on Attitudinal and Financial Outcomes: A Field Experiment," *Journal of Applied Psychology*, 1996.

J. Churchill, "To the Bitter End," *Registered Rep.,* March, 2006.

J. Collins, *From Good to Great*, New York: Harper Collins, 2001.

J. Davidson, "The Business of Ethics." *Working Woman,* February, 1998.

J. Hewett, "Office Politics," *Australian Financial Review,* September, 2003.

J. Newman and D. Grigg, "Vancity's Robbery Intervention Program Wins Award," *Vancouver Sun,* October, 2004.

J. Ott, "United No More," *Aviation Week and Space Technology,* May, 2005.

J. Pfeffer, *Managing with Power: Politics and Influence within Organizations*, Boston: Harvard Business School Press, 1992.

J. Porterfiled and B.H. Kleiner. "A New Era: Women and Leadership," *Equal Opportunities International*, 2005.

J. S. Ott, *The Organizational Culture Perspective*, Pacific Grove, CA: Brooks/Cole, 1989.

J. Thottam, "Reworking Work," *Time,* July 25, 2005.

J. Tupponce, "Listening to Those Inner Voices," *Richmond Times-Dispatch,* May, 2003.

J. Van Maanen, "Breaking In: Socialization to Work," in *Handbook of Work, Organization, and Society,* ed. R. Dubin, Chicago: Rand McNally, 1976.

J.A. Bargh and M.J. Ferguson, "Beyond Behaviorism: On the Automaticity of Higher Mental Processes," *Psychological Bulletin*, 2000.

J.B. Rosener, "Ways Women Lead," *Harvard Business Review*, November-December 1990.

J.C. Quick et al., *Preventive Stress Management in Organizations*, Washington, DC: American Psychological Association, 1997.

J.J. van Muijen, "Organizational Culture," in *A Handbook of Work and Organizational Psychology: Organizational Psychology*, 2nd ed., ed. P.J.D. Drenth, H. Thierry, and C.J. de Wolff, East Sussex, UK: Psychology Press, 1998.

J.P. Meyer, "Organizational Commitment," *International Review of Industrial and Organizational Psychology*, 1997.

J.S. House, *Work Stress and Social Support*, Reading, MA: Addison-Wesley, 1981.

J.Z. DeLorean, *On a Clear Day You Can See General Motors*, Grosse Pointe, MI: Wright Enterprises, 1979.

K. Brooker and J. Schlosser, "The Un-CEO," *Fortune,* September, 2002.

K. Danna and R.W. Griffin, "Health and Well-Being in the Workplace: A Review and Synthesis of the Literature," *Journal of Management,* Spring, 1999.

K. Lewin, *Field Theory in Social Sciences: Selected Theo-retical Papers*, New York: Harper Brothers, 1951.

K.B. Clark and S.C. Wheelwright, *Managing New Product and Process Development*, New York: Free Press, 1993.

K.B. Clark and T. Fujimoto, "The Power of Product Integrity," *Harvard Business Review,* November-December, 1990.

L. Festinger, *A Theory of Cognitive Dissonance*, Evanston, IL: Row, Peterson, 1957.

M Doehrman, "Anthropologists-Deep in the Corporate Bush," *Daily Record*, Kansas City, MO, July, 2005.

M. Alvesson, *Understanding Organizational Culture*, London: Sage, 2002.

M. Beer, *Organization Change and Development: A Systems View*, Santa Monica, CA: Goodyear Publishing, 1980.

M. Cooke, "Humiliation as Motivator?" *Meetings A Conventions*, July 2001.

M. Fan, "Cary, N.C., Software Firm Posts Steady Growth without IPO," *San Jose Mercury News,* July, 2001.

M. Hannah and J. Freeman, *Organizational Ecology*, Cambridge, MA: Harvard University Press, 1989.

M. Tripsas and G. Gavetti, "Capabilities, Cognition, and Inertia: Evidence from Digital Imaging," *Strategic Management Journal*, 2000.

M. Washington and M.J. Ventresca, "How Organizations Change," *Organization Science*, 2004.

M.T. Hannah and J. Freeman, "Structural Inertia and Organizational Change," *American Sociological Review*, 1984.

N:, Wasserman, B. Anand, and N. Nohira, *When Does Leadership Mat-ter?* Harvard Business School Working Paper, 2001.

N.M. Ashkanasy, "The Case for Culture," in *Debating Organization,* ed. R. Westwood and S. Clegg, Maiden, MA: Black-well, 2003.

O. Port, "Moving Past the Assembly Line," *Business Week,* Special Issue: Reinventing America, 1992.

P. Guenzi and O. Pelloni, "The Impact of Interpersonal Relationships on Customer Satisfaction and Loyalty to the Service Provider," *International Journal of Service Industry Management*, 2004.

P. Ohemawat, *Commitment: The Dynamic of Strategy*, New York: Free Press, 1991.

P. Roberts, "The Empire Strikes Back," *Fast Company,* February-March, 1999.

P. Salovey, and J. Mayer, "Emotional Intelligence," *Imagination, Cognition, and Personality*, 1990.

P. Szuchman, "The Job-Share Advantage," *Working Mother*, May, 2002.

P.O. Northouse, *Leadership: Theory and Practice,* 3rd ed., Thousand Oaks, CA: Sage, 2004.

R,M. Stogdill. *Handbook of Leadership*, New York: The Free Press, 1974.

R. Basch, "Doing Well by Doing Good," *Searcher Magazine,* January, 2005.

R. Craver, "Dell Thinning Out List of Job Candidates," *Winston-Salem Journal,* April, 2005.

R. Drago, D. Black, and M. Wooden, *The Persistence of Long Work Hours,* Melbourne Institute Working Paper Series, Melbourne: Melbourne Institute of Applied Economic and Social Research, University of Melbourne, August, 2005.

R. Jacobs, "Using Human Resource Functions to Enhance Emotional Intelligence," in *The Emotionally Intelligent Workplace,* ed. C. Cherniss and D. Goleman, San Francisco: Jossey-Bass, 2001.

R.B. Zajonc, "Emotions," in *Handbook of Social Psychology,* ed. D.T. Gilbert, S.T. Fiske, and L. Gardner, New York: Oxford University Press, 1998.

R.E. Quinn and N.T. Snyder, "Advance Change Theory: Culture Change at Whirlpool Corporation," in *The Leader s Change Handbook,* ed. J. A. Conger, G.M. Spreitzer, and E.E. Lawler III, San Francisco: Jossey-Bass, 1999.

S. Keer and J.M. Jermier, "Substitutes for Leadership: Their Meaning and Measurement," *Organizational Behavior and Human Performance*, 1978.

S. Lieberson and J.F. O'Conner, "Leadership and Organizational Per-formance: A Study of Large Corporations," *American Sociological Review*, 1972.

S. Sackmann, "Culture and Subcultures: An Analysis of Organizational Knowledge," *Administrative Science Quarterly*, 1992.

S. Schachter, *The Psychology of Affiliation*, Palo Alto, CA: Stanford University Press: 1959.

S.D. Parley and M.F Stasson, "Relative Influences of Affect and Cognition on Behavior: Are Feelings or Beliefs More Related to Blood Dona-tion Intentions?" *Experimental Psychology*, 2003.

S.E. Taylor et al., "Psychological Resources, Positive Illusions, and Health," *American Psychologist*, January, 2000.

S.E. Taylor, R.L. Repetti, and T. Seeman, "Health Psychology: What Is an Unhealthy Environment and How Does It Get under the Skin?" *Annual Review of Psychology*, 1997.

S.G. Harris, "Organizational Culture and Individual Sensemaking: A Schema-Based Perspective," *Organization Science*, 1994.

S.L. Bellar, M. Helms, and D.E. Arfken, "The Glacial Change: Women on Corporate Boards," *Business Perspectives*, 2004.

T. DeCotiis et al., "How Outback Steakhouse Created a Great Place to Work, Have Fun, and Make Money," *Journal of Organizational Excellence*, Autumn, 2004.

T. Hamilton, "RIM on a Roll," *Toronto Star,* February, 2004.

T. Lester, "Performance at Hugo Boss," *Executive Briefing (Economist Intelligence Unit),* May, 2006.

V. Schultz, "Reconceptualizing Sexual Harassment," *Yale Law Journa,* April, 1998

VL. Goodwin, J.C. Wofford, and J.L. Whittington "A Theoretical and Empirical Extension to the Transformational Leadership Construct," *Journal of Organizational Behavior*, November, 2001.

W. Bennis, *Why Leaders Can't Lead*, San Francisco: Jossey-Bass, 1989.

W.C. Kim and Mauborgne, "Tipping Point Leadership," *Harvard Business Review*, 2003.

W.G. Bennis and R.J. Thomas, *Geeks and Geezers*, Boston: Harvard Business School Press, 2002.

W.M. Ensel and N. Lin, "Physical Fitness and the Stress Process," *Journal of Community Psychology*, January 2004.

WM. Bulkeley, "Kodak Scales Back Short-Term View but Sees Revival," *The Wall Street Journal,* September, 2005.

Index

D

E

F

G

H

I

J

L

M